FLORIDA STATE
UNIVERSITY LIBRARIES

SEP 27 1993

TALLAHASSEE, FLORIDA

Women Prime Ministers
and Presidents

Women Prime Ministers and Presidents

by
Olga S. Opfell

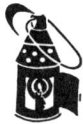

McFarland & Company, Inc., Publishers
Jefferson, North Carolina, and London

D
839.5
O64
1993

British Library Cataloguing-in-Publication data available

Library of Congress Cataloguing-in-Publication data available

Library of Congress Catalog Card Number 92-56675

ISBN 0-89950-790-5 (lib. bdg.; 50 # acid-free natural paper) ∞

©1993 Olga S. Opfell. All rights reserved

Manufactured in the United States of America

McFarland & Company, Inc., Publishers
 Box 611, Jefferson, North Carolina 28640

for Dylan Rose

Contents

Introduction	ix
SIRIMAVO BANDARANAIKE *Prime Minister of Ceylon (later Sri Lanka): 1960–65, 1970–77*	1
INDIRA GANDHI *Prime Minister of India: 1966–77, 1980–84*	14
GOLDA MEIR *Prime Minister of Israel: 1969–74*	33
ISABEL PERÓN *President of Argentina: 1974–76*	51
ELIZABETH DOMITIEN *Prime Minister of the Central African Republic: 1975–76*	62
MARGARET THATCHER *Prime Minister of the United Kingdom of Great Britain and Northern Ireland: 1979–90*	68
MARIA DE LOURDES PINTASILGO *Prime Minister of Portugal: 1979*	82
EUGENIA CHARLES *Prime Minister of Dominica: 1980–*	88
VIGDIS FINNBOGADÓTTIR *President of Iceland: 1980–*	95

GRO HARLEM BRUNDTLAND
Prime Minister of Norway: 1981, 1986–89, 1990–   101

MILKA PLANINC
Prime Minister of Yugoslavia: 1982–86   112

MARIA LIBERIA-PETERS
Prime Minister of the Netherlands Antilles: 1984–86, 1988–   121

CORAZON AQUINO
President of the Philippines: 1986–92   127

BENAZIR BHUTTO
Prime Minister of Pakistan: 1990–91   141

ERTHA PASCAL-TROUILLOT
President of Haiti: 1990–91   154

KAZIMIERA PRUNSKIENE
Prime Minister of Lithuania: 1990–91   161

VIOLETA CHAMORRO
President of Nicaragua: 1990–   169

MARY ROBINSON
President of Ireland: 1990–   181

KHALEDA ZIA
Prime Minister of Bangladesh: 1991–   189

EDITH CRESSON
Prime Minister of France: 1991–92   200

HANNA SUCHOCKA
Prime Minister of Poland: 1992–   212

Selected Bibliography   223

Index   229

INTRODUCTION

Since Sirimavo Bandaranaike of Ceylon (later Sri Lanka) stepped into prominence in 1960 as the world's first female prime minister, 20 women have followed as heads of government or state, each a political pioneer in her country. In 1975, Isabel Perón became the world's first female president.

Now is a propitious time to look at them all. Their numbers, of course, will grow; in 1990 alone, five new names came to the front, although only two stayed prominent.

Several women became public figures because of a husband's or father's prominence or position (the Appendage Syndrome, in Antonia Fraser's apt term). Tragedy, however, cast long shadows. Four suffered a husband's assassination and one, a father's execution. Each appalling event left the survivor with a sense of mission. Less dramatically, other women steadily climbed party ladders to arrive at the top. One president and one prime minister were appointed on interim bases.

Among heads of state, power has varied considerably. Certain presidents have wielded much authority; some have been apolitical, acting rather as cultural ambassadors and national symbols. Successes contrast with disappointing performances, one of which caused an outright coup.

On their way to high office or after leaving it, five women suffered imprisonment or house detention. One prime minister was struck down by bullets. Complex social and political forces have washed over many. Wars have intruded.

Chronologically arranged, this book of profiles briefly unfolds the careers of the famous and the lesser known and shows sharp differences in political affiliation, character, charisma, vision, and fervent advocacy. Since a few careers are ongoing, more remains to be told. My aim has been to provide objective accounts; the reader is invited to make comparisons and assessments.

Few of these pioneers have labeled themselves feminist, but as a pioneer each is important. By virtue of being first in her post, each leader, whatever her accomplishments or length of term, is assured a niche in her country's history.

I should like to express my deep appreciation to my husband John B. Opfell for wide-ranging help and encouragement. My special thanks go to Ruth Loring, who asked pertinent questions and made valuable suggestions. I am also grateful to Jenny Erickson and Dorrit Grina for supplying me with many articles I might otherwise have missed and to Bernard Kouzouma, Victor Nakas, Sara Lessley, Michael Parks, Hanne E. Ban, T. W. Maciejowski, and Radio Free Europe for providing various details. Finally I thank those embassies in Washington, D.C., that graciously responded to my requests for biographical information and photographs.

Olga S. Opfell
Torrance, California

SIRIMAVO BANDARANAIKE

Prime Minister of Ceylon (later Sri Lanka)
(1960–65, 1970–77)

A devastating family tragedy in 1959 thrust a relatively unknown widow into the international spotlight. Because of a murder, Sirimavo Bandaranaike became the world's first woman prime minister. Ten months before she took office in 1960 in Colombo, Ceylon, she had seen her husband, Prime Minister Solomon Bandaranaike, stagger into their villa, his body pierced by bullets. So with stunning immediacy began the active political career of which she had never dreamed.

The family lineage included many members of the old Kandyan ruling aristocracy. Sirimavo, the eldest daughter of Barnes and Kumarihamy Ratwatte, was born on April 17, 1916, at her great-aunt's house in Ratnapura, a city in the foothills surrounding the old capital of Kandy. The Ratwatte home was in Balangoda, 33 miles away on the Horton Plain, Ceylon's highest plateau. But because the young mother had already lost two infants, a soothsayer had advised her to have her third child in another place.

Kumarihamy and her baby spent a couple of months in the ancestral mansion of her father, the old chieftain of Balangoda district, the Ratemahatmaya Mahawalatenne, who on his death would bequeath his post to his son-in-law, Barnes Ratwatte. Over the next few years at Balangoda, Kumarihamy would bear another daughter and three more sons.

Sirimavo attended a private nursery school in Balangoda. Then she was sent to Ratnapura to live with her great-aunt while she went to kindergarten. A year later, she began her formal schooling at St. Bridget's Convent in Colombo, where she would stay for 11 years. Eventually her three brothers joined her there. It was a memorable occasion for the family when their father, dressed in colorful, ceremonial robes for the impending governor's levy, came to visit.

In 1934, just as a malaria epidemic struck Ceylon, Sirimavo came back home. Often she accompanied her father on his circuit of the area. "I learned we were on the same wave length," she said later. "I began to understand how he felt about the people he had looked after for years and how his heart yearned for their welfare." During the crisis the Ratwattes operated a convalescent home, where the tall, grave-eyed girl worked tirelessly with her mother. By the end of 1935 the epidemic was under control, and Mrs. Ratwatte turned over the household duties to her daughter so she could practice the natural healing techniques she had learned from her father, the old chieftain Mahawalatenne.

Away from domestic duties, Sirimavo learned to do exquisite embroidery; grew prize roses with her father; and, like him and her sister, became a keen tennis player. She also took time to work for the Balangoda Service League, a group of young volunteers.

In 1940 her parents arranged a marriage they hoped would bring their daughter both happiness and success. Their choice was Solomon West Ridgeway Dias Bandaranaike, a bespectacled, pipe-smoking lawyer and politician 17 years her senior. His father, Sir Solomon Dias Bandaranaike, a wealthy landowner, had once been the chief Ceylonese aide to the British governor. The younger Solomon was definitely a "political animal." Fresh from Oxford and the English bar, he had been elected in 1931 to the newly formed Legislative Assembly, or State Council.

Europe had entered Ceylonese history with the Portuguese invasion of 1505. The Dutch had taken over by 1658. British rule, begun in 1796, had dotted the island with coffee, tea, cinnamon, coconut, and rubber plantations and benefited both the Ratwatte and Bandaranaike families. But as the 20th century brought increasing demands for independence, Solomon had taken up the cause.

His dream was tied to a fervid devotion to his Sinhalese heritage. Descendants of immigrants from northern India, the Buddhist Sinhalese constituted about 70 percent of the Ceylonese population. Especially proud of their ancient language and culture, they were fiercely resented by the Hindu Tamils, about 20 percent of the population. Sprung from southern Indian immigrants, the Tamils had a far different language and religion. In 1937, Solomon formed the Sinhala Maha Sabha, an organization pledged to make Buddhism the national religion and Sinhalese the national language.

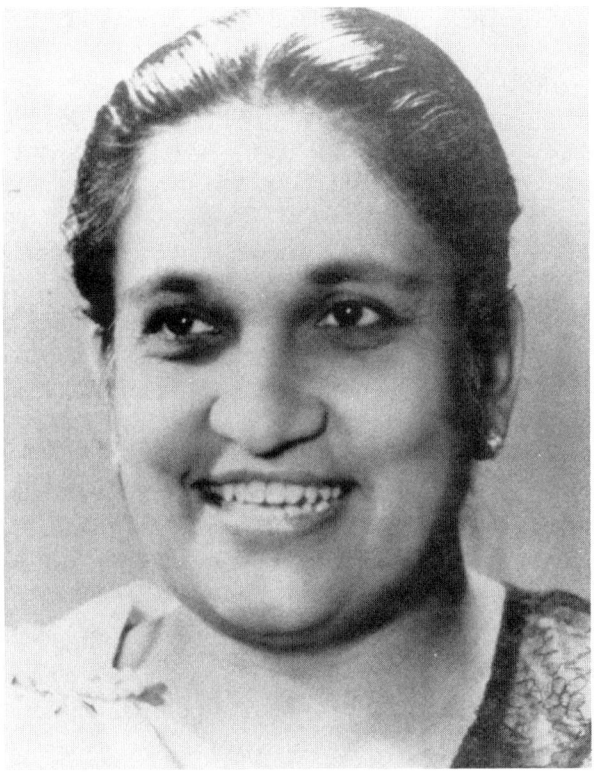

Sirimavo Bandaranaike: courtesy Embassy of Sri Lanka, Washington, D.C.

Before any engagement between the Ratwattes' daughter and the volatile politician could be announced, soothsayers were consulted and pronounced all the omens auspicious for a union between a first-rank family of the lowlands and a first-rank family of the Kandyan highlands. The wedding was a lavish affair, but the bridegroom chose to appear in a hand-loomed outfit, emulating his hero, Mohandas K. Gandhi.

A year after her marriage, Sirimavo joined the Lanka Mahila Samiti, the Ceylon Women's Association, pledged "to ameliorate rural conditions and improve the social and economic life of the people, particularly in the rural areas." Village institutions were set up in various places. Sirimavo would later write, "There were many occasions when we would travel through narrow jungle paths, ridden with leeches and serpents, wade through floods, ford rivers, climb hills and dales, find our way over almost impossible trails. Such visits were necessary to see for ourselves that the women were maintaining the standards of hygienic living, cultivating their home gardens, giving a simple but balanced diet to their families, taking an active part in community self-help schemes."

The Bandaranaikes' first child Sunetra was born in 1943. Chandraka arrived a few years later, and a son, Anura, was born in 1949. Like their mother, the children would be sent to Catholic schools. Like her father, Sunetra would attend Oxford.

After World War II, political groups could finally look forward to the first parliamentary election promised by the British. In 1946, Solomon's Sri Lanka Freedom party (SLFP), the Ceylon Muslim League, and the Tamil-influenced Ceylon National Congress formed the United National party (UNP) under the leadership of D. D. Senanayake. In 1947, Solomon was elected to the new House of Representatives and appointed minister of health and local government.

Ceylon's role as a crown colony ended the next year when it gained Dominion status and became an independent member of the Commonwealth. It was, however, still tied to the British Crown through a governor-general.

While Solomon gained prominence in the UNP, Sirimavo held various offices in the Lanka Mahila Samiti. Meanwhile, as her husband's confidante, she was receiving a special kind of political education.

To Solomon, who was one of the few cabinet members not related to Senanayake, the UNP seemed too Western oriented. So in 1951 he resigned from the government and the UNP and, under his old party banner, was reelected to the House of Representatives, where he became leader of the opposition.

Senanayake was killed in a fall from his horse in 1952 and was succeeded by his son Dudley. The elder Senanayake had instituted a policy of providing a free ration of rice to every Ceylonese. But in 1953 the "rice issue," an attempt to increase the price of the grain, led to mass riots, many deaths, and the declaration of a state of emergency. Citing ill health, Dudley Senanayake resigned; his uncle by marriage, Sir John Kotelawa, followed him in office.

In 1956 Solomon Bandaranaike formed the People's United Front (Mahajana Eksath Peramuna, or MEP), an alliance of his SLFP with independent and leftist parties, both Trotskyites and Communists. The purpose was to topple Kotelawa and the UNP. To gain money for the election, the Bandaranaikes mortgaged their house at Rosmead Place.

Sirimavo canvassed for her husband in the Ratnapura-Balangoda area. Waging the campaign largely on nationalistic issues, the MEP achieved a stunning victory, and Solomon became prime minister. But the Bandaranaikes chose to remain at Rosmead Place rather than live at Temple Trees, the official residence, which they intended to use only for formal entertaining.

The new leader would bring about significant changes. Quickly he introduced legislation to make Buddhism the national religion and Sinhalese the national language, replacing English. The Sinhalese Only Act, however, set off bloody riots in the Tamil-speaking Hindu population to the north.

In 1957 terrible floods destroyed crops and led to unemployment and serious labor troubles. As Solomon faced mounting tensions, he eased back from his decision about the Sinhalese language and assured the Tamils that they would be allowed "reasonable use" of their native tongue. In May 1958, communal strains broke out again, and gangs of thugs and looters entered the fray. After five days of fierce fighting, the government declared a state of emergency that would last until 1959.

Internationally, the MEP advocated a neutralist policy, but the prime minister was actually busy establishing ties with the Communists. To show his colors, he turned to a huge program of nationalization and the establishment of state monopolies. The press was openly critical of his plans to nationalize the tea and rubber plantations, banks, and insurance companies. It further deplored his Ceylon Transport Board, which took over every private bus line on the island with chaotic results. Better received was his agreement with the British to relinquish their military bases in Ceylon.

Sirimavo had remained active in the Lanka Mahila Samiti; she had already served as treasurer and vice-president and was now president. Her concerns were family planning and political rights and education for women. Speaking at one institute in 1958, she disclaimed any political ambitions for herself: "Knowing how difficult it is to cater to all the requirements of a nation and to solidify them I would not accept the post of premier even if it were offered to me."

Then the unexpected happened. On the morning of September 25, 1959, she was busy with preparations for Solomon's trip to the United States, where he was to address the United Nations General Assembly in New York and meet with President Dwight D. Eisenhower in Washington, D.C. A small group of well-wishers gathered on the Bandaranaike veranda, hoping to catch a glimpse of the prime minister, who was inside the villa chatting with the new American ambassador. Sirimavo stepped into the side garden to speak with her brother.

In the waiting group stood Talduwe Somorama, a disgruntled young Buddhist monk. Bandaranaike emerged from the house to see the ambassador to his car and then returned to the veranda. At that moment, the yellow-robed monk lunged forward and fired, hitting his target four times. Shouting, the prime minister stumbled into the house. Hearing the commotion, Sirimavo rushed in from the garden and saw her husband half lying in a chair, stoutly insisting that he was all right. After his sister-in-law, a physician, examined him and found no wounds near his heart, he was carried to his car and driven to the hospital.

Before being taken to the operating room, Solomon Bandaranaike dictated a statement to the nation, asking for forgiveness and compassion for his attacker. Afterward he talked freely with Sirimavo and her brothers, who thought he would recover. But by morning he was dead. His widow would later say that it would have been impossible for her to live through the nightmare without the help of her mother, sister, and brothers. She was to wear traditional white mourning saris for three years.

Solomon Bandaranaike was briefly succeeded by the minister of education, Wijayananda Dahanayake; then new elections were set for March 1960. As the widow of a national hero who had brought the government back to the common people, Mrs. Banda, as she was affectionately dubbed, was asked to campaign on behalf of the SLFP. Wanting to perpetuate Solomon's memory, she traveled tirelessly through Ceylon, delivering speeches and playing tapes of her husband's speeches. At times she seemed so emotional that opponents dubbed her the weeping widow. She had not agreed to become a candidate.

The SLFP won 46 seats in the House of Representatives, four fewer than the UNP. Dudley Senanayake, the UNP leader, then formed a minority government, only to lose his first vote of confidence. He stayed on in a caretaker capacity because elections were scheduled for July.

In May, Sirimavo was unanimously appointed head of the SLFP. Years later, she would say, "I would personally have preferred to keep away from politics, giving more of my time to my fatherless children, who needed my care and attention and to whom I had to play the part of both father and mother. My fate was to be different from what I thought." But she believed she must work for the welfare of the millions who had loved Solomon.

One of her first actions, based on Solomon's 1956 strategy, was to enter an agreement with Ceylon's two Marxist parties, the Trotskyites and the Communists, that none of the three groups would contest a seat the others were campaigning for. She firmly declined to run in July, explaining that she had no wish to be leader of the opposition party in case the SLFP did not win.

It turned out that the party won 75 out of 151 seats in the House of Representatives. In July, as party leader, Sirimavo was appointed prime minister. Independent candidates brought the SLFP six more seats, and as head of government she could suggest six other names to the governor-general. That working majority made it unnecessary to depend on Marxist supporters, at least for the present.

Still, she was in the peculiar position of not being a member of the parliament. To remedy the situation, Sir Oliver Goonetilloke, the governor-general, named her to one of the 15 appointed seats in the Senate, the upper legislative house.

To her high post Sirimavo brought a resolute commitment to follow through on Solomon's socialism and nationalization program and his encouragement of Buddhism and the Sinhalese language and culture. One of her early moves, which angered the United States, was to assume control of the oil companies.

In August, the government took over seven Ceylonese newspapers and transferred them to corporations in which the government and the public held shares. By December, Sirimavo announced a huge takeover of private state-aided schools run by religious groups.

Her most controversial measure was to enforce the use of Sinhalese. When 2 million Tamils revolted against her decree, Sirimavo sent troops into the Tamil provinces, where they remained until 1963.

Having reserved the portfolios of minister of defense and minister of external affairs for herself, Sirimavo declared a policy of neutrality in international affairs. In March 1962 she attended the Commonwealth Prime Ministers' Conference in London, becoming the first woman to sit at the Commonwealth table.

That same year, a plot to overthrow the government by force was discovered just in time. It was evidence that the SLFP did not enjoy great popularity. The country suffered from an alarming economic situation. There always seemed to be a food crisis; with an exploding population, Ceylon had to import one-third of its food and be dependent on the vagaries of the world market. When opponents taunted her with the remark that a woman's place was in her home, in her kitchen, Bandaranaike replied, "A woman's place is everywhere and anywhere duty requires her to be and also in her kitchen." (She was a fine cook.)

To strengthen her hold, Sirimavo Bandaranaike in 1964 formed a coalition with the Trotskyites, who demanded more press curbs and tighter trade controls. Her decision to put newspapers under governmental supervision led inexorably to her downfall. The SLFP lost a vote of confidence in the House of Representatives, and elections were scheduled for 1965. Voters returned UNP's Dudley Senanayake to office. But Bandaranaike won the Attanagalla seat for herself and became the leader of the opposition. Once in power, Senanayake seemed surprisingly reluctant to turn the nationalization program about. Every year his problems grew. By 1970, unemployment, inflation, and a bungled irrigation project made for a critical situation.

Once again Bandaranaike turned to her old allies, the pro–Moscow Communist party and six Trotskyite parties—the United Front—and swept Senanayake out of office. During a vigorous campaign, she had contended that it was not possible for the UNP to seek a fresh mandate because it had not solved Ceylon's problems. Instead, she charged, it had sold out to the United States and the International Bank for Reconstruction and Development.

Back at her old desk, clearly savoring her electoral triumph, a two-thirds majority, Sirimavo Bandaranaike appointed a 21-member cabinet, including six Trotskyites and one Communist.

Now the SLFP set its course on ending the 22 years of British Dominion status. Full independence became its battle cry. Defiantly Sirimavo Bandaranaike announced that the 157 members of the House of Representatives had approved the establishment of a constituent assembly to draft a new constitution making Ceylon "a sovereign and independent republic pledged to recognize the objectives of a socialist democracy."

The prime minister's ties to the Communists grew ever closer. She extended recognition to North Vietnam, the Viet Cong's provisional revolutionary government of South Vietnam, North Korea, and East Germany. At the same time she severed diplomatic relations with Israel.

Now the nationalization program extended to foreign banks. Several Ceylonese banks were set up to finance the development of industry, agriculture, and trade. But the Bandaranaike government provided no incentives for acquiring wealth. No business firm was allowed to pay dividends of more than 12 percent annually, and no Ceylonese could receive a monthly salary of more than $600.

As Bandaranaike proceeded confidently on the nationalization program, she met opposition for not moving quickly enough. Violence broke out in the southern and central provinces. Youthful leftists and unemployed workers, calling themselves Marxists or Guevarists (for the Cuban revolutionary, Che Guevara) led the bitter revolt, seizing roads and bridges and attacking governmental installations. In 25 separate incidents they called for the overthrow of the government.

Bandaranaike gave the army full authority to use search-and-seizure techniques, to set 24-hour curfews, and to impose martial law. Handicapped by limited military equipment, she sought arms from the Soviet Union, Egypt, Yugoslavia, Palestinian groups, Britain, and the United States.

The rebels, using jungle cover, were hard to defeat. By September 1971, however, 9,000 had turned in their weapons, and 5,000 captives were placed in special detention camps. The death toll was estimated at about 3,000. Many had been executed by military firing squads.

Like her predecessors, Bandaranaike had advocated a small defense budget, but now she was forced to double it to purchase expensive weapons from the Soviet Union, China, and the United States. She also had to spend over $16 million to repair roads and damaged installations.

After the trauma of the rebellion, it was good to anticipate the full independence Britain had finally promised. Bandaranaike presided over ceremonies on May 22, 1972, when Ceylon became the Socialist Republic of Sri Lanka. The proud new name meant "great and beautiful island." The governor-general, William Gollapawa, was declared president, and Bandaranaike remained prime minister.

Following 22 months of deliberation, the Constituent Assembly approved the new constitution, which provided for a unicameral National Assembly with six-year terms. The last link to Britain disappeared when lawyers were denied appeal to the Privy Council in London. In keeping with Socialist dogma, the constitution excluded the rights to private property and called for the collective ownership of property, including land.

Meanwhile, Bandaranaike still felt shocked by the ultraleftist rebellion of the previous year, and she kept her country on military alert. Her political troubles were far from over. The coalition became shaky when the Communists withdrew their support after the adoption of a bill that permitted the courts to use normally inadmissible evidence in confessions.

Economically, the news stayed worrisome, too. A trade deficit of

$625 million resulted from a depleted coconut crop and a drop in world coconut prices, while a severe drought affected the rice crop. Tea plantations were nationalized, and legislation was introduced to limit personal income to about 2,000 rupees (approximately $300) per month. The year 1973 proved equally disastrous. Basic foods had to be put on wartime rationing, and political officials took control of agriculture.

All the while, steady streams of intellectuals and professionals were leaving the country. To stem the tide, the Bandaranaike government made all emigrants sign bonds obliging them to send back to Sri Lanka up to 10 percent of their earnings. It was, a government spokesman explained, a way of paying for some of the free education the emigrants had received.

The same year, Bandaranaike lost her longtime opponent when Dudley Senanayake died. Senanayake's successor as leader of the UNP was Junius R. Jayewardene, who seemed unable to lead the parliamentary opposition effectively.

Constantly, Bandaranaike's leftist allies pressed her to nationalize more banks and plantations, but she argued that doing so might mean welfare aid, which she felt her pauper state could not afford.

Late in 1974, when she was visiting Moscow, Trotskyites called for a union rally and street demonstrations. Angrily she balked and told her government that the rally must be banned. Her order was carried out, but she was not happy over the showdown. She knew she had to remain dependent on the far Left to prevent demands for higher wages. Food stayed in short supply. Only a shipment from China averted a grave crisis; then, following the Chinese lead, other governments began sending food.

Special courts now thought it was time to release some of the youths imprisoned for the 1971 riots. But the students continued to show their restlessness, and the more than 750,000 unemployed grew more desperate. Bandaranaike doubled the size of the army. Throughout 1975, Colombo buzzed with rumors of an imminent breakup of the United Front. On September 1, President Gollapawa sent letters to the ministers who belonged to the Trotskyite Equality party, telling them they had been fired.

The prime minister had disagreed with the Trotskyites' new demands. She agreed with them about nationalizing some 400 estates left in private hands, but could not accept their insistence on controlling the people there. With their domination of key unions and university campuses, she thought they already controlled enough. On the other hand, she retained her alliance with the pro–Moscow Communists.

After the Trotskyites were expelled, Bandaranaike was expected to steer a more middle course to rescue the almost-bankrupt nation and to quell rising discontent. A black market flourished; unemployment and underemployment grew daily. Meanwhile thousands of the 1972 protesters remained in jail. Again the students were restless. After police shot at them in demonstrations, the students declared boycotts, which Bandaranaike assailed, charging that political elements were behind them. From then on she forbade all public demonstrations on public highways.

The next year the country's woes were set aside when she played hostess to thousands of diplomats who gathered in Colombo for a summit of nonaligned nations. Under her watchful eye, luxury hotels and new buildings had sprung up, the airport road had been whitewashed, and thousands of beggars had been trucked out of Colombo. Austerity was indeed thrown to the winds, and expenditures were put at $30 million.

Behind the temporary facade of prosperity, the per capita income was $129 a year. A rationing system tried to keep malnutrition at bay. But to compound the misery, a severe drought brought on water rationing in Colombo and reduced the harvest. By now, more than one-third of the rice crop had to be imported. The prices of tea and rubber, Sri Lanka's two main crops, were fluctuating.

Bandaranaike's enemies charged that her family held too many key posts. Her son Anura headed the youth wing of the SLFP, one daughter acted as official adviser to her mother, and the other took charge of the board that controlled the tea and rubber plantations.

And the Tamils were restive again, demanding a separate state to be called Eelam. When Bandaranaike ordered several Tamil leaders arrested, she unwittingly precipitated electoral disaster.

Signs of great discontent appeared everywhere. Each morning at daybreak, women lined up at shops that sold fish, bread, and red pepper for curry. Only through the black market could they get matches, spices, or kerosene for lamps. Every fifth worker was unemployed, and prices went sky high.

Disregarding the warning that this was no time for elections, Bandaranaike called one for July 1977. Again her chief opponent was Jayewardene of the UNP. This time, in opposition, the pro–Moscow Communists and the Trotskyites formed a new United Front.

Jayewardene's promises appealed to the voters: a ration of rice and flour for each person each week at subsidized prices, at least one j(every family, a huge free port area to encourage foreign investments the end of the nationalization program. His victory was overwhelming. Sirimavo Bandaranaike barely kept her seat. Early in 1978, Jayewardene gave up the premiership to become president with greatly expanded powers granted by the National Assembly. Sirimavo warned of impending dictatorship.

Two years later, the government declared an emergency to forestall a "bloodbath" allegedly planned by the SLFP. Bandaranaike's civil rights were revoked, and she was expelled from the National Assembly for having abused her power while prime minister. Though barred from running for any office, she was allowed to remain nominal head of the SLFP.

The Sinhalese and the Tamils had remained bitter enemies, and excessive rioting and violence in 1981 drove the Jayewardene government to declare a state of emergency. In this tense atmosphere, a bomb exploded at a political meeting where Bandaranaike was speaking, but she escaped unharmed.

Jayewardene called for early elections the next year, and the restoration of Sirimavo Bandaranaike's civil rights turned into one of the prime issues in the campaign. With Jayewardene's victory, however, the issue became moot.

The SLFP boycotted "amity talks" between the Tamils and the Sinhalese in 1984, but later reconsidered. Also in 1984, left-wing elements of the SLFP, led by Bandaranaike's daughter Chandraka and son-in-law, Vijaya Kumaranatunga, broke away to form the Sri Lanka People's party.

On the first day of 1986, Sirimavo's civil rights were restored, and she immediately decided to run for president. Tragically, before the elections of 1988, Chandraka, like her mother, suffered the trauma of a husband's assassination. Kumaranatunga, who had supported an India-brokered peace accord between the Sri Lankan government and the Tamils that promised greater autonomy for the Tamils, was shot to death outside his home in suburban Colombo.

Failing to win the presidential race, Bandaranaike then geared up for the National Assembly elections in 1989, the first in 12 years. She won back her seat, and the SLFP took 66 other places. Still outspoken and combative at 73, the former prime minister headed the opposition.

Once again the legislators were preoccupied with the Tamil crisis. Over the years, the demand for a separate state had only increased. A terrorist campaign had begun in 1983, lasting until 1987, when India signed an accord with the Sri Lankan government to call a cease-fire and to create an autonomous state from the predominantly Tamil Northern Province and the ethnically mixed Eastern Province. But the most powerful rebel group rejected the agreement. Peacekeeping Indian troops found themselves attacked by guerrillas. Nevertheless, in 1988 the Northern and Eastern Provinces merged, and elections were held.

In March 1990 the Indian soldiers withdrew. By June, the cease-fire broke down. Militants fought Sri Lankan government troops again, and resolution seemed far off. Aside from the Tamil conflict, violence had broken out in 1987 when the Sinhalese Liberation Front sought to overthrow the Colombi government. The uprising had ended only with the capture and execution of its leaders. In the National Assembly Sirimavo and the other legislators continued to feel the social stresses of the ethnic battles.

INDIRA GANDHI

*Prime Minister of India
(1966–77, 1980–84)*

Destiny intertwined Indira Gandhi and her family with the history of modern, independent India. From early childhood, she found herself caught up in the nationalist politics of her grandfather, Motilal Nehru, and her father, Jawaharlal Nehru, India's first prime minister. She became prime minister herself, and after her violent end her son Rajiv succeeded her. Thus the Nehru-Gandhi lineage was often called India's royal dynasty.

Indira was born on November 19, 1917, at her grandfather's palatial home, Anand Bhavan (Abode of Peace), in Allahabad in the state of Uttar Pradesh in northern India. Spacious lawns and gardens surrounded the gleaming white villa, with its long verandas, columns, colonnaded arches, and balconies. In its opulence, the estate attested to the success of the proud Brahmin lawyer, Motilal Nehru.

The only surviving child of Jawaharlal Nehru and his teenage bride, Kamala Kaul, the daughter of a Kashmiri businessman from Delhi. Indira was named for Motilal's mother and received the middle name Priyadarshini (beautiful to behold) from her parents. Usually she was called Indu. She spent her first years at Anand Bhavan in the midst of a doting extended family. But although they spoiled the child, Motilal's wife, Swarup Rani, and her elder daughter, Vijaya Lakshmi (later Mrs. Pandit), taunted and insulted Indu's adored mother, the shy, unsophisticated Kamala, considering her their inferior in education, social standing, and knowledge of Western ways. Krishna, the younger daughter, was more sympathetic.

Motilal and Jawaharlal, both trained in the law, were members of the Indian National Congress, which though founded under British auspices as a "talking union," had developed into an organization that pressed for democratic reform. But at the time of Indira's birth, her father and grandfather often quarreled over Jawaharlal's devotion to the ascetic Mohandas K. Gandhi and his program of nonviolent civil disobedience through the instrument of noncooperation. *Satyagraha,* as Gandhi called his movement, advocated the nonpayment of taxes and sitting in the streets to protest British rule, which had begun more than a century earlier in 1805.

The 1919 massacre at Amritsar, when British troops fired on a public meeting called by the congress to protest the repressive Rowlett Acts, changed Motilal's feelings about Gandhi. After 379 of his countrymen were killed and 1,200 wounded, Motilal Nehru persuaded the congress to support the inspiring new prophet, a bespectacled, skinny, little figure who would later take to wearing a simple loincloth.

Jawaharlal had left the law, and Motilal now closed his own practice and began dismissing servants, selling carriages and horses, and giving up his Anglicized way of living, symbolized by his pin-striped suits and silk ties. Gandhi had called for a boycott of all imported textiles, the better to support India's cottage industries of spinning and weaving. As an adult, Indira said that her earliest memory was watching the Nehru family make a huge bonfire of silks, satins, velvets, and chiffons on the terrace when she was almost four. The family had pledged themselves to wear *khadi,* or coarse, white, homespun cloth.

As Jawaharlal and Motilal were drawn into the Gandhi orbit, Anand Bhavan swarmed with politicians and intellectuals. But the affiliation with Gandhi had a darker side—imprisonment. In 1921, Motilal went on trial for disobedience, and Indu sat on his lap during the proceedings, which sent him behind bars for a brief period. She also sat in on her father's trial after he was arrested for picketing shops that sold foreign goods. Found guilty, he was incarcerated for 87 days. Since the Indian National Congress would not pay fines for its arrested members the police often came to Anand Bhavan to carry away furniture and silver.

In 1922 the men of the family once again sat in prison, Jawaharlal for 265 days. At that time Kamala, Krishna, and Swarup Rani accepted Gandhi's invitation to visit him at his ashram at Ahmadabad and they brought Indu with them. The little girl soon learned to accept the fact that devotion to Gandhi's ideals meant the frequent disappearance of her beloved father. Nehru, mayor of Allahabad until 1925, served his briefest sentence, 12 days, in 1923.

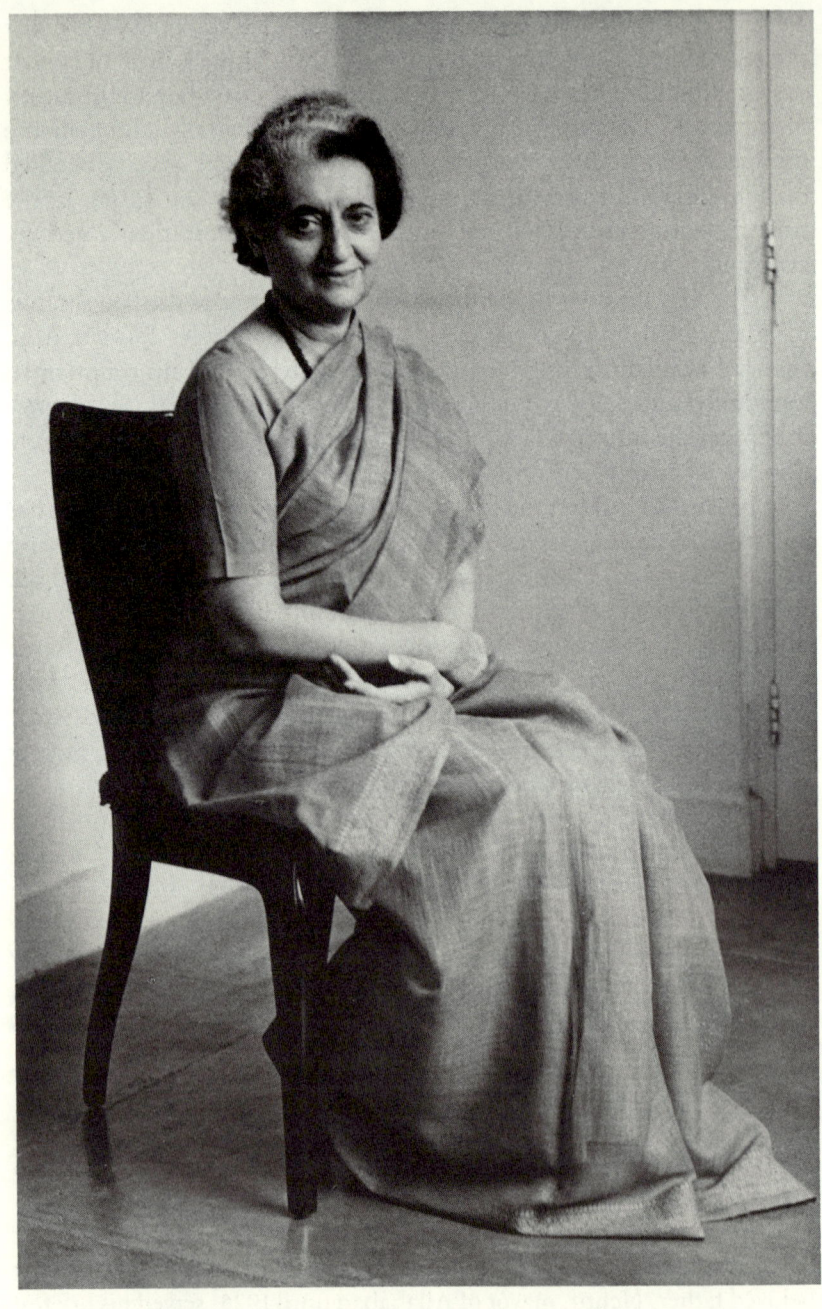

Indira Gandhi: photograph by T. S. Nagarajan, Bangalore, India.

Gandhi and the congress had called for a boycott of government-aided schools. Jawaharlal supported it, but having been educated at Harrow, Oxford, and the Inner Temple in London, he did not give up his long-range plans to have his daughter attend an English university. After a brief period at a kindergarten in Delhi, Indu was sent to the Modern School of Allahabad. Motilal, however, thought that the school's educational program was inadequate and peremptorily moved his granddaughter to St. Cecilia's, a private school run by three English sisters. Out of loyalty to the congress, Jawaharlal withdrew Indira from the school. Father and son compromised by having the girl taught by a private tutor at home.

The abrupt change completely deprived the lonely, aloof child of playmates. By herself she became a tomboy, running freely through the huge estate and climbing trees. When she played alone with her dolls, she pretended they were fighting nationalist battles, which the freedom fighters always won. Often she identified herself with Joan of Arc.

She had always sympathized with her mother's unhappiness in the face of family taunts, and now a new anxiety arose. In 1925, Kamala fell gravely ill, and doctors told Jawaharlal that she had pulmonary tuberculosis, which required treatment in a Swiss sanatorium. Jawaharlal acted immediately, bringing Kamala and Indira to Geneva, where the girl was enrolled in the International School and later was sent to L'École Nouvelle at Bex. Sometimes she accompanied her father on his visiting rounds and thus was introduced to such men as Albert Einstein, Romain Rolland, and Ernst Toller. She did not go with him on a trip to the Soviet Union, a tour that perked his interest in Marxist economy.

After Kamala was pronounced cured in the fall of 1927, the Nehrus returned to India. Suddenly Jawaharlal ended his opposition to placing his daughter in a non–Indian school and allowed her to enter classes at St. Mary's Convent in Allahabad. Still he insisted that she learn Hindi from a tutor.

The next summer, when Indira was spending a long vacation at Mussoorie, a hill station, her father, now general secretary of the Indian National Congress, of which Motilal was president, took time off from his work in Allahabad to write her a series of letters about prehistoric times that were later published as *Letters from a Father to a Daughter: Being a Brief Account of the Early Days of the World, Written for Children.*

Motilal Nehru gave Anand Bhavan to the congress in 1929, having built another home, almost as large, on other grounds of the estate. Since he wanted to use the name Anand Bhavan, the old house became known as Swaraj Bhavan (Freedom House).

That year Jawaharlal Nehru succeeded his father as head of the congress and presided over a historic session at Lahore that proclaimed the goal of complete independence for India. Meanwhile, Kamala began picketing the shops that sold foreign cloth. Longing to be active, Indira organized a Monkey Brigade for youngsters her own age whose mission was to smuggle messages, address envelopes, and spy on police stations to learn about possible arrests of congress members.

All India was talking about Gandhi's new campaign of civil disobedience, highlighted by a 200-mile march from his ashram to the sea to protest the Salt Acts, which made it a crime to possess salt not purchased from the British government. Once at their destination, Gandhi showed the hundreds who followed him how to extract salt from seawater.

In the same year, Jawaharlal landed behind bars for 99 days. From his cell he began a second series of letters to Indira, so comprehensive that they amounted to a correspondence course in world history.

About this time Kamala acquired her most devoted follower. One day while picketing a government college, she fainted. Among the youths who rushed to aid her was Feroze Gandhi, a stocky, handsome student, not related to Mohandas Gandhi, known as the Mahatma (Great Soul). Kamala's fragility, coupled with her quiet determination, affected him so strongly that he followed her wherever possible. Now she was also demanding equality for women. Indira would support female emancipation, too, but with less fervor than did her mother.

In January 1931, Kamala was put in jail for picketing. During such a bleak spell, with her father still a prisoner, Indira sadly watched her grandfather's rapid physical decline. As Motilal's death approached, his son and daughter-in-law were freed from jail, and their return helped Indira bear the loss of a loving mentor. A month later, beset by grief over his father and distress over Gandhi's declaration of a truce between himself and the British viceroy Lord Irwin (later Lord Halifax), Jawaharlal took his wife and daughter to Ceylon for a seven-week vacation to restore their spirits. It was the year the British moved the seat of government from Delhi, the capital since 1912, to New Delhi, a suburb.

On their return, at Gandhi's suggestion, the thin, somber-eyed Indira was sent to the Poona School, which had been founded by followers of the poet-philosopher Rabindranath Tagore. Soon Kamala was ailing again, the Gandhi-Irwin truce was broken, and Gandhi and Nehru were thrown in jail, Jawaharlal for 612 days. The solitude set him to writing more letters to Indira that would later be pubished as *Glimpses of World History: Being Further Letters to His Daughter Written in Prison and Containing a Rambling Account of History for Young People.*

Indira was overjoyed when her father came to visit her at Poona in 1933. But when she left the school the next year, he was again sent to prison—this time for 569 days. For a while, she joined her mother, who was undergoing treatment in Calcutta. By fall, Kamala accompanied Indira to Visna-Bharati, the university founded by Tagore at Shantiniketan. The university was a different world of Spartan living and constant exposure to the arts. Harmony reigned among students and teachers, who were always receptive to the uplifting presence of the saintly Tagore, with his white locks, white beard, and sensitive poet's face.

Less than a year later, in May 1935, with Nehru still in prison, Indira left with her mother for Badenweiler, Bavaria, where the sick woman was admitted to a sanatorium. One of her most frequent visitors was Feroze Gandhi, who had enrolled at the London School of Economics.

Kamala was subsequently moved to Lausanne in January of the new year, 1936, and Indira rejoined L'École Nouvelle in Bex. Agatha Harrison, Gandhi's representative in England, wrote of her: "What a pathetic figure, old beyond her years in experience and suffering." Mrs. Harrison helped obtain Jawaharlal Nehru's release from prison on compassionate grounds, and to Indira's immense relief he rushed to Kamala's bedside. Within a month, however, Kamala was dead. She did not live long enough to see Britain grant India a constitution that provided for future autonomy. Indira, who had been more attached to her mother than to anyone else, was deeply shaken.

But she had to fill the void. Jawaharlal had decided that she should be educated at Oxford, and she left Bex for England. While she was in London preparing for her entrance examinations, she counted on Feroze Gandhi for sympathy and companionship. Feroze also brought her to several meetings of left-wing organizations in London. Recurrent periods of depression, however, made studying so difficult that she failed her exams.

Indira came home in the spring of 1937 and accompanied her father on a tour of Southeast Asia. Reluctantly she then returned to England because he had asked her to try again to enter Oxford. Following a brief stay at Badminton School near Bristol, she passed the exams and in February 1938 went to Somerville College to read modern history.

Nehru arrived in Europe that summer and, after a visit to the leaders of the Spanish Republic in Barcelona, came to London. Indira begged to accompany him on further trips to France, Czechoslovakia, and Hungary, and he acquiesced. By November she decided to return with her father to India to regain her health, which had again deteriorated.

Back at Oxford in April 1939, she still could not settle down to studying and was depressed by the academic atmosphere. On frequent trips to London, however, she enjoyed Feroze's courtship, which increased in ardor as World War II began. Lord Linlithgow, the British viceroy, committed India to war, but the Indian National Congress demanded immediate self-government and refused to participate in the war effort.

On a walk through the woods in October, Indira was caught in a downpour and soaked to her skin. The resultant chill developed into pleurisy. After leaving the hospital, she was sent to Leysin, Switzerland, where she heard that her father was in prison for the eighth time for starting a new but limited civil disobedience campaign. He would remain behind bars for 398 days. Her convalescence lasted until November 1940. Returning to London by a circuitous route at the height of the blitz, she did some relief work, then with Feroze made another roundabout air journey, finally sailing for Bombay. To her joy, her father was free again. She felt no regrets that she had not taken a degree. During the six years since her mother's death, she had greatly matured and had learned a remarkable self-possession.

In her independent way, Indira stood firm when the fiercely proud Nehrus objected to her plans to marry Feroze, a Parsi. Although the Parsis had been successful in commerce, the Nehrus, typical Brahmins, looked down on these descendants of Persian refugees with their Zoroastrian beliefs. Mahatma Gandhi had named Jawaharlal his heir-apparent, and it seemed singularly inappropriate to bring a lower middle-class Parsi, whose family owned a general store, into the aristocratic Nehru family, mixing race and religion. On top of everything else, the Nehrus found it hard to accept a love marriage instead of the arranged marriage dictated by Hindu custom. But after the Mahatma indicated his approval, Jawaharlal gave his consent, and the wedding was held at Anand Bhavan in March 1942, with the usually serious-faced bride showing the dazzling smile she had inherited from her mother. The couple spent their honeymoon in the high green valleys and snows of Kashmir, the home of Jawaharlal's ancestors.

As they settled down in a small house in Allahabad in 1943, new political problems arose. India had become a huge base and training center for the Allies, and the Japanese threatened to invade. Thereupon the Mahatma called on the British to leave so that a free India could stand up to the enemy. In August, Jawaharlal Nehru moved a "Quit India" resolution at a meeting of the All Congress Committee. Two days later he, Gandhi, and the other congress leaders were arrested, and the leftist members initiated a massive revolt in protest. Indira watched her father taken away for the ninth time. It would be his longest detention, 1,040 days.

Soon Feroze went underground, and Indira returned to Anand Bhavan, which was under British surveillance. When she attended a ceremony to hoist the congress's tricolor, a young man holding the flag passed it to her as the police began dragging him away. She continued to carry the flag even though she was beaten with a *lathi,* or metal-topped pole.

When Indira heard of her own imminent arrest, she decided to speak at a public meeting in the center of Allahabad. Before she could begin, the British took her into custody. Afterward, she considered her arrest to have been one of the most meaningful moments of her life because it brought her full circle with her parents.

She joined her aunt Mrs. Pandit and cousin Lekha in Naini Prison, where Jawaharlal had spent so many years. He was still at a fortress in Ahmednagar, 100 miles to the south. The living conditions at Naini could only be described as foul, but Indira and the Pandits endured them for nine months. Later she asserted that the difficult period had toughened her character.

Feroze, who also had been imprisoned, was released three months after his wife and went to work as an insurance agent. On the side he wrote articles for various magazines. In the sweltering summer of 1944, Rajiv Gandhi was born.

During the war, the British tried to reach some agreement on independence, but always seemed thwarted by Muslim demands that a separate Muslim country, Pakistan, be carved out of India. Nehru was vehemently opposed to partition. In 1945 he was back home and involved in the congress's affairs, but he did not know how to solve the Muslim problem. Then, in 1946, Britain offered independence as soon as Indian leaders could agree on a government. Before long, they chose Jawaharlal Nehru as head of an interim regime. Feroze succeeded his father-in-law as managing editor of the *National Herald,* a paper Nehru had founded in Lucknow. Indira's second son Sanjay was born in December of that exciting year.

After Hindu-Muslim tensions exploded into riots and bloodshed, British and Indian leaders agreed to divide India. There seemed no other way to end the violence. Lord Louis Mountbatten, the new viceroy, oversaw the partition into two dominions within the British Commonwealth of Nations, India as an independent dominion, Pakistan as a British dominion. August 15, 1947, was proclaimed Independence Day; temple bells rang out, fireworks burst noisily, and crowds danced and sang in exuberant celebrations. As leader of the Constituent Assembly, which would govern India for the next few years, Jawaharlal was sworn in as the first prime minister of the Government of India (Independent). The ceremony in New Delhi was a proud moment for him and his daughter.

Partition saddened both Gandhi and Nehru, who had worked for a united country. The situation grew more painful with continuing civil war between the Hindus and Muslims. As religious rioting escalated, the wizened Mahatma began a fast in January 1948 to end the bloodshed that had wiped out entire villages. Five days later, the fighting stopped, and he ended his fast. But within 12 days, a Hindu fanatic, who hated Gandhi's program of political and religious tolerance, shot him to death.

The tragedy numbed Indira and her father. Hardly had they recovered from their grief when Pakistan invaded Kashmir, claiming that most of its people were Muslims. For protection, its Hindu ruler made it part of India, and fighting between Pakistan and India continued until a United Nations cease-fire was arranged in 1949. After the war with Pakistan, Nehru had to deal with more problems: Hindu refugees were streaming into India, and the princely states had to be integrated into the federal structure.

Meanwhile, in November 1948, the Constituent Assembly adopted the new constitution, which declared that India was an independent, democratic republic. The constitution was to take effect at the beginning of 1950.

With her father in office, Indira first commuted between Lucknow and New Delhi, sharing hostess duties with her aunt Krishna. But Nehru soon decided he needed her full-time companionship and support. In 1949, Indira and her children joined the prime minister at Teen Murti House, once the official residence of the commander in chief of the British-Indian armed forces. Her roles were those of chatelaine, hostess, and confidante. One of her tasks was to take charge of the family zoo, for

Nehru, who was particularly fond of animals, kept a panda, tiger cubs, numerous dogs, and birds. Remembering her own lonely childhood, Indira arranged to spend a lot of time with her sons. It was Feroze who had to commute.

Extending over five months, the first general election in India was held from October 1951 to March 1952. The Indian National Congress had become the Congress party, with Nehru as its leader. Indira and Feroze were both members. Feroze, who had joined his family at Teen Murti Bhavan on a full-time basis, won election to the Lok Sabha, or lower house of Parliament. But he could not easily adapt to Teen Murti Bhavan, where life revolved around an often-temperamental prime minister, and he took an apartment to receive his constant stream of visitors.

Ambitious to bring India into the modern age of scientific, technological development, Nehru launched the first of several five-year plans. At the same time he considered himself an apostle of socialist, secular democracy with a special concern for the poor and the outcasts.

Internationally, he stood for nonviolence and world peace. With these ideals, espoused by Mahatma Gandhi, he became the high priest of nonalignment in the developing world. Indira accompanied him on important trips to the United States, China, and the Soviet Union, using each one to learn more about social welfare programs.

Two men who pushed Indira toward public service were M. O. Mathai, Nehru's special assistant, and V. K. Krishna Menon, chief adviser on foreign policy, whom Indira knew from her student days in London. By 1955 she was ready to take political steps herself. Becoming a member of the working committee of the executive of the Congress party, she was given special responsibilities for the women's department and the youth organization. She was elected to the party's central election committee in 1957 and to the Congress Parliamentary Board in 1958. Once she entered public life, she never again appeared in Western dress.

One year later, somewhat to her father's concern, she was elected president of the Congress party. But Nehru's worries lessened when he saw her determination to forge unity and bring new blood into the party ranks. Shrewdly she took advantage of the Hindu tradition, which extolled powerful women in religion, literature, and history. Her aunt, Vijaya Lakshmi Pandit, had led India's first delegation to the United Nations and had been elected president of the General Assembly in 1953. After her one-year term ended, she had served as India's ambassador to the United States, Britain, the Soviet Union, and Spain.

The president of the Congress party found that her biggest problem lay with the Communists in the state of Kerala, who did little to advance the party's policies. She went to Kerala and proved so effective a speaker that the Communists left and the Congress party ruled Kerala once more. But again she was in frail health, and within a year she resigned.

After regaining her strength, Indira gave her attention to social welfare even as she remained her father's indispensable hostess. Always uncomfortable in Teen Murti Bhavan, Feroze Gandhi not only worked but now lived in a separate apartment, managing, however, to remain a devoted father to his sons. There was no talk of divorce, only recognition that Indira was fully occupied with helping her father bear the burdens of his office. After Feroze recovered from a heart attack in 1959, Indira brought him to Kashmir for a holiday to recapture some of their honeymoon memories. When he died of a second heart attack in 1960, throngs turned out for his funeral procession. He had won great popularity in the Lok Sabha for exposing corruption in an insurance corporation.

Indira was elected a member of the executive of the Congress party in 1961. That year Nehru's policy of nonviolence lost credence in the Western world when he sent Indian troops into the Portuguese colony of Goa, the last remaining colonial outpost in India.

Nationally, his popularity was tarnished the next year when the Chinese, capping long-term border disputes, invaded Assam and Kashmir, and the proud Indian army suffered defeat after defeat. The prime minister called on Western help, and on the eve of victory the Chinese withdrew. Indira had acted as chair of the Citizens' Central Council to consolidate civil defense.

Nehru, the tall, slender aristocrat, who always appeared in a Gandhi cap and with a rose in his buttonhole, was now 73 and clearly in ill health. He suffered one stroke at the end of 1963 and a second one in January 1964. During his convalescence, Indira was virtually the acting prime minister. Following a third stroke, he died in May. His grief-stricken daughter and her sons moved out of Teen Murti Bhavan into a big house at One Safdarjung Road.

Nehru's successor, the sparrowlike Lal Bahadur Shastri, wanted Indira Gandhi to become foreign minister, but she told him that she needed time to recover from her loss. For a while she considered joining her sons in England. Rajiv was at the Imperial College in London, and Sanjay was at a Rolls-Royce factory at Crewe, learning about car manufacturing.

She gave up this plan, however, to make a successful run for the Lok

Sabha. Then she finally agreed to become Shastri's minister of information and broadcasting. At once, she set about doubling the amount of broadcasting time and opening radio and television to the opposition and independents. Beyond India, she had long been active in the United Nations Educational, Scientific, and Cultural Organization (UNESCO) and now was elected to its executive board.

In September 1965, Pakistan once again invaded Indian-held Kashmir, and another war began. The two countries had clashed in April over the Rann of Kutch, where oil was the suspected prize, but British Prime Minister Harold Wilson had brought about a truce. For the war over Kashmir, which proved to be without victors, the United Nations arranged a cease-fire.

Shastri died of a heart attack in Tashkent in January 1966, the day after he had signed a peace accord with Pakistani President Mohammed Ayub Khan. With many possible successors standing in line, Home Minister Gulzarilal Nanda was named interim prime minister. Kumaraswamy Kamaraj, head of the Syndicate, a caucus of party bigwigs, believed that he was acting in the interests of national unity when he convinced Nehru's daughter to run for the party leadership. Since the Congress party held a majority, the post of prime minister would fall to its chief. One candidate, Morarji Desai, the former prime minister, was an anathema to the Syndicate, which believed that Indira was more malleable.

Indira defeated Desai by a vote of 355 to 169. On January 24, wearing a red rose — Nehru fashion — in her homespun sari with shawl, she became prime minister, assuming as well the portfolio of minister of atomic energy. One political journal commented: "A woman ruler is under a special handicap until she has been able to consolidate her position. In the beginning every group leader wants to advise and control her." To reporters, Indira Gandhi insisted that her sex was irrelevant and immaterial: "I am not a woman. I am a human being."

She faced an economic crisis, brought on by still-unpaid costs from the Chinese border war of 1962 and an unparalleled drought that hit at the same time as the Indo-Pakistani War. To make matters worse, the United States had stopped all economic aid during the war.

Making her first appearance as prime minister before the Lok Sabha on March 1, Indira felt strained and jittery, and, sensing her plight, opposition members constantly interrupted her. She sounded so inarticulate that one politician gave her the nickname "Dumb Doll," an epithet that stuck despite her later effective speeches.

At the end of the month she left for a goodwill trip to Washington. Small and slender, with her jet black hair showing a dramatic streak of white, she completely charmed President Lyndon B. Johnson, who warmed to her elegance and gracious bearing. During their talks, she learned that the United States was deeply interested in the devaluation of the rupee and in getting American money invested in fertilizer production and other enterprises. Gandhi made the wished-for concessions and, in return, received pledges of tons of food grains and assurances of loans. She also agreed to mute her criticism of the Vietnam War. Returning to New Delhi, she was accused of selling out to the United States.

In June she informed the full cabinet that she had devalued the rupee to boost sagging exports and to curb the thriving black market. An angry Kamaraj demanded a meeting of the Congress party's working committee, but she refused to call one.

Food supplies from the United States often proved to be irregular, and Indira soon believed that Washington had humiliated her. She began speaking about Vietnam again and deplored the bombing of Haiphong and Hanoi. Since the Soviets had been unhappy about her trip to Washington, she went to Moscow in July to give reassurances of friendship. There she condemned "imperial aggression" and signed a communiqué demanding an immediate halt to the bombing of North Vietnam.

The shortage of food caused galloping inflation, and food riots erupted in various provinces, especially Kerala, where the imposition of regional food zones had led to a short supply of rice. Although pressed by both the Left and the Right to abolish the zones, Gandhi gave in to Kamaraj and the Syndicate, which could not brook the idea of amending the resolution that had set them up.

There were further troubles. When Punjab state was divided between Sikhs and Hindus, protests and violence broke out. Demonstrations against the slaughter of cows provoked street battles. Students churned up unrest.

Nonetheless, Gandhi campaigned vigorously for the upcoming election in 1967. During one stormy meeting, somebody hurled a stone at her nose, fracturing it. After her nose was set, she jokingly complained that since it was too long, the doctor should have used the opportunity to make it beautiful. Kamaraj and two of his cohorts lost their legislative seats, and their defeat allowed Gandhi to hold on to her post. She also gained some strength when her rival Desai accepted the job of deputy prime minister and finance minister. Still, the Congress party held only 200 of 500 seats in the lower house. Gandhi expected the radical Left to take advantage of the situation, but its members were deeply divided. Although total food production had increased, endless labor strife resulted in strikes and lockouts of management. The Gandhi government did little to curb the unrest.

In typical seesaw fashion, food production worsened again in 1968, and the nation's birthrate continued to soar. Gandhi initiated a birth control program and made contraceptives available in distribution clinics throughout India.

Her work schedule was always full, 12 to 16 hours a day, and there were frequent and strenuous tours of state. Despite her diligence, Indira Gandhi sensed that her power was eroding. The Syndicate of old party bosses had already decided to get rid of her, and when President Zakir Husain died in May 1969, it nominated Neelam Sanjiva Reddy, speaker of the lower house, whom Gandhi regarded as her enemy. This act emboldened her. Defiantly she supported Varahagiri Venkata Giri, a trade union leader.

Before the election was held in August, she outplayed the bosses. She pushed through a law nationalizing 14 of the nation's commercial banks and fired Desai as finance minister. Giri won, but only by a small margin.

The president of the Congress party, Siddavanahalli Nyalingappa, belonged to the old guard and continued to oppose Gandhi. That December there were two Congress parties, Nyalingappa's and Gandhi's. The bosses "expelled" Jawaharlal Nehru's daughter from the party Nehru had helped build, but most members supported her. This political battle was fought against the background of week-long riots as the everbelligerent Hindus and Muslims kept slaughtering each other.

The old party bosses joined the rightist parties, but Gandhi stayed on because of leftist backing. As elections in Kerala loomed in September 1970, she decided to enter them in coalition with the pro–Moscow Communists and the Muslim League. Her victory crushed the Syndicate and set back the machine of the Marxist Communists. Early in 1971, Gandhi won absolute control of the Lok Sabha and felt ready to speed ahead with her program of moderate socialism.

Only a few days after her election triumph, the Pakistani army struck brutally against Sheikh Mujib-ur Rahman's Awami League, which demanded independence for East Pakistan, separated from West Pakistan by more than a thousand miles of Indian territory. The "independent sovereign republic of Bangladesh" was proclaimed in April. Through the next half year, refugees, many suffering from cholera and dysentery, clogged the roads of escape into India.

Gandhi hoped that Pakistani President Agha Muhammad Yahya Khan would sit down at a conference table with Mujib, but no negotiations took place. In December, the Indian army carried out a pincer attack on Dacca and defeated the Pakistani defenders in 12 days. India was the first to recognize the new nation of Bangladesh. Soon after, the Pakistani army surrendered, and Mujib, who had been under arrest, returned as prime minister of Bangladesh. Meanwhile, Gandhi signed a 20-year treaty of peace, friendship, and cooperation with the Soviet Union. Having called up more than 600,000 reservists, she went to the United States and its Western allies, asking them to pressure Yahya Khan to negotiate. In spite of her efforts, a war broke out in December.

The war lasted only two weeks, and India won a total victory and a reputation as Asia's major military power. Gandhi, often compared to the goddess Durga riding on her tiger, had never been more popular. She used the war triumph to make a sweep in provincial elections, driving out any old party bosses who were left. Still, landowners and well-to-do peasants controlled crucial sections of the Congress party, and Gandhi's plan to give land to perhaps 100 million peasants went nowhere.

Far more unsettling, the old problems returned in 1972. The lack of monsoon rains brought severe drought and grain shortages. There was no help from the United States, which had cut off aid after tilting toward Pakistan in the recent war. Along with the other problems, industry stagnated.

Its economy failing to improve, India was restless through much of 1973. Food riots over lean rations often ended violently. As one form of relief effort, the government put people to work building roads or crushing rocks. It also nationalized the grain trade, a move that prompted severe criticism.

Although relations with the United States improved gradually, distrust remained. Ties with the Kremlin grew stronger, and when Leonid Brezhnev, general secretary of the Communist party, came to New Delhi in November, he and Gandhi signed an agreement providing for greatly increased aid over the next 15 years.

The rains of 1974 brought relief to some states but devastating floods to others. Prices rose rapidly; the nation, which needed oil so badly, suffered from the Arab oil squeeze. When 2 million railroad workers walked out, the prime minister fought back by arresting strikers, firing some, and evicting many from their company-owned homes.

But even her enemies recognized that Gandhi probably had dealt better with the plethora of terrible problems than any other leader could have done. Yet there remained a hard core of disillusioned Indians who accused her of trusting no one and of being too autocratic, as well as being amorally indifferent to dishonesty and corruption, even financial scandals. Cronies and cliques had a rapid turnover.

Soon a powerful opposition movement, led by a respected politician, Jayaprakash Narayan ("J P"), began gathering against her. The "J P Movement" became a rallying point for all who questioned Gandhi's moral authority.

Feeling the same pride they had shown during the war, Indians wildly applauded the atomic test that made India the sixth member of the nuclear club. But the under-the-sands explosion, which the prime minister said was for peaceful purposes, brought worldwide condemnation.

Gandhi received the shock of her life on the morning of June 12, 1975, when the high court in Allahabad, considering a suit by a defeated opponent, Raj Narain, ruled that she had won her parliamentary seat in 1971 by corrupt means. She was ordered to give up the seat and was barred from seeking elective office for six years. On the same day, her candidates in a provincial election were beaten by a party coalition led by her old enemy Desai.

Two weeks later, at her bidding, President Fakhruddin Ali Ahmed ordered a state of emergency owing to internal disturbances. Desai was among those rounded up. To the dismay of her aunt Mrs. Pandit, a member of the opposition, Gandhi's majority in Parliament approved the emergency laws in July.

One law allowed her to rule by proclamation. Another declared that the courts could not review her actions. The day before Gandhi was to begin her appeal to the Supreme Court, the election law was changed retroactively so that she was absolved of any past offenses. In November the court reversed her conviction.

Now she made sure that she was beyond all legal challenges. The Lok Sabha passed a set of constitutional amendments allowing the president to follow the prime minister's instructions and to amend the constitution single-handedly for two years. These amendments took away the courts' right of review of those amendments except for procedural reasons. Now the government could disregard the individual rights of a person engaged in "antinational activities." Thousands were arrested. Permanent censorship of all newspapers was ordered in January. It was little wonder that many designated Indira Gandhi the most powerful woman in the world and perhaps one of the most powerful in history.

Her older son Rajiv, who had become an airplane pilot, showed no inclination for politics, but the younger, Sanjay, had become his mother's closest adviser. It was widely believed that Gandhi was grooming him to follow her as prime minister. As a member of the Congress party's youth wing, Sanjay acted arrogantly and impulsively. He was constantly attacked on grounds that, trading on his mother's name, he mixed politics and business deals, one connected to the manufacture of a small India-made car.

Few people understood why in 1977 Gandhi suddenly called for the elections she had earlier postponed. Intelligence sources warned of defeat for the Congress party, but Sanjay reportedly told her to disregard them. He appeared unaware of the anger he had aroused in the north of India after he ordered thousands of men to undergo vasectomies. Other advisers also reported that the time was ripe for victory, and when astrologers confirmed this opinion, Indira swept ahead. Both she and Sanjay were badly beaten. The Congress party gained only 153 seats, losing by more than half. Desai and his Janata party were the victors, and he became prime minister.

Over the next month Desai kept predicting Gandhi's detention and trial for her behavior. As she stood before cheering crowds, she defied him to do his worst. In early October 1977, police came to her door and arrested her, but the next morning a magistrate set her free. A higher court, however, received a governmental appeal.

Indira Gandhi was down, though not out. In January 1978, her devoted followers left the Congress party to form the Congress-I (I for Indira) party, which a few months later was recognized as the official opposition party in Parliament.

The Janata party remained weak and loose; internal dissension was beginning to wreck it. Desai failed to deal with hunger, unemployment, labor unrest, and the conflict between untouchables and members of the higher castes over the opening of more civil service jobs.

But while rejoicing that Indira had regained power in the Lok Sabha, the Gandhi family had new worries. Criminal charges had been lodged against Sanjay for his business dealings. Then a governmental commission reported that during the 18-month emergency rule, the Gandhi government had carried out illegal and repressive acts and violations of human rights.

As soon as Indira was elected in the state of Karnataka in November, Desai took away her seat and ordered her jailed for contempt because she had blocked a probe of Sanjay's affairs in 1975. Her supporters staged such violent protests that she was released from jail on December 26. Six months later, fearful of not receiving a vote of confidence in the Lok Sabha, Desai resigned. With the fatal splintering of the Janata party, Indira Gandhi became a kingmaker. Two rivals fought for the succession, Charan Singh, finance minister, and Jagjivan Ram, defense minister and leader of the untouchables. With support from the 71-member Congress-I party, Singh formed a cabinet that mixed pro–Moscow Communists and Conservatives. Gandhi, however, demanded a steep price for her support: All charges against herself and Sanjay had to be dropped. Singh refused to do so, and his cabinet fell. At this juncture Gandhi persuaded President Reddy to order elections for January 1980. She and the Congress-I party swept to a landslide victory, and she was again prime minister. Quickly she dismissed hostile governments in nine provinces, and Sanjay handpicked the replacement candidates for a new election.

Next, Gandhi had to call out the army against a general strike staged by a dissident movement in Assam protesting the influx of Bengali immigrants from Bangladesh.

Then in June a family tragedy struck. Sanjay was at the controls of a sophisticated stunt plane when it crashed over New Delhi. Gandhi almost collapsed, but forced herself to carry on. As her adviser, she turned to Rajiv, who gave up his flying career to answer her call to enter politics.

Following Sanjay's death, she began to emphasize foreign policy initiatives. She signed a joint declaration of cooperation with the Soviet Union, then turned to seeking closer ties with the United States. In 1982 she visited Washington, resolving a dispute over atomic fuel, and made a trip to Moscow.

Although busy with election preparations, Gandhi took time in March 1983 to host a summit conference of 101 Third World nations and organizations in New Delhi; she was credited with returning the movement to a more moderate stance.

It was an especially turbulent year. The Congress party had controlled two southern states, Andhra Pradesh and Karnataka, since 1947; to Gandhi's dismay, she lost them both in the election. Her entire cabinet and council of ministers felt forced to resign. All the while, Sikh nationalists staged violent demonstrations in Punjab state, where they demanded greater autonomy. During elections in Assam, Hindus rioted to prevent Muslim Bangladeshi immigrants from voting, and 3,000 died.

With Rajiv, his Italian-born wife Sonia, and their daughter and son, Gandhi's relations remained close and loving. It was otherwise with Sanjay's widow, Maneka; Maneka formed a party to oppose Rajiv, who had won Sanjay's seat. Rajiv's rise was swift. He was soon secretary-general of the Congress-I party.

The massacre of 1919 had burned the name of Amritsar into Hindu memory. Sixty-five years later, Amritsar again became the scene of tragedy. Sikh extremists occupied the Golden Temple, and Indian troops invaded it in June 1984. The incident led to smoldering hatred among the Sikhs, some of whom were members of Gandhi's security guard.

On the morning of October 24, 1984, as she was on her way across her garden to a television interview with actor-playwright Peter Ustinov, two Sikh security guards shot her to death. A horror-stricken Ustinov beheld her crumpled body, draped in the vivid saffron sari she had chosen for the cameras.

Rajiv was immediately appointed prime minister. He, too, was destined for a tragic end. Ousted in 1989, he campaigned again in 1991. During a rally in May, a Sri Lankan Tamil woman, with explosives strapped around her waist, threw herself on him; the blast tore away his face and part of his body. When Rajiv's devastated widow declined to finish his campaign, it was clear that the Nehru-Gandhi political dynasty had run its course.

GOLDA MEIR

Prime Minister of Israel
(1969–74)

When Golda Meir became prime minister of Israel in 1969, her political adviser, Simcha Dimetz, assured the press that she possessed "the best qualities of a woman—intuition, insight, sensitivity, and compassion—plus the best qualities of a man—strength, determination, practicality, purposefulness." Much of the world would come to accept that judgment.

What mattered most to Golda Meir throughout her life was the fact that she was a Jew. She was born on May 3, 1898, in Kiev, the Ukraine, Russia, to Moshe Yitzhak Mabovitch and his wife Blume, née Naiditch. Their first child, Sheyna, had arrived in 1886, and between that date and Golda's birth year the Mabovitches had buried five infant sons.

Golda, named for her stubborn and bossy great-grandmother, was called Goldie almost at once. Her earliest memory, from the age of four, was seeing her father nail boards across the door of their house in anticipation of a Cossack-led pogrom, which fortunately did not materialize. That same year, 1902, her sister Zipke was born.

As a superior craftsman, Moshe had been permitted to live outside the Pale of Settlement for Jews. But he was often discriminated against because of his religion and was always underpaid or not paid at all. To escape the battle for survival, he booked passage for the United States in 1903, leaving his family temporarily behind. With his departure, the Mabovitches moved back within the Pale. Blume took her three daughters to Pinsk to live with her father, who ran a tavern. After a time, she began selling homemade cakes and bread to rich customers; soon she did so well she was able to rent a little house for her family.

By now Sheyna had joined a group of teenagers involved in the revolutionary movement against the czarist regime. Often she led meetings in the Mabovitch kitchen when her mother was out. Squeezed on a shelf above the big coal stove, her younger sister listened intensely to the passionate rhetoric.

Like Kiev, Pinsk would leave Goldie with bitter memories of the pain of being a Jew in Russia. Once when she and Zipke were playing in the muddy street, a small band of Cossacks, thundering by on horseback, leaped over their heads, barely missing them. Another time, a drunken peasant terrified Goldie and one of her friends by banging their heads together and shouting that all Jews needed to be so treated.

If Blume was unaware of the kitchen meetings, she at least knew about Sheyna's associates and considered them dangerous. She appealed to her husband for help; when Goldie was eight, Moshe Mabovitch sent for his family. He had settled in Milwaukee, Wisconsin, and worked as a railroad carpenter. Soon after the immigrants arrived, Blume opened a little grocery store serving their predominantly Jewish neighborhood to supplement the family income.

Enrolled in the Fourth Street Elementary School, Golda was a bright, cheerful, independent child, who quickly mastered English and showed leadership qualities. At age ten she effectively organized the America Young Sisters' Society, which bought textbooks for poor children.

About this time Sheyna, who had a spot on her lungs that was diagnosed as tuberculosis, left for Denver, Colorado, and the Jewish Hospital for Consumptives. She had argued incessantly with her parents, usually about her radicalism. Ultimately Golda also became rebellious, complaining that her parents were too strict. For her the final straw came when she was 14, an age Blume considered eminently marriageable. Golda learned that her mother was secretly negotiating with an "old" prospect, a relatively successful businessman in his early 30s.

After her recovery, Sheyna married Shamir (Sam) Korngold, her boyfriend from Kiev, who had followed her to Denver. The young couple operated a dry cleaning shop. Golda decided that her opportunity lay with them in Denver, and one January morning in 1913 she stole off on a train, having plotted her flight after months of secret correspondence with the Korngolds. Left behind was a note informing her parents where she had gone. Living with the Korngolds, Golda attended high school and worked for her brother-in-law.

She had blossomed early, with a slim figure, expressive eyes, and

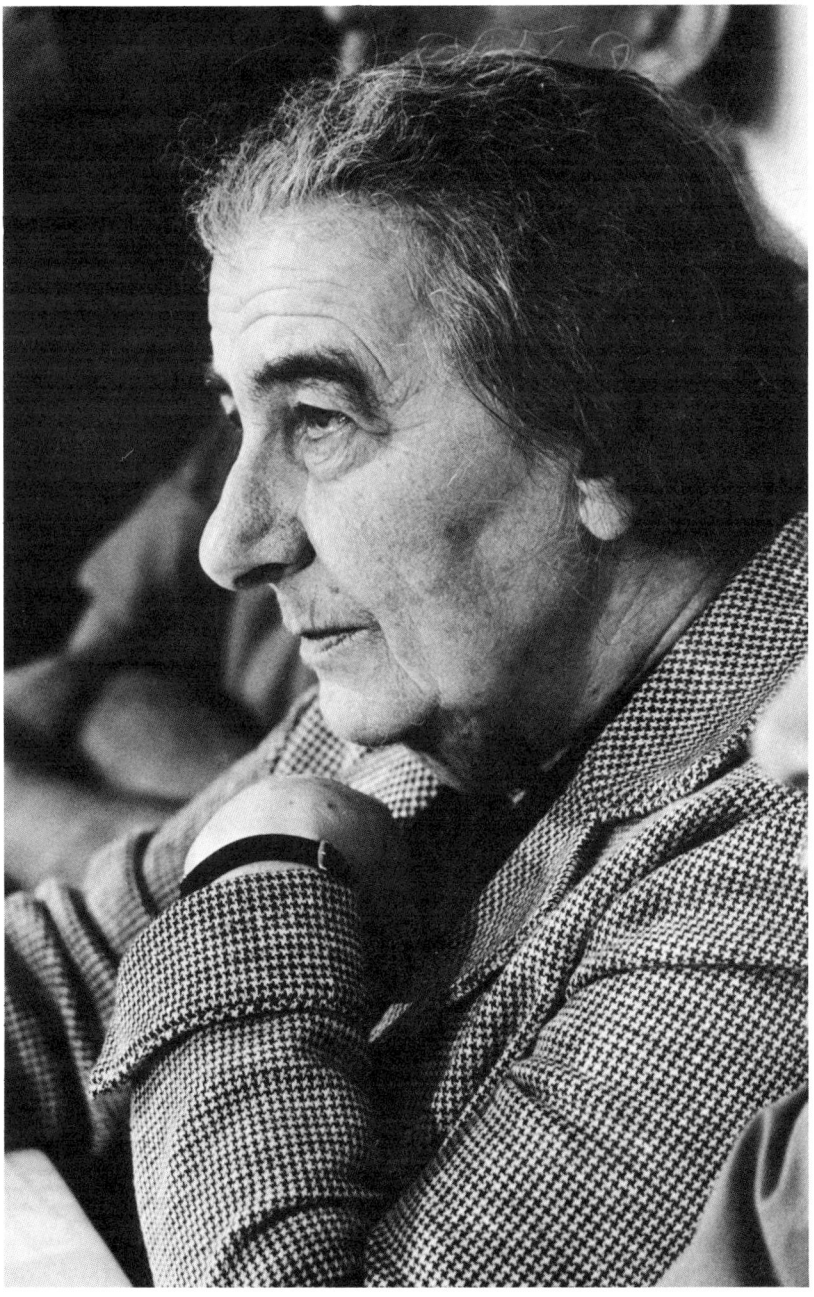

Golda Meir: courtesy Consulate General of Israel, Los Angeles.

glowing dark hair. Her good looks attracted so many young men that Sheyna scolded her about having too active a social life. Of all those who swarmed about her, Golda felt most drawn to Morris Meyerson, a shy, studious sign painter, who was far from handsome. His attraction was that he introduced her to a new cultural world she found fascinating. Whenever he could afford tickets, they attended plays and concerts. But in the midst of this rewarding companionship, quarrels with the Korngolds grew so frequent that Golda left their apartment and employ, quit school, took a room of her own, and worked both in a laundry and a library.

By 1914 she decided to return home. She had long wanted to become a teacher, and she believed opportunities would be better in Milwaukee. Before leaving Denver, she became secretly engaged to Morris. The home atmosphere she found much improved, and her feelings toward her parents warmed even more as they began making their house a haven for Jewish Legion volunteers. Golda finished high school, began teaching Yiddish at a *folkschule,* and in the fall of 1916 enrolled at the Teachers' Training College in Milwaukee. But she did not stay a whole year because she found her time taken up with her activities in the Poale Zion (Labor Zionist) organization, dedicated to finding a homeland for the Jews.

Once there had been an independent Jewish state in the area called Palestine. Through the centuries the Jews had suffered the Babylonian Captivity, Roman rule, and various invasions, but had never given up hope of gaining political independence. Escaping from the rampant anti–Semitism of eastern Europe, the first settlers from Russia and Romania arrived in Palestine in 1881, followed by more colonists. In 1897 the Austrian journalist Theodor Herzl formally founded modern Zionism at an international congress in Basel, Switzerland. He tried to obtain a charter to set up a separate state, but the Turks, who ruled Palestine, gave him no encouragement. In 1906 a second aliyah, or homecoming, took place, with 400,000 emigrants arriving from Russia. Since then, Jews all over the world had kept up a drumbeat for a Jewish state.

Herzl was one of Golda's heroes, and she could think of little else than going to Palestine. Morris, who had moved to Milwaukee, was less enthusiastic, and they quarreled frequently. Putting principle above love, she broke their engagement and plunged into action, beginning a recruiting job in Chicago for the Poale Zion Midwest. She worked evenings for the movement and afternoons at a public library.

The United States entered World War I in April 1917, but Morris was not drafted because of his poor eyesight. Suddenly he yielded to Golda's wishes and promised to accompany her to Palestine after the war.

That November the Jews harbored new hopes of success. The Russian-born Zionist Chaim Weizmann, a teacher of chemistry in Manchester, England, had discovered an improved method for making acetone, used in the manufacture of explosives, and thereby had won such acceptance at Whitehall that he persuaded the British government to issue a paper favoring the establishment of a Jewish state in Palestine. (Bitterly the Arabs there remembered that in 1915 the British, while fighting the Turks, had promised that Palestine would become an Arab state.) This declaration bore the name of the British prime minister, Arthur Balfour. More hope came in 1918 with news that British troops had finally driven out the Turks.

On December 24, 1917, Golda and Morris were married by a rabbi at the Mabovitch home. To her father's dismay, she quickly began going on the road for Poale Zion. Meanwhile, doggedly persistent, she scrimped and saved for the journey to Palestine. More than ever, she was an activist, thrilled to exuberance over attending in Philadelphia in the winter of 1918 the first American Jewish Congress, which demonstratively called for a Jewish homeland.

Jewish euphoria was somewhat dampened in 1920 when Britain received a League of Nations mandate over Palestine. The next year Britain divided the country at the Jordan River. East of the river it created Transjordan and installed as its emir Abdullah ibn Hussein, a member of the Hashemite family of Arab leaders.

Even with the dream darkened, the Meyersons were ready to emigrate. Golda had also persuaded Sheyna and her two children and her childhood friend, Regina Hamburger, to come with them. Sam Korngold would arrive later.

During the 53-day journey, almost everything that could go wrong went wrong. Even the baggage was temporarily lost. But finally the party arrived in Tel Aviv, where the Meyersons and Sheyna rented a two-room apartment. More than anything, Golda wanted to settle on a kibbutz, where members owned all the property in common and pooled their labor to cultivate crops in a former desert wasteland. But she and Morris could not go immediately to the Kibbutz Merhavia, her choice, and had to stay in Tel Aviv waiting to hear if they had been accepted. While Golda gave English lessons and learned Hebrew, Morris worked as a bookkeeper for a British firm in Lydda and came to Tel Aviv only on weekends.

When their acceptance papers arrived after worrisome delays, Golda expected to find an enthusiastic reception at the kibbutz. Instead, she met disapproval of her American background, perceived as fostering softness, indulgence, and spoiled behavior. Morris gained a transient popularity because of his records and his phonograph without a horn. Before long, Golda won over the colony with her exuberant personality, her determination, and her remarkable vitality. She thought that her link to the phonograph also helped. Eagerly she pitched into any task assigned her in the fields or the chicken house. Suggestions she made about better kitchen management were first rejected, then gratefully accepted.

But within a few months Morris was clearly unhappy. Hard physical labor was taking a toll on his never too robust health. While Golda thrived, he suffered. Soon she had progressed so far in kibbutz favor that she was sent as a delegate to a convention of the Histadrut (the General Federation of Jewish Labor), which also served as a shadow government. There she impressed David Remez, the head of Histadrut's contracting and public works enterprise.

Morris's pleas to leave Merhavia fell on his wife's deaf ears until an attack of malaria sapped all his strength, and Golda realized they must get out. They had hardly arrived in Tel Aviv when Morris was offered work as a bookkeeper in Remez's offices in Jerusalem, where Golda was a part-time cashier.

A son Menahem was born in November 1924. After six months, Golda returned to Merhavia to try kibbutz motherhood. She had hoped to work the land, but was put in charge of five additional children. Within half a year she was ready to go back to Jerusalem.

Morris earned little money, and the next years were full of privation. Following the birth of a daughter Sarah in 1926, Golda did laundry at home to pay for her son's nursery school and sometimes gave private English lessons. It was a period of despair for the restless young mother, who desperately wanted to be a moving force in the Zionist movement.

But Golda did not lack for sympathy; her family was close by. Sheyna often helped her. Moshe and Blume Mabovitch had emigrated to Israel in 1926 and lived in Herzliah. Only their youngest daughter Zipke, who called herself Clara, remained in the United States.

While Golda took on the duties of motherhood, Remez had not forgotten her. In 1928 he again stepped in, feeling she was perfect for the job of secretary to the Histadrut's Women's Labor Council in Tel Aviv. The job involved going on many speaking tours, as well as setting up training farms for Jewish girls who emigrated to Palestine to work on the land.

Golda could not resist the challenge, although it meant renewed separation from Morris except on weekends. The children lived with her in Tel Aviv, attended nursery school, and were looked after by a helper till their mother, often tardy, came home from work. Years later, Golda said that the type of woman who cannot remain at home cannot let children narrow her horizons. Yet she was always painfully aware of the price of breaking away from domestic duties. As she wrote: "My children have a very close relationship with me, but if I am to be honest with myself there is a little—maybe more than a little—pang of conscience over the injustice I have done to them. I know that when they were little they suffered a lot on my account."

In 1930, David Ben-Gurion, longtime general secretary of the Histadrut, merged two major labor parties and founded the United Labor party, also called Mapai. Golda became a loyal member, never deviating from its principles. Politically middle-of-the-road, it would be known as the establishment party for statehood.

She was on a speaking tour of the United Kingdom in 1932 when Morris wired her that their daughter Sarah was gravely ill with kidney disease. Golda rushed back to Tel Aviv, where she learned that Sarah would get the best possible treatment in the United States, a therapy that might take two years. So she asked for an assignment as national secretary of the Pioneer Women, an organization that worked among American women to spread the Zionist cause. Menahem accompanied his mother and sister and stayed with friends while Golda traveled about making speeches that won over audiences with their plain style.

Sarah was cured at a New York hospital and returned with her mother and brother to Tel Aviv. By this time the Meyersons recognized that their marriage was in serious trouble. The two had long lived in different worlds, and there seemed to be no bridge for their incompatibility. Golda's star rose higher that same year of 1934 when she became a member of the Histadrut Executive Committee as director of the tourism department. Her chief duty was to escort important visitors around the kibbutzes and cooperatives.

By the next year she reached the inner circle when she was elected to the secretariat of the Histadrut Executive Committee. At this time, Ben-Gurion became chairman of the executive for the Jewish Agency of Israel, which directed all Jewish affairs in Palestine.

Capably Golda filled various posts, managing a mutual aid program of the Histadrut and then becoming chair of the board of directors of the Workers' Sick Fund for Histadrut members and their families. Often she attended international conferences. To collect money for the Histadrut's new maritime enterprise, which envisioned a fleet of Jewish ships and well-trained young seamen, Golda, whose approach to people was direct and unaffected, was sent to the United States on a speaking tour and again proved her reputation as a dazzling fund-raiser. On her return, working for Nachshon, as the project was called, she became an expert on shipping matters. Hers was also a forceful voice in defending Histadrut's policies to disgruntled workers.

She and Morris saw each other only on weekends and grew increasingly alien. She was far happier in the company of her Histadrut colleagues. Although she was by now a public figure, she kept her private life behind a veil. Still, there were flying rumors of intimate relationships with Remez and Shneur Zalman Shazar (Rubashov). Historian, editor, and spellbinding orator, Shazar would later take the largely ceremonial role of president of Israel from 1963 to 1973. Whispers of her intimacy with Shazar caused a jealous Remez to break with her, but before long he was back, guiding her career. As secretary-general of the Histadrut, he was now one of the most powerful Jewish leaders. Later there would be stories of Golda's relationships with Zalman Aranne, who helped her organize a labor college for workers, and Yaacov Hazan, who deviated from the Mapai party's principles.

For Golda Meyerson, the dream of an independent homeland had persisted, but it was disrupted by the Peel Commission, which issued a report in 1937 calling for the partition of Palestine into a larger Arab and a much smaller Jewish state. Meanwhile in Germany the Nazis under Adolf Hitler began a campaign of terror against the Jews, thousands of whom desperately wanted to go to Palestine despite British obstinacy.

An international conference convened at Évian-les-Bains, France, in 1938, was expected to take care of the refugee crisis. Although chosen to represent Israel, Golda was classified as an observer, not a delegate. She was stunned and then explosively angry when the various nations declared there was nothing they could do.

By now she and Morris had formally separated, but for the sake of their children did not want a divorce. When Morris saw the children, he was a most caring father.

Side by side with the Jewish dream of independence, a feeling of nationalism was growing among the resident Arabs, who could not tolerate the thought of a Jewish state in Palestine. Guerrilla fighting, which had begun in 1936, lasted for three years. At its end the British, who had often seemed helpless to control it, issued the White Paper of 1939, which limited Jewish emigration to Palestine to a total of 100,000 over the next five years, and then stopped it altogether. To Golda Meyerson and her fellow Zionists, it seemed a complete repudiation of the Balfour Declaration.

Still, when World War II began in September 1939, the Jews forgot their bitterness and joined forces with the allies. Golda was appointed to the War Economic Advisory Council and was assigned as a liaison between British authorities and the Jewish people of Palestine, which was placed on a war economy. She played a double role because she also acted as chief spokesperson for the *Yishuv*, the Jewish community. In 1940 she became head of the political department of the Histadrut. When some Palestinian Jews were convicted of stealing arms for Haganah, the Yishuv's fighting arm, in 1943, she was summoned to give testimony in their behalf. It proved to be impressive.

By this time her children were grown. Sarah joined a kibbutz in 1944, and Menahem, who had studied the cello, was dreaming of a professional career. Their relationship with their mother remained close even though they had spent so little time with her. In pursuit of her goals, Golda seemed endowed with tireless energy. Sometimes, however, she suffered from migraine headaches. Later, when ill health plagued her, she carefully concealed several hospital stays from the public.

Once the war was over, the Jews renewed their struggle against British policy. When Golda attended the 22nd Zionist Congress in Basel, Switzerland, in 1946, she found the delegates apprehensive over the growing number of refugees whom the British still would not allow into Palestine. When one ship was indefinitely detained in port, in La Spezia, Italy, its desperate passengers responded by going on a hunger strike. Golda and other leaders in Jerusalem showed their support by fasting for several days, too. Finally, the British allowed the ship to sail.

Golda's friend Remez recommended that she be named head of the political department of the Jewish Agency after its director, Moshe Sharett, was detained in England. Ben-Gurion, however, still determined major policy. One of Golda's most heartbreaking duties entailed visiting refugees who were being held in internment camps in Cyprus. She wept when a child who had never seen a live flower handed her a bouquet of paper blossoms. The plight of babies behind barbed wire was urgent, and with all her powers of persuasion, Golda managed to get many adults to turn over their places on the quota list to the infants.

Jewish-Arab problems grew so intense by 1947 that the British Labour government of Clement Atlee turned for help to the recently founded United Nations. The UN General Assembly sent a special commission to Palestine to study the situation and make recommendations. In 1946 Britain had recognized the complete independence of Transjordan, and its emir had been proclaimed king. Twelve days before the UN report was to be voted on, Golda Meyerson met with King Abdullah ibn Hussein of Transjordan at the border and felt heartened by his disclosure that he did not care to join the Arab League if it invaded the contemplated new state of Israel.

On November 19 the General Assembly accepted the UN commission's proposal that Palestine should be divided into an Arab state, Transjordan, and a Jewish state, Israel, with Jerusalem under international trusteeship. The Arabs, however, were angry about Jerusalem and mounted more riots.

Gradually the British began to relinquish control over the section of Palestine that lay west of the Jordan River. Just in case hostilities should break out with the Arabs despite King Abdullah's promise, Golda, Israel's best fund-raiser, was sent to the United States at the end of January 1948 to get money for arms. Speaking without eloquence but always with persuasion, she brought back the astonishing sum of $60 million.

On her return in May, she met again with King Abdullah, traveling to Amman wrapped in Arab shawls and veils. To her shock, he reneged on his promise that he would not be a party to Arab hostility against the Jews.

The new state of Israel was scheduled to be born on May 15, 1948. In fear of inciting an immediate Arab attack, Ben-Gurion called a secret meeting at the municipal museum for members of the Jewish National Council to sign the declaration of independence. When Golda wrote her name, she was wet eyed. It was the proudest and most fulfilling moment of her life.

That same day, armies from Transjordan, Syria, Egypt, and Lebanon invaded Israel. Iraq and Saudi Arabia also joined in the fighting. It was imperative to get more arms, and at the invitation of the head of the United Jewish Appeal, Golda flew to the United States. Her tour grew complicated when a taxi accident in New York City fractured her leg, but she managed to raise a sizable sum for the Israeli army anyway.

The Soviet Union was the second country after the United States to recognize Israel. Golda wanted to remain close to the fledgling Israeli state in its time of peril, but accepted Ben-Gurion's decision to send her as Israel's first diplomatic representative to Moscow. She asked to take along her daughter Sarah, who would act as a radio operator, and Sarah's new husband, Zechariah Rehabi, a code expert. It had been decided that French would be Israel's diplomatic language, and Golda had in her entourage Lou Kaddar, a young woman whose French was impeccable and who would become her "indispensable assistant" and close friend. It was a joke that Golda ran the legation like a kibbutz, with everybody on equal terms and on an equal work basis.

Her first months in Moscow, however, were fraught with anxiety because of the war even though Israeli troops seemed to have gained the upper hand. Despite being still short of arms, Israeli soldiers drove the Arabs out of Galilee, the Negev, and a strip of land that connected Israel to Jerusalem. They also held the new part of Jerusalem.

The UN General Assembly named Count Folke Bernadotte, a Swedish diplomat, as mediator, but before he could offer his peace plan, he was assassinated in Jerusalem. His successor, Ralph Bunche, soon persuaded Israel and Egypt to begin armistice negotiations. When the war ended early in 1949, Transjordan was renamed Jordan.

In Israel's first election in January 1949, the Mapai party won 35 percent of the vote. Weizmann became the first president and Ben-Gurion, the first prime minister. At once, Weizmann invited Golda home from Moscow to become minister of labor because he knew her amazing capacity for hard work. The White Paper of 1939 had been rescinded, and thousands of immigrants streamed into Israel. Full of plans, Golda made housing and jobs her first priorities. She also declared that there would be no restrictions on immigration; Israel would provide for any Jew who wanted to come.

The new state of Israel hoped to start on a firm economic basis, and a master plan was conceived to raise one third of the budgeted $1.5 million by taxes and the rest by floating a bond issue. In 1950, Golda went to the United States to convince American Jews to invest in Israeli bonds. She succeeded brilliantly.

On her return home, she presented the Meyerson program, which called for 30,000 new housing units. Massive public works were planned to bring down unemployment. As she went everywhere, suggesting and demanding, people called her "Golda-on-the-spot." Meanwhile Israel began building a modern industrial nation. Innovative agricultural measures made the desert bloom.

Solitary to the last, Morris Meyerson died in 1951, never having expressed bitterness about their long separation. Sarah and Menahem remembered him as an exemplary father, but Golda said little about her feelings.

By 1953 her housing program was doing so well that she began other projects, such as a code of labor laws and a national insurance bill that included maternity benefits. Her office also issued a women's labor law and various vocational programs.

Ben-Gurion left office in 1953, only to return two years later in the face of a new Arab threat from Lieutenant Colonel Gamal Abdel Nasser. The young officer who had helped overthrow Egyptian King Farouk two and a half years earlier was encouraging guerrilla raids on Jewish villages.

Ben-Gurion and his foreign minister, Moshe Sharett, could not agree on how to deal with the Arab threat. Along with most of the cabinet, Golda sided with the prime minister, who proposed attacking the Arabs. Sharett, voice of the opposition, resigned, and Ben-Gurion turned to Golda, who had supported him openly during all the stormy cabinet sessions. But if she accepted Sharett's post, he told her, she must Hebracize her name to Meir. She did so and threw herself into new challenges.

Because of unexpected developments, a war scenario soon unfolded. In July 1956 the United States and Britain announced that they were withdrawing their previous offers to help finance the Aswan High Dam across the Nile River. An angry Nasser, fueled by nationalist sentiment, then seized the internationally controlled Suez Canal and announced that its tolls would be used to pay for the dam.

The Arabs were openly gathering against Israel. Ben-Gurion now learned that Jordan and Syria had placed their forces under a unified Syrian command. Meir sat in on the briefings in which Brigadier General Moshe Dayan outlined a plan for Israel to invade the northern Sinai peninsula, held by Egypt.

Dayan struck with lightning speed on October 29. Two days later, Britain and France dropped bombs on Egypt. Israel occupied the Gaza Strip and in a matter of four days drove the Egyptians from the Sinai.

Meanwhile, a British-French armada had been steaming toward

Egypt, and forces landed there on November 5 and 6. In Washington, D.C., President Dwight D. Eisenhower, facing an election, grew furious at this rush of events and asked the UN Security Council to obtain a cease-fire. After one was arranged on November 6, a UN police force took over the canal.

At the United Nations in March 1957, Israel's foreign minister gave a speech that she later said marked the nadir of her career. She announced that, compelled by the big powers, Israel would withdraw from the Sinai and Gaza, leaving a UN force in place there, too.

The war behind her, Golda decided that her role offered a unique opportunity to tell the world about Israeli aspirations. She was especially interested in the newly independent and the soon-to-be-independent countries of Africa and adopted a motherly, protective attitude toward them.

Her brand of friendly diplomacy was certainly something new. Sometimes it meant leading her entourage in a spirited hora (Israeli circle dance) and asking the Africans to join in. Her visits to Liberia, Ghana, Nigeria, and the Ivory Coast in 1958 resulted in the Israeli International Program, which called for Israelis, usually one or two, to teach the natives how to carry out various projects while working side by side with them.

A second African tour in 1960 brought Golda back to Ghana and then to Guinea, Sierra Leone, Togo, and Dahomey and resulted in more projects. Meir also visited Asia, but always thought that her African diplomacy was the most successful part of her tenure as foreign minister. The number of African missions in Jerusalem grew to 39. With the war of 1967, however, most of the states she had won over would sever ties with Israel.

She was never too happy with her old ally, Ben-Gurion, who she thought was too active in foreign affairs. Shimon Perez, the defense minister, also stepped on her toes.

All the while, she kept a wary eye on Syria and Egypt, which in 1958 had formed a union, called the United Arab Republic (UAR). Syrian rebels ended the union in 1961, but Nasser kept the UAR name for his country.

Now stocky, with thick legs, a severe hairdo, and a warm smile, Golda built on her grandmotherly image and charmed the nation. Sarah had two sons and a daughter, and Menahem had three sons from his second marriage. His retarded daughter from a first unhappy marriage lived with her mother, and the girl's handicap was kept from the public; Golda never mentioned her. On the whole, she was satisfied with her children's lives. Sarah thrived at the kibbutz; Menahem taught cello at a conservatory of music and played with the Israeli Philharmonic Orchestra. Meir still seemed indefatigable, but illnesses occurred more frequently.

Ben-Gurion abruptly resigned as prime minister in 1963, and Levi Eshkol was appointed to fill out his remaining two years. At the climax of the long-festering Lavon Affair, which concerned a serious breach of security that resulted in the arrest of Israeli intelligence agents in Egypt, Ben-Gurion turned on Eshkol for refusing to set up judicial hearings. Helplessly, Meir watched their bitter quarrel. Already exhausted from a punishing schedule, she suffered a minor stroke, from which she quickly recovered. But an examination had revealed an enlarged lymph node, and doctors made a preliminary diagnosis of lymphoma. From then on, they watched her carefully.

In 1965, Ben-Gurion stunned Israel by announcing that he had founded a new political party named Rafi. After her years of loyalty, Golda sorrowed over breaking with him, but she was now committed to serving Eshkol, who had asked her to remain as foreign minister, at least until the elections. When he won handily, she felt she could gracefully retire in 1966.

She looked forward to pursuing her private inclinations to read, to cook, and to enjoy her grandchildren, but her retirement lasted only a few months. Israel could not do without her, and Mapai drafted her to become its secretary-general.

Again the nation, battling difficult economic conditions, was being threatened by its Arab enemies. Syria was demanding aggressive action against Israel. A unified Arab command was formed at the same time that the Palestine Liberation Organization was set up to supply guerrillas for acts of terrorism against the border.

Although she was no longer in government, Meir, as secretary-general of Mapai, sat in on many crucial decisions, some of them made in her kitchen, where she brewed coffee for Israel's leaders. Egyptian and Syrian troops were lined up on the southern and northeastern borders, and border raids increased; Meir warmly supported Eshkol when he declared that Israel stood ready to defend itself. In May 1967, Nasser demanded that the United Nations withdraw its peacekeeping troops from the Gaza Strip and from the Sinai. Without informing Eshkol, Secretary-General U Thant complied. Nasser next declared a blockade of the Gulf of Eilat; 90 percent of Israel's oil passed through the port of

Eilat. While Eshkol appealed for help from the United Nations, Nasser and King Hussein of Jordan signed a five-year mutual defense treaty, placing the Jordanian forces under Egyptian command. Troop units from Iraq and Saudi Arabia also moved toward the eastern border.

Eshkol, who had named Dayan, the hero of Suez, minister of defense, concluded that Israel must strike first. On June 5, Israeli planes hit ten airfields in the Sinai. Other waves of strikes against Syria and Jordan destroyed vast amounts of war material. Without air power, the Arabs were helpless. Dayan's fighting strategies, based on surprise, were masterful, and after six days Israel occupied the entire Sinai Peninsula up to the Suez Canal, the Golan Heights, and the old city of Jerusalem.

Golda Meir said, "We don't want wars, even when we win." Still she called the Israeli soldiers "the most victorious army in history." When the defeated Arabs bowed to a series of cease-fire demands by the UN Security Council, the flash war ended. The Israelis were determined to occupy Arab land until the Arabs agreed to recognize the state of Israel.

During the winter of 1967–68, Meir carried out an assignment Eshkol had given her: to merge Mapai, Rafi, and Achdut Ha'avoda, which had split from Mapai in 1944. Thus the new Israel Labor party was formed.

That August, Meir resigned, but retirement was all too short. In February 1969, Eshkol suffered a fatal heart attack. Several replacements, including Dayan and Yigal Allon, the deputy prime minister, were suggested. In the end, however, overlooking objections that Golda Meir was an "old, sick woman," the Labor party picked her as the only political figure who could be the necessary unifying force.

In March a huge majority of the Central Committee voted to appoint her. But since the Labor party held only a bare majority in the Knesset (Parliament), it formed a coalition with the moderate liberal Mapam party, the ultranationalistic Gahal party, and two conservative religious parties.

As interim prime minister, Meir was blunt, businesslike, and firm, not above thumping the table to restore order or to make a point. Still, she was prudent and careful; dry wit enlivened her plain speaking. "Anyone who wants this job," she said, "deserves it."

She continued to show her tough though flexible posture toward the Arabs. In October elections the Labor party lost five seats, whereas the Gahal party, which was implacably opposed to negotiations over the conquered areas, gained five. Yet, when Meir presented her new coaliti' government in December, she won a huge vote of confidence. She stood as a woman of commanding dignity.

Again there was growing aggression by Nasser's forces along the Suez Canal, quickly followed by Israeli reprisals. Nasser's death from a heart attack in 1971 removed a formidable enemy. The UAR name was dropped, and once more the country was called Egypt. But Anwar Sadat, the general who replaced Nasser, was not conciliatory, and the Israeli government kept up costly military preparedness.

Since 1966, Israel had held firm to its demand that a formal peace treaty recognize its territorial integrity behind secure frontiers before it would withdraw from occupied Arab territory. It insisted on control of the Golan Heights and Sharm-el-Sheikh at the tip of the Sinai, as well as a demilitarized peninsula. The Meir government gave residents of the Gaza Strip some special considerations, abolishing entry permits and building some new homes. At the same time, it continued to set up Jewish settlements in the occupied areas.

A ruling by Israel's Supreme Court brought on a cabinet crisis in January 1970. The court declared that Jewish nationality did not require one to belong to the Jewish religion. After a tense two months, the atmosphere cleared when the Knesset passed a law that only those who were born of Jewish mothers or were formally converted could be considered Jews and that citizenship rights could be offered to non-Jews in a Jewish family.

Two acts of terrorism in 1972 shocked not only Israel but the world. In May, three gunmen sprayed Lod Airport near Tel Aviv with bullets, killing 26. An Arab guerrilla attack in September left 11 members of the Israeli Olympic team dead in Munich.

When Israel celebrated its 25th anniversary of independence in May 1973, it simultaneously decried 25 years under Arab siege. Israelis well understood why they had to devote more money to defense than did any other nation. But on this anniversary they could count noteworthy achievements in many areas, especially agriculture and industry, often based on awesome technologies. Still, for all the successes, there were complicated social problems spawned by the diverse social, cultural, and ethnic backgrounds of the Jewish immigrants. There was also constant religious controversy between the Orthodox minority and the non–Orthodox majority.

Five months after Israel paraded its military might in Jerusalem during the anniversary celebration, a fourth Arab-Israeli war broke out with dramatic suddenness. On October 8, Arab armies began attacking everywhere. Jews were celebrating Yom Kippur, their most holy festival. Because of the feast day, mobilization was delayed, and the Israelis lost precious time. The Arab forces had benefited from Soviet technical training, and surface-to-air missiles obliterated Israeli tanks. In short order Iraq, Tunisia, Kuwait, Algeria, Morocco, Jordan, Sudan, and Saudi Arabia signaled their intentions to pitch in against Israel. The Egyptians crossed the Suez Canal and destroyed Israeli defense positions in the Sinai, and Syria attacked on the Golan Heights. Only the United States came to Israel's aid. Gradually, under Dayan's command, Israeli troops stopped the advances and then began to push the Arabs back.

Displaying impressive energy and will power, Golda worked ceaselessly at her desk and at her telephone; she even flew to Washington to meet with President Richard Nixon, who dispatched Secretary of State Henry Kissinger to Israel.

The UN Security Council proposed a cease-fire on October 22 and sent in a UN Emergency Force three days later. But Egypt and Israel waited until November to sign the agreement. Most fighting had stopped by then.

For Golda Meir, the Yom Kippur War was a tragedy. It was far costlier than the Six Day War, which clearly had established Israel as the victor. This time neither side won, and there were no decisive advantages in either camp. Arabs, however, got a psychological lift from their ability to meet the Israelis on equal terms. Israel lost about 2,000 men and much equipment.

The Labor party gained only a narrow margin in the national elections that had been postponed because of the war. After much political infighting, based on Israel's economic difficulties and Meir's agreement to withdraw from Suez, the 75-year-old prime minister won a vote of confidence.

Yet the Israeli army's poor performance in the early days of the war still rankled many. Demands were made for Dayan's resignation, although the Aganat Commission cleared him of negligence and fixed the blame on faulty intelligence and an inaccurate estimate of Egypt's capabilities. Meir responded by ordering a wholesale shake-up of the military command.

Drawn and exhausted, she resigned in April 1974 and gave up her Knesset seat as well. Warmly she congratulated Yitzhak Rabin, her successor, and Shimon Perez, who replaced Dayan as defense minister.

Through the years she had always shaken off her numerous serious bouts of illness. She did so once again after a short rest. Responding to an English publisher's often-repeated request that she write her memoirs, she finished *My Life,* which became a best-seller in 1975.

Even out of office, she kept constantly busy. She received several honorary doctorates and was in great demand as a speaker and counselor to government officials. Anxious for some peaceful solution, she eagerly followed Sadat's new overtures.

In 1977 she saw the Labor party, which had ruled Israel for 29 years, defeated by the Likud party, headed by Menahem Begin, former leader of a Zionist guerrilla group that had fought British occupation troops and Arabs in Palestine.

Sadat's highly dramatic move in traveling from Cairo to Jerusalem to meet with Begin in November 1977 gave Meir a chance to come face to face with the enemy. Highlighted on television was a brief encounter, during which she and Sadat chatted amiably and joked about grandchildren. The homely repartee struck a hopeful note, but unfortunately Sadat's diplomatic trip divided the Arab world, at least temporarily.

Finally, Golda Meir gave in to constant pain and extreme exhaustion. In 1978, doctors said her lymphoma was so extensive it could not be stopped. She was hospitalized in Jerusalem for the last 15 days of her life. With few exceptions, only members of her family were allowed to see her. Sheyna was dead, but her sister Clara came from the United States to sit by her bedside. The Begin administration had to rely on daily hospital briefings. The 80-year-old stateswoman lost consciousness on December 7 and died the next day.

Since she had requested that there be no epitaph, dignitaries who crowded the Knesset's Chagall Hall had to pay wordless tribute. But the actress Orna Porat read from the last paragraph of *My Life*:

> I believe that we will have peace with our neighbors, but I am sure that no one will make peace with a weak Israel. If Israel is not strong, there will be no peace. . . . I have only one desire left: never to lose the feeling that it is I who am indebted for what has been given to me from the time that I first learned about Zionism in a small room in czarist Russia all the way through to my half century here, where I have seen my five grandchildren grow up as free Jews in a country that is their own. . . . Our children and our children's children will never settle for anything less.

ISABEL PERÓN

President of Argentina
(1974–76)

Solely because of her married name, she came to power. As the third wife of Argentina's charismatic Juan D. Perón, she often was haunted by the image of her predecessor, the flamboyant Eva Duarte Perón, Wife Number 2. Isabel Perón, however, reached a station denied Eva. She became the first woman president of her country, the first, in fact, in the world.

Her unusual story began in La Rioja, a provincial capital in the mountains northwest of Buenos Aires. There María Estela Martínez was born on February 1, 1931, the youngest of the six children of Carmelo Martínez, a bank clerk, and the former María Josefa Cartas. When María Estela was three, the family moved to Buenos Aires. Carmelo died four years later, leaving his wife to provide for her young family by working at various jobs.

In 1930, army officers, in league with conservative party leaders, had seized control of the government and established a long pattern of military rule over Argentina. María Estela was 12 when a dashing army colonel, Juan Domingo Perón, led a right-wing military coup that overthrew President Ramón S. Castillo. In the junta that was set up, Perón became minister of labor and social welfare, a post that gave him ample opportunity to forge ties with the labor movement and the *descamisados* (shirtless ones), the poorest of the working class, who cheered the social legislation he sponsored. After a year he also became vice-president and minister of war, his three offices making him the most powerful member of the junta. A widower, he now acquired a decorative mistress in Eva Duarte, who was a politically ambitious radio and movie actress.

About this time, to defray household expenses, María Estela went to live with José and Isabel Cresto, who practiced spiritism. She had left school after the sixth grade and was studying piano and ballet. Eagerly she now absorbed lessons in the occult from the Crestos.

By 1945, Perón had aroused so much jealousy that rival military factions conspired to seize him and imprison him on the island of Martín García. Massive demonstrations by the descamisados, however, soon won his freedom. Eva Duarte was also given credit for speaking out, and soon after his release Perón married her. They lost no time in organizing a labor party.

An impressionable María Estela, who had a taste for romantic Spanish poetry, could not have been unaware of Eva Perón, who turned up everywhere. Blond and flashy, often overloaded with mink and jewelry, she inspired both love and hate. The descamisados especially adored her, won over by her passionate, persuasive speaking style and her promises of land, higher wages, and social security.

When María Estela was 15, Perón was elected president, and he and his wife took up residence in the pink palace known as the Casa Rosada. Eva, called Evita by the masses, became his unofficial minister of health and labor. In effect, she was his co-president. Evita genuinely concerned herself with welfare and educational reforms—she herself had little schooling—and worked harder than anyone else to achieve the vote for Argentine women.

During his first term, Perón carried out his campaign promises by carefully blending economic nationalism with private ownership. As one of its first moves, the government took over British-held railroads and the telephone system that belonged to U.S. investors.

Perón's determination to make Argentina the preeminent political, military, and economic power in Latin America led his enemies to charge that he operated within a totalitarian framework inspired by Adolf Hitler and Benito Mussolini. They could not dispute his good luck. The postwar world's desperate need for Argentine beef and wheat helped fuel the country's prosperity, and the Roman Catholic church enthusiastically supported the regime. Always behind him, urging him on, was Evita, "the woman with the whip," who could be ruthless to opponents.

In 1951, María Estela Martínez enrolled in the National School of Dance, but stayed only one year. Meanwhile Señora Cresto had died, and the young dancer took the name of Isabel to honor the woman she considered her surrogate mother.

That year of 1951, Juan Perón was reelected president because a

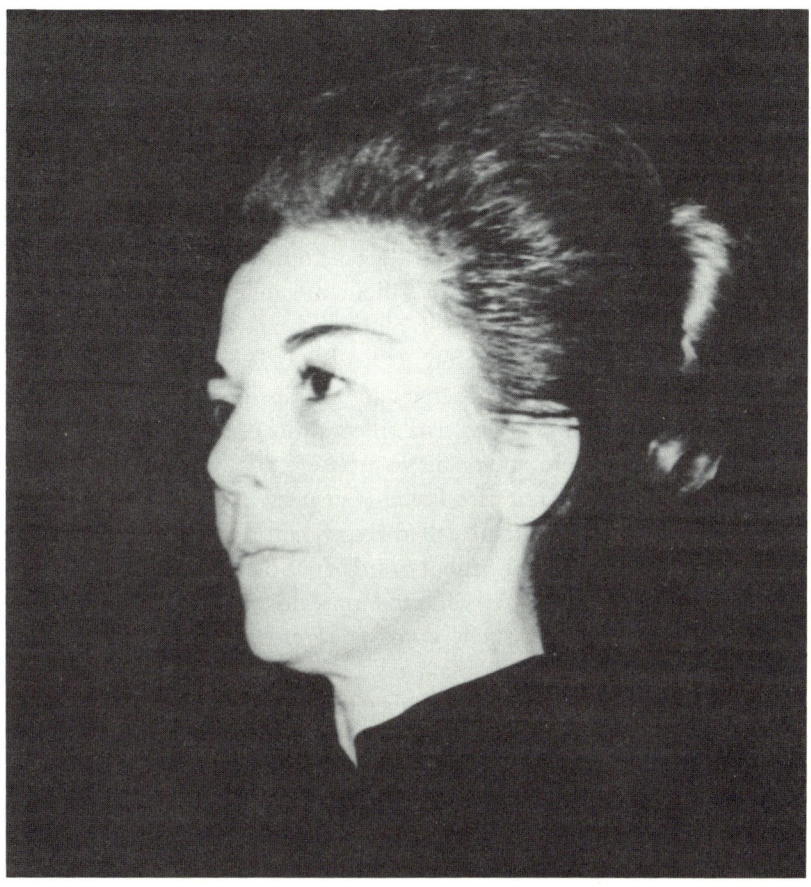

Isabel Perón: courtesy Embassy of Argentina, Washington, D.C.

constitution written two years earlier allowed him to succeed himself. He had proposed Evita as vice-president, but the military forced him to withdraw her name. The opposition did not know that doctors were deeply concerned about her deteriorating health. Finally the doctors diagnosed her condition as uterine cancer, and surgery was performed in November, five days before Perón was reelected. The cancer, however, could not be contained. Though desperately ill, Evita applied heavy makeup when she made several public appearancs, the last one for Perón's second inauguration. She died in July 1952 to wild mourning by the descamisados, and things began to fall apart for the widower.

Gossip was rife about the sports camp for girls he established at the presidential *quinta* in Olivos although there never was any substantial proof of "orgies." Rather, the childless Perón assumed a kind of paternal role over the girls he hoped to convert to Peronism.

The camp, however, was a minor issue. Argentines were growing angry over Perón's suppression of speech and the fast-tumbling economy. Most ominously, a schism was developing between the church and the president, who accused its officials of fostering agitation and proposing measures to separate church and state. Angrily the Vatican excommunicated him. Before long, the Catholic hierarchy in Argentina threw its support to dissident elements in all three branches of the armed services, which together ousted Perón in October 1955 and sent him into exile aboard a Paraguayan gunship that had been sitting in the Buenos Aires harbor. Three days of civil war had killed almost 50.

By November, Perón made his way to Colón, Panama, where chance brought about his meeting with Isabel Martínez, who was then performing in a Panama City nightclub called Happy Land. Since 1952, when she had left the National Dance School to strike out on her own, she had progressed from a Spanish dance group in Montevideo, Uruguay, to a troupe that was scheduled to tour the west coast of South America. In Medellín, Colombia, in 1955 that ensemble had fallen on hard times and had been dissolved. At this juncture Isabel met a Cuban dancer named Joe Herald, who asked her to join six other girls in his group. He took them to Panama City.

Perón needed some cheering up as the Christmas season of 1955 approached, and a woman friend suggested that the Joe Herald troupe from Happy Land be invited to a party at the ex-president's hotel. Of all the nightclub dancers, Isabel most attracted Perón, and she, in turn, found him to her liking. At 60, with dyed black hair, he retained his handsome and forceful appearance. Within days, the wide-eyed, auburn-haired Isabel gave up dancing to become his private secretary, although she could not type. In January she began living with him. Seemingly unsophisticated, she exuded an air of domesticity that Perón found most agreeable. She was an excellent cook, and her piano playing and singing relaxed him.

Hotel Washington, where they lived, was owned by the Canal Zone, an agency of the U.S. government. Feeling uncomfortable about Perón's presence, the U.S. State Department was just about to remove him when he and Isabel checked out. They took a small apartment in Panama City, but within three months returned to Colón and rented a house.

Events in Buenos Aires merited Perón's rapt attention. Major General Eduardo Lonardi, leader of the coup that had toppled him, lasted only two months as provisional president. In turn he was overthrown by Major General Pedro Eugenio Aramburu, who was widely criticized for his unwillingness to suppress Peronism among the workers and in the military. In answer, he crushed a Peronist revolt in the summer of 1956, arresting thousands and executing its leaders. The Peronists were forbidden to function as a party.

From Panama, Perón tried to direct the resistance against Aramburu, but found communication difficult. Venezuela was under the control of a dictator, Marcos Pérez Jiménez, and Perón believed that he could operate better from Caracas. He and Isabel flew there and settled in a small house.

Matters seemed to be looking up. Argentine elections were scheduled for February 1958, and one of the presidential contenders, Arturo Frondizi, seeking Peronist support, made conciliatory overtures toward Perón.

In Venezuela, however, the climate was changing fast. At the beginning of the new year, a failed coup against Pérez Jiménez was followed by a series of strikes. During a period of great unrest, army and navy officers warned Pérez Jiménez that there would be civil war if he did not leave. The dictator departed, nonetheless leaving anarchy behind him. Since Perón was suddenly considered an enemy of the people and faced physical danger, he and his party took temporary refuge in the unguarded Dominican embassy. The next day the new government gave him permission to leave for Ciudad Trujillo, but insisted that he travel alone. After his departure, Isabel stayed in the embassy for several days, then happily rejoined him.

The Dominican Republic was also ruled by a dictator, Rafael L. Trujillo, who exerted strict surveillance over the exiled leader. At length, Perón realized that Ciudad Trujillo was not a satisfactory place of exile. At least during the Dominican interlude, Isabel acquired two new skills. Under her lover's tutelage she learned to fence and to ride a motor scooter. When the Venezuelan government grew hostile toward Trujillo, who had also given refuge to the ousted Cuban president Fulgencio Batista, Perón decided it was time to leave for Spain with Isabel and his beloved poodles.

In 1960 the government of Generalissimo Francisco Franco gave him permission to enter Spain and suggested Torremolinos as a place to reside. But it did not object when a friend offered Perón the use of a house in a Madrid suburb, El Plantío. Sharing quarters was Américo Barios, a journalist who had become Perón's private secretary, a title Isabel no longer used. Perón, who was somewhat hard pressed for funds, wanted to get his hands on Evita's Swiss bank deposits, whereabouts unknown. Before long, he sent Isabel to Geneva to investigate, but she returned empty handed.

Late in the year Isabel had to prepare for another move, this time to a fashionable apartment on Dr. Arce Street, one block from the Plaza de la República Argentina. Here a new circle of Spanish friends gathered around the couple. Among them was Perón's personal physician, Dr. Francisco Flores Tascón whose wife was particularly disturbed that Perón and Isabel, called Chabela by their friends, had been living together for almost six years without benefit of clergy. The excuse was that Isabel as a practicing Catholic could not wed the excommunicated Perón. Finally, after continuous pressure from Señora de Flores Tascón, a bishop sanctioned a marriage of convenience. Isabel Martínez, aged 30, and Juan D. Perón, aged 66, became man and wife on November 15, 1961, in the Flores Tascón living room.

The new Señora Perón, still faithful to the occult, began to study Zen Buddhism, but did not neglect her kitchen. Often the American movie actress Ava Gardner, who lived in the same apartment complex, came to the Peróns' door to sample Isabel's delectable empanadas (meat pies).

While Isabel was busily occupied, Perón began to float the idea of returning to Argentina. As a first step, he succeeded in obtaining a Vatican decree that invalidated his excommunication, making him again constitutionally qualified to become president. Under Frondizi, who had been elected in 1958, the Peronist party was still proscribed, but neo-Peronist parties existed at the provincial level; moderate Peronist union leaders were interested in negotiating with the government. Elections in March 1962 for provincial officials brought the Peronists a big victory and angered military leaders, who arrested Frondizi. Thereupon José María Guido, president of the Senate, became provisional chief executive and dissolved all political parties, which were ordered to organize under new rules.

Arturo Illía, the next president, preached a policy of national conciliation, and many of Perón's followers came to Madrid to urge him to move quickly. Appearances, however, suggested that he planned to stay permanently in Spain because he was supervising the construction of a new house, in the Puerta del Hierro neighborhood on the outskirts of Madrid, that was finished in six months.

In December 1964, leaving Isabel behind, Perón departed for Buenos Aires with a small entourage. Operation Return had begun. In Rio de Janeiro, however, the plane was detained after the Brazilian government received a request from Buenos Aires not to allow the Perón group to proceed farther. The plane then went on its scheduled flight without its passengers, but on returning to Rio, the pilot was instructed to take the exile to Madrid.

Although Isabel had not participated in Operation Return, Perón decided in 1965 to cast his good-looking young wife in a political role. He could not enter Argentina, but she could. Her first mission in May was to Asunción, Paraguay, to see Jorge Antonio, a Perón follower, whom Franco had expelled from Spain after Operation Return. Some stories ran that Antonio and his circle suggested to Isabel that she had the potential to become a second Evita.

That fall Isabel set off on her second mission, going to Buenos Aires to help loyalists stem the tide of "Vandorism." In the gubernatorial election in the province of Mendoza, scheduled for spring 1966, a candidate loyal to Perón was facing one supported by Augusto Vandor, a powerful union leader, who wanted to prove that Peronism could prevail without Perón. Vandorist and loyalist candidates were pitted against each other for other offices as well. Isabel's arrival in Buenos Aires set off demonstrations and scuffles between the rival groups, and she was forced to switch hotels several times.

But when Isabel traveled to western Argentina, she was treated almost like a saint because the magic of Perón's name had not dimmed. The loyalist candidates won, and the revolt her husband had feared was suppressed. While Isabel was touring the country, Illía was ousted in a coup and replaced by another interim president, General Juan C. Ongania.

When she returned to Madrid in July, Isabel brought with her a new attendant. José López Rega, a retired police corporal, had introduced himself to her as a former gatekeeper for Perón at the Casa Rosada, and Isabel had been immediately impressed by his pledge of loyalty. Installed at the Puerta del Hierro villa, he soon became handyman and valet. What really attracted Isabel was his "literary" background. López Rega had published several books on spiritism in which she still was interested. By this time, Perón himself was curious about occultism, and he rapidly took

López Rega into his inner circle. It was not long until the ex-corporal became private secretary. He and Isabel worked closely together, gradually extending their influence by controlling access to Perón through the telephone and the mail.

No government lasted long in Buenos Aires. Another coup in 1970 deposed Ongania and installed an unknown army attaché, Roberto M. Levingston. Juan Perón, who by now had various health problems, was still biding his time.

Levingston proved highly ineffectual. One more coup, and he was replaced by Alejandro Lanusse, who promised an orderly transition to civilian rule and scheduled elections for 1973. So, in 1972, Juan Perón sent his wife back to Buenos Aires to negotiate with the Lanusse government over Peronist participation in the congressional elections and Perón's rehabilitation as a presidential candidate. Unfortunately for Isabel, no fast agreement could be reached.

Eva Perón's carefully embalmed corpse had mysteriously disappeared in 1956. Sixteen years later the Peronists were still clamoring for it. Finally it was returned to the Perón villa in Puerta del Hierro, reportedly from a cemetery in Milan, where it had been taken on Aramburu's orders lest a mausoleum become a shrine. After a doctor examined the remains and found only minor damage that could be repaired, Isabel washed the body and arranged the hair. At López Rega's orders, the coffin was kept in a room on the second floor.

Lanusse still wanted smooth elections, and because the Peronist movement remained the greatest political force in Argentina, he pressed on with his goal of coming to some kind of understanding with Perón. Talks in Madrid again proved inconclusive, however. In an unexpected challenge, Lanusse announced in July that all presidential candidates would have to become permanent residents by August. Unable to do so, Perón rejected the ultimatum.

He and Isabel turned up in Buenos Aires in November for a month's stay, and he immediately set about building a workable agreement among the Peronists, the anti–Peronists, and the military. Before heading back to Madrid, he rejected a nomination as presidential candidate of the Justicia party.

But he kept on with his carefully detailed plans. In March 1973 his handpicked candidate, Hector Campora, won 49.6 percent of the vote, and Peronists swept the elections. But before Campora could be inaugurated in May, the military government, responding to an extremist killing-kidnapping binge and soaring ransom demands, declared a state of emergency in the federal district and some of the more populous provinces. The immediate cause was the assassination of a former chairman of the joint chiefs of staff.

With the advent of a civilian government, Perón was permitted to return permanently. Jamming the Eziza Airport, supporters greeted him and his wife with wild enthusiasm after they stepped off an airplane in June. Then tensions between the leftist and rightist factions in the airport crowd erupted into ugly violence, and almost 400 persons were killed. All signs pointed to irreconcilable differences among Perón's followers.

At Perón's bidding, Campora resigned on July 13 to prepare the way for new elections, but remained in a caretaker capacity. Perón openly sought the presidency again, but nobody knew whom he would select as his running mate. A proper choice was imperative because he was 77 and in frail health. Many Argentines reacted with shock when he named Isabel, who modestly said, "I am only a disciple of Perón."

Criticism came from all sides. His enemies thought he was scheming to concentrate more power in his hands. Some Peronists were unhappy at what they considered an attempt to present a new version of Evita. Others suspected the influence of the supposedly ultrarightist José López Rega, who often had Perón's ear.

Both Peróns accepted their nominations at a party convention in August. The aging general made few public appearances, leaving Isabel, attractive and modish but far more subdued than Evita, to appear at hospitals, universities, and even in remote areas. She felt buoyed by success after left-wing Peronists began coming over to her. Backing for the Peróns widened from labor to students and to much of the middle class, wooed by the old man's promise of restoring prosperity and ending terror and violence. This message proved irresistible, and September 23, 1973, brought a landslide victory.

Two days later, Argentina's principal labor leader, a strong Peronist ally, was assassinated, and Perón threatened to crack down on Marxists and urban guerrillas. During his first months in office, the economic picture brightened, but a high level of political violence continued, coming principally from the Marxist People's Revolutionary Army.

Once installed in her vice-presidential suite, Isabel Perón began championing the cause of Argentine women as Evita had done, but she lacked Evita's charisma. She tried to recapture Evita's compelling image, however, by dying her hair blond and wearing a chignon.

Before Christmas, Perón became seriously ill, and Isabel assumed the duties of head of state, presiding over the cabinet for the next six months and traveling to Paraguay as her husband's stand-in. By June he urged her to make her most ambitious trip, to Geneva to address the International Labor Organization and then on to Madrid and Rome, where Pope Paul VI gave her an audience.

Returning, she found Perón suffering from infectious bronchitis. Within a day he turned over full executive power to her. On July 1, 1974, she tearfully appeared before television audiences to announce that he had died of heart failure. She was now president, and for a brief moment the people of Argentina took her to their hearts.

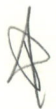
But reality quickly asserted itself. The country appeared out of control with intractable problems: the Peronist movement divided between left and right; a battered economy characterized by strikes, a black market, and severe inflation; and overwhelming political violence marked by daily bombings and assassinations.

In the midst of the chaos, Isabel sent López Rega to Madrid to bring Evita's corpse home. The coffin was placed beside Perón's in a mausoleum in Palermo Park.

Widely resented and considered a Svengali figure, José López Rega, who had emerged as the victor in the tussle betwen right- and left-wingers in the Peronist camps, remained at Isabel's side. Now presidential secretary and minister of welfare, he dictated a cabinet reshuffle that put several of his conservative cronies into key positions. He was reputed to be the guiding light behind the Argentine Anti-Communist Alliance (Triple A), a rightist terrorist force. The Trotskyite People's Revolutionary Army and the left-wing Peronists also contributed to the worsening climate with killings and kidnappings for ransom. As the cost of living rose by 335 percent, strikes and demonstrations multiplied.

For the first eight months of 1975, Argentina appeared to be on the verge of anarchy. Isabel Perón, thin, brittle, and increasingly uneasy whenever she had to appear in public, was often close to physical and nervous breakdowns and took prolonged absences from the Casa Rosada. Labor called a general strike in July, and the cabinet resigned. The thoroughly detested López Rega was pushed out of office by pressure from labor, old-time Peronists, and the military.

Desperate for a new strong man, President Perón picked young Colonel Vincente Damasco as her minister of the interior, thereby infuriating conservative generals, who less than gently encouraged her to take another holiday. While she was gone, the interim president fired Damasco. Meanwhile the Monteneros, the most radical Peronist youth wing, staged a new series of kidnappings and then blew up military barracks and attacked a frigate.

Isabel did not stay away as long as the generals had hoped. But by November she suffered a serious gall bladder attack. During her convalescence, she found herself fighting charges of corruption. Repeated calls were made for her resignation. One cabinet crisis succeeded another, but, though nagged by doubts, she hung on desperately.

It was all over for Isabel Perón on March 24, 1976. That day she had planned to go to the presidential quinta in Olivos. But her helicopter was diverted, and she was placed under arrest and informed that a coup by the army commander, General Jorge Raphael Videla, had ousted her. Within minutes she found herself whisked to a remote government-owned resort in the lake region of the Andes, where she remained under house arrest.

Quickly the military junta, which had dissolved the legislature and imposed martial law, proceeded to investigate the corruption charges against her. New allegations declared that she had transferred more than a million dollars from Peronist party charities to her own bank account.

The junta saw to it that the coffins of Juan and Eva Perón were removed from the mausoleum and separated. Perón was buried in his grandfather's tomb in a Buenos Aires suburb, Evita in the Ricoleto, a cemetery reserved for the wealthiest. Long ago she had purchased a tomb there for the Duarte family.

Isabel Perón was released in 1981 and went into exile in Spain, where she kept herself from public view. When Argentina returned to civilian rule in 1983, she came back almost secretly, determined to remain in the shadows, and there she has stayed.

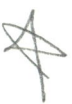

ELIZABETH DOMITIEN

*Prime Minister of the Central African Republic
(1975-76)*

Those who live in the Central African Republic describe their country as the heart of Africa. Poverty stricken and extremely backward, it is little known on other continents except perhaps for photographs of pygmies and Ubangi women, who wear ivory platters to stretch their lower lips.

But in the 1970s its ruler, Jean-Bedel Bokassa, an erratic soldier of Napoleonic ambition, attracted world attention. Involved in his giddy-paced political life, Elizabeth Domitien became Africa's first and so far only woman prime minister. But her tenure was short. Under Bokassa, the Central African Republic won a reputation as a place where anything could happen at any time and in the most unpredictable manner.

Since Domitien remains persona non grata to the government of General André-Dieudonne Kolingba, who took over in 1982, information about her life is scarce. She was born around 1920 in Samba, a village in the territory of Ubangi-Shari, which together with Chad, Gabon, and Middle Congo comprised the administrative grouping, French Equatorial Africa.

As a child she accompanied her father to the colonial capital, Brazzaville, in Middle Congo, where he worked in a crew setting telephone and telegraph poles. There she met Jean-Bedel Bokassa, an orphan about her age, from Ubangi-Shari. His father had been caned to death by a colonial administrator, and his mother had committed suicide; he was living with a brother in Brazzaville while being educated by Catholic missionaries. A friendship was formed that would later propel Elizabeth Domitien to temporary high office.

In Ubangi-Shari she grew up to become a skilled seamstress. She married Jean Baka and bore a daughter, but Baka would not be around when she was named prime minister. She was also politically active, joining the independence-oriented Mouvement d'Évolution Speciale d'Afrique Noire (MESAN), which had been founded in Bangui in 1949 by Jean-Bedel Bokassa's uncle, Barthélmy Boganda, a former priest. Ubangi-Shari had been under French domination since early in the 20th century. MESAN's program was "to defend the liberty of the African people, to ensure equality among all men, respect of each African's human dignity, and the individuality of each community or tribe."

MESAN members rushed to avail themselves of Elizabeth's sewing skills. Meanwhile she built up a trading enterprise, SOCACOM (Societé Centrafricaine de Commerce), which bought coffee beans for export. As leader of the Association of Male and Female Sellers of the Central Market in Bangui and of an association called Operation Wali Garass, she was a familiar figure amid the colorful stalls. In addition, she operated bars and liquor warehouses.

In 1958 under the leadership of Boganda and his nephew, David Dacko, Ubangi-Shari became an autonomous republic within the French Community and took the name Central African Republic. Bangui was the capital. Two years later the CAR achieved full independence, as did Chad, Gabon, and Middle Congo. Boganda, however, had been killed in an airplane crash, and Dacko had become the country's first president and also leader of MESAN, where Elizabeth Domitien had developed into an effective orator.

The same year of 1960, her childhood friend Lieutenant Jean-Bedel Bokassa arrived in Bangui after 20 years of service with the French army, which he had entered as a private at the outbreak of World War II. After the fall of France he had joined an African unit of the Free French force; later he served with distinction in the colonial army in Indochina. He cut an impressive figure, and quickly Dacko asked him to organize a 400-man army. Having retired from the French army as a captain in 1961, Bokassa became a major in the CAR army and was designated commander in chief in 1963.

The newly promoted Colonel Bokassa ousted his cousin in a military coup on New Year's Eve, 1965, and declared himself president and leader of MESAN. His immediate steps were to dissolve the national assembly, to abrogate the constitution, and to announce that he ruled by decree. Political opponents were executed or given long prison sentences. Some who were accused of treason against the state were expelled. The presi-

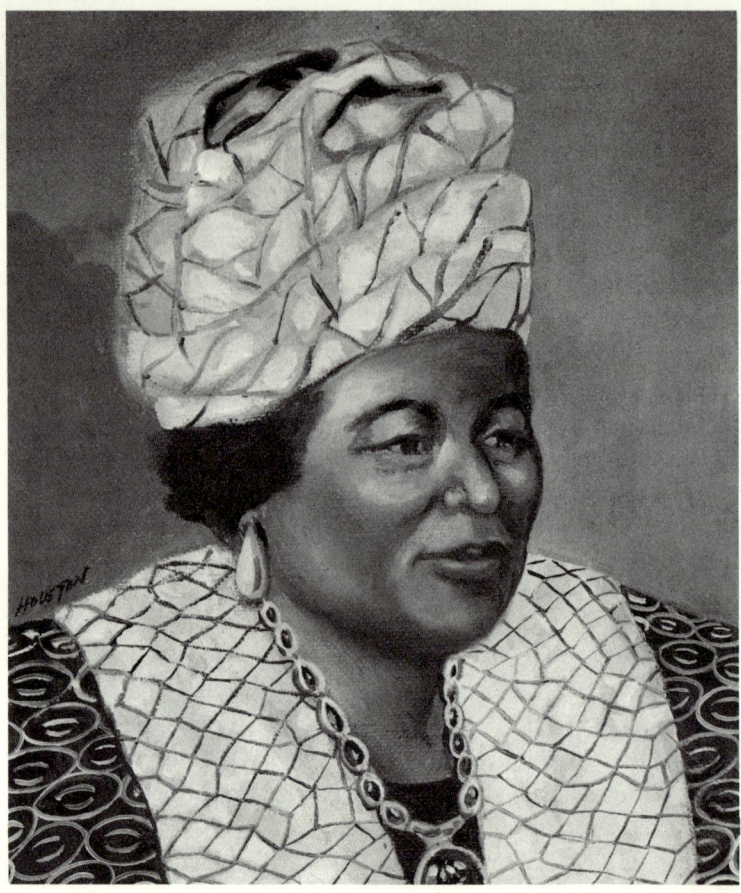

Elizabeth Domitien: oil portrait by John Houston.

dent made frequent cabinet changes and was fast earning a reputation as an overly temperamental leader.

Bokassa was prime minister, as well as president, and took on a bewildering variety of other posts. Among his many portfolios was that of trade and industry, and undoubtedly Domitien's business prospered, particularly from the expansion of coffee exports. In his first years, he tried to establish a sound economy with French help.

Recognized as a militant within MESAN, Domitien became its vice-president in 1969. Grasping for more power, Bokassa convened a national congress of MESAN, and Domitien helped proclaim him president for life in 1972. Two years later he gave himself the title field marshal. Over the next few years he was saved by French military intervention from being ousted in several coups. Domitien, his close friend, accompanied him on many trips abroad, where he ingratiated himself with his hosts by showing charming manners and freely dispensing diamonds. The foreign press, however, carried reports of his personal savagery to his opponents, to beggars, and particularly to thieves.

On January 1, 1975, bestowing on himself the new title of president of the government, Bokassa named Domitien prime minister. But the stout, forceful favorite, seen as arrogant by her enemies, had to swallow the fact that she was only a puppet.

Though smarting under her inauspicious role, prime minister only in name, Domitien was grateful for Bokassa's intense interest in reducing the high cost of transport for commercial enterprises. The Ubangi and Congo rivers were not adequate. The president for life had great plans to build a railroad that would be linked with lines in Cameroon and the Congo, and Domitien hoped to benefit from it.

In March Bokassa hosted a summit between France, represented by President Valéry Giscard d'Estaing, and the Francophone countries in Africa. As Giscard and Bokassa drove through the streets of Bangui, they were greeted by chanting, dancing, drum-beating throngs. The host threw a gala dinner for 3,000 at his white palace. His prime minister, however, remained in the background among other women clad in brocade or silver lamé evening gowns. She was never mentioned in any newspaper dispatch of the event. Rather, reporters focused on the entertainment — stomping pygmies and grass-skirted dancers and fireworks exploding overhead. Giscard also went hunting elephants on Bokassa's 200,000-acre private preserve.

Twenty countries had been invited; 14 were represented, but only seven heads of government or state showed up. Bokassa's point in holding the gathering was to get aid for development. Diamonds and an array of valuable minerals, especially uranium deposits, were waiting to be exploited. But Giscard could do no more than promise that his government would study Bokassa's economic proposals. The summit, however, made history; for the first time a former colonial master country and its subjects were brought together on an equal basis.

Bokassa escaped unharmed from an attempted assassination in February 1976. Among those sentenced to death for complicity in the plot was one of his sons-in-law. Bokassa's near brush with death made him more volatile than ever, and he ordered cabinet changes again. He dismissed Domitien in April. Rumor had it that his associates considered her business activities too much of a threat to them. Briefly, Bokassa put himself in the post, only to relinquish it to Ange Patasse and to establish a 31-member Council of the Central African Revolution with himself as president again: To general amazement, he appointed Dacko his closest personal adviser. Domitien, still active in MESAN, was not a member of the council.

By autumn, Bokassa's unpredictability had increased. When Libyan leader Muammar Qaddafi came to Bangui in October, the president announced that he had converted to Islam and taken the name of Salah Addem Ahmad Bokassa. In December a special congress of MESAN approved a new constitution that proclaimed the Central African Empire. Henceforth the president was Emperor Bokassa. At that point, Bokassa abandoned his Muslim name, claiming it was incompatible with his new majesty. He was concentrating on his hero, Napoleon.

Back in favor as an imperial adviser, Domitien witnessed Bokassa's lavish, Napoleon-style coronation. Clad in ermine and velvet robes with a jewel-encrusted, 39-foot train, he placed a $2 million dollar diamond crown on his head. The gown of the Empress Catherine, first in rank of his three wives, had been ordered from Lanvin in Paris. The whole spectacle cost $22 million. After the ceremony at the sports stadium, Domitien joined a procession along a flag-bedecked route to the cathedral of Notre Dame de Bangui for a High Mass.

Behind the imperial glitter, the elaborate protocol, and the huge gilded eagle throne, the economy was in miserable condition, with a bankrupt treasury and heavy foreign debts. The emperor himself, however, was rich. A large part of his personal fortune was based on the ivory trade, which had decreased the elephant population from about 40,000 to 10,000.

Meanwhile Bokassa's foreign policy was confusing observers. At the same time, he was making a cautious but steady rapprochement to South Africa and encouraging the Soviet Union to become involved in the Central African Republic. He said he would not mind getting money, even from the devil.

Amnesty International issued two chilling reports in 1979. Bokassa, who doted on uniforms, had ordered that all schoolchildren wear uniforms made by the Bokassa family. The first report said that when some of the children protested, he ordered his troops to fire on them, and about a dozen were killed. The second report stated that after another group of children threw stones at Bokassa's car, they were rounded up and thrown into sweltering prisons, where several suffocated, and that Bokassa himself slit open six small heads with his imperial ebony cane. When a judicial commission confirmed the reports, Bokassa ordered arrests and even some executions for all who had appeared as witnesses before the commission.

The world reacted with outrage to Amnesty International's disclosures, and in Paris, Giscard decided that Bokassa must be removed. When the emperor visited Qaddafi in Libya in September, French paratroopers surrounded the palace and seized the radio station. Dacko was told he was president again. The new cabinet, however, included several who had been prominent in the Bokassa empire. But other cohorts were arrested, among them Domitien. Bokassa tried to fly to France, but was not admitted into the country. Instead, arrangements were made for him to be a guest in President Houphouët-Boigny's palace in Abidjan, the Ivory Coast.

An election was held, and Dacko won 50.23 percent of the vote. But with reports of widespread balloting irregularities, violence flared. In 1980 "le grand monstre" was tried in absentia and sentenced to death on eight charges, including the massacre of the children and the embezzlement of diamonds. He was also accused of cannibalism, but the evidence was not conclusive.

Domitien was freed in 1981. In the fall, General André-Dieudonne Kolingba deposed Dacko in a bloodless coup and took over as president.

Toward the close of 1983, a group of supporters tried to pick up Bokassa in Abidjan, take him back to Bangui, and restore him to power. It was his dream of Napoleon returning from Elba. When apprised of the attempt, Houphouët-Boigny threw Bokassa out of the country. With 15 of his children and 20 women in his entourage, Bokassa flew to France and settled in his rundown chateau at Haudricourt. After four years, saying he was miserable in the cold weather, he returned voluntarily to Bangui. At a new trial he was condemned to death, but Kolingba commuted his sentence to life imprisonment in solitary confinement.

Domitien remained out of politics. Her "trading empire" had collapsed. In 1992 she was reported to be selling firewood.

Margaret Thatcher

*Prime Minister of the United Kingdom
of Great Britain and Northern Ireland
(1979–90)*

Since 1979, when she first went to Number 10 Downing Street, she had been up and down in British opinion polls, but public opinion never mattered much to Margaret Thatcher, who always described herself as a conviction, not a consensus, politician. Toward the close of 1990, however, the polls mattered to the mavens in her party. After another sharp drop in her popularity, an extraordinary Tory coup took place at Westminster, and the Iron Lady was forced to resign as party leader and then as head of government. For days, her precipitous fall made international headlines because the grocer's daughter from Grantham had become one of the most powerful women in the world. In the United Kingdom of Great Britain and Northern Ireland she had given her name — as Thatcherism — to an era and a pervasive political philosophy.

Although she had revamped herself in a stylish, somewhat aristocratic pattern, she never attempted to hide her lower middle-class origin. Following a sister Muriel by four years, she was born Margaret Hilda Roberts on October 13, 1925, to Alfred Roberts, a hardworking grocer, and his wife, Beatrice, née Robinson, a former dressmaker. Her birthplace, Grantham, was an unexciting market town in Lincolnshire.

The family lived above Alfred Roberts's grocery shop, where he and his wife both waited on customers. When the daughters were old enough, they, too, had duties in the store. In the Spartan household, which lacked indoor plumbing and hot water, life revolved around work, thrift, church attendance, and strict morality. Deprived of a carefree childhood, young Margaret Roberts was cherub faced, well behaved, neat, somewhat prissy, but self-assured.

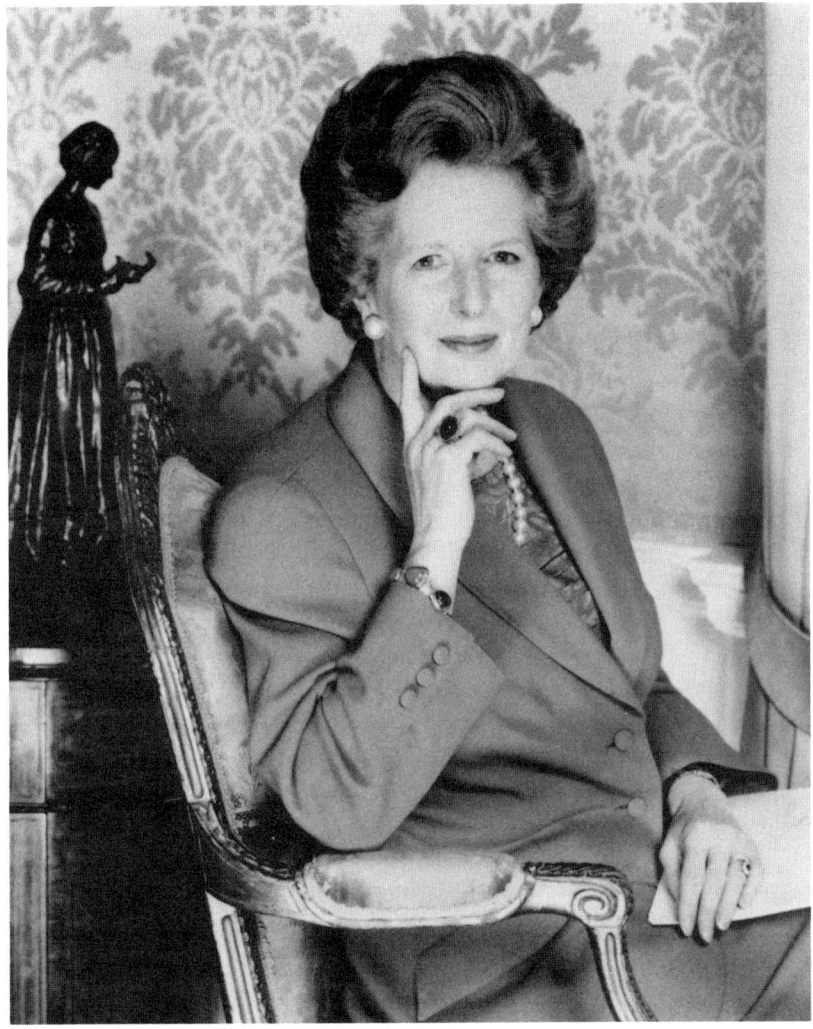

Margaret Thatcher: courtesy Embassy of the United Kingdom of Great Britain and Northern Ireland, Washington, D.C.

Alfred Roberts was also a lay preacher in the Methodist church and a local politician who belonged to the Conservative party. Although a great reader, he was conscious of his lack of formal education and therefore strove to acquire a second shop, so he could give his daughters the best schooling.

Muriel, however, was not bookish and eventually chose to train in physiotherapy. Margaret, her father's favorite, was studious and at an early age seemed obsessed with details. From elementary school she went on to Kesteven and Grantham Girls' High School, a prep school, where she joined a debating society. To acquire a more polished accent, she also began taking elocution lessons. A proud Alfred Roberts paid for lessons in Latin and the classics to prepare her for the university. All the while, she was imbibing his philosophy. "He brought me up to believe almost all the things I do believe," she later said.

She was 14 when World War II broke out. Since Grantham had a considerable weapons industry, it became a prime target for Nazi bombers once the blitz began, and during raids the Roberts family often huddled under their dining room table. For a time, an Austrian Jewish girl, a pen pal of Muriel, lived with them as a refugee.

In her last year at Kesteven, where she did well in mathematics, chemistry, and biology, Margaret decided she wanted to follow a classmate to Oxford and pursue a chemistry major, which she thought would guarantee her a job. Alfred Roberts had become a part-time justice of the peace, and Margaret often accompanied him to the courthouse where she was so fascinated by the unfolding legal dramas that she thought she had erred in choosing a future in science. But one of his lawyer friends told her to get a chemistry degree before she studied law.

Margaret was admitted to Somerville, one of the oldest women's colleges, which Indira Gandhi had attended earlier. There she had as her principal tutor Dorothy Crowfoot Hodgkin, a crystallographer and future Nobel laureate.

Feeling somewhat an outsider in the Oxford milieu, Margaret tried to gain status by talking a bit grandly about "Daddy, the mayor." After serving as councilman and alderman, Alfred Roberts, founder of the local Rotary Club, had been elected to a short mayoral term. By the next year, Margaret's visits home became more comfortable because her father had at last bought a semidetached house with indoor plumbing.

The Nazis never bombed Oxford, but volunteer war work was plentiful. Margaret served on the fire watch brigade and dispensed coffee and biscuits to soldiers at a canteen one night a week. More important for her future, at this time she joined the Oxford Union Conservative Association. From childhood, when she had been on the fringe of local politics because of her father, she had felt her political juices running. Quickly she became an important member of the union and in her junior year was elected its first female president. In 1945 when Winston Churchill, head of the wartime government, called for elections, Margaret campaigned vigorously for a Conservative candidate, but Clement Atlee and his Labour party crushed most of their Tory opponents. At the very moment of Britain's military triumph, its inspiring architect, Churchill, was turned out. The Labour victory had a decisive effect on Margaret Roberts; whereas Atlee proceeded to implement a welfare state, dismantling it would become one of her overriding goals.

After graduating from Somerville in 1947, she took a job as a research chemist with a plastics firm in Colchester. Helping develop adhesives in the laboratory, she frequently had to step out on the shop floor, where the men resented her laboriously learned upper-class accent and her constant political talk.

The next year, as representative of the Oxford Graduate Conference Association, the pretty, smart, well-dressed Miss Roberts caught the attention of officials at the Conservative party's annual conference. With their help, she became the youngest parliamentary candidate in Britain early in 1949. The seat was Dartford, Kent, an industrial town east of London. In the past it had been considered solidly Labour.

One night, following a reception to celebrate her formal adoption by the Tory constituency of Dartford, Margaret needed a ride back to Colchester. The party chairman obtained one for her with a businessman named Denis Thatcher. Ten years her senior and staunchly Conservative, Denis was doing well running his family's paint and chemicals firm. Having given her the lift to Colchester, he kept calling her for dates. Usually he took her out to dinner before they attended political meetings.

When elections were scheduled for February 1950, Margaret Roberts meticulously planned her political campaign. First, she quit her job with the plastics firm so she could live closer to her intended bailiwick. Since she could find no employment in Dartford, she accepted an offer from a food conglomerate in Hammersmith to test cake fillings and develop an artificial ice cream. Her evenings she devoted entirely to campaigning. Despite all her effort, she lost the election, but took comfort in a respectable showing that gave her the credentials to run again from Dartford in October 1951. She lost that election, too, despite a Conservative win, which brought Churchill back to Downing Street. As the returns came in, Denis proudly announced that he and the unsuccessful candidate would soon be married.

Because he was divorced, they kept their December wedding small and simple, possibly out of deference to Margaret's strait-laced parents.

the bride made a certain splash in her velvet gown of sapphire blue, the Tories' official color, and her matching hat with a great white ostrich feather sweeping down to her shoulder. The honeymoon in Portugal, Madeira, and Paris was her first visit abroad. Soon after, she left Methodism and joined the Anglican church.

With a moderately wealthy husband, the new Mrs. Thatcher could afford to quit her job in Hammersmith and take up the study of law full time. Displaying her usual concentration, she plunged into her books and did not stop when she found herself pregnant a year later. To her and Denis's surprise, twins, Mark and Carol, were born by Caesarean section, in October 1953, seven weeks ahead of schedule. Despite the extra work the premature babies demanded, she would not consider postponing her finals in December. She hired a nanny-housekeeper, who stayed on when Margaret went to work as a clerk for a tax lawyer, specializing first in patent law and then in tax law. Eventually her name was on the office door.

She was still committed to her goal of becoming a member of the House of Commons, but because she had two babies, selection committees turned her down, saying she should stay home and rear them. Reluctantly she postponed her parliamentary dream, but continued her legal career. Finally in 1959, when the twins were six, she found what was considered a safe seat from Finchley, a London suburb close to Fainborough, where the Thatchers had moved. She campaigned with her customary unstoppable energy and reaped her reward in a Tory landslide. So she took her seat as the youngest woman in Parliament, where 24 other women occupied the back benches.

Thatcher made a stunning debut with an incisive maiden speech, presenting a bill to allow the press to attend local government council meetings. Headlines blazoned her name, although the bill, heavily amended, did not pass until later.

Harold Macmillan had been prime minister since 1957, when Anthony Eden, ill and censured for the Suez Canal fiasco of 1956, resigned. Margaret, the comely young MP, had no access to the upper class, old-boy network in Parliament. But impressed by her intelligence and hard work, Macmillan suddenly offered her a junior post in the ministry of pensions and national insurance, and she accepted on the spot. The Conservatives had left intact much of the social insurance introduced by Atlee a decade earlier.

Domestically, she had smooth sailing. She and Denis agreed perfectly on each other's right to pursue independent interests. She was dedicated to government work; he combined business and sports. When the Thatcher family firm had been sold to an oil company, Denis joined its board. If he was not traveling on business, he golfed, refereed rugby matches, and attended sporting events. Always, however, his wife knew she could count on his full support. After 29 years of marriage, she would tell the *Daily Mail*: "He has his rugger cronies, and I have a circle of political friends. We have a life together and a life apart, and I think that's very important." Even in her busiest years, whenever he was home, Margaret Thatcher cooked her husband's breakfast.

The twins had graduated from nannies to boarding schools. For several years the family enjoyed some skiing holidays in Switzerland. But usually Mark and Carol did not see too much of their parents, who, although loving, always acted in a somewhat formal manner toward them. Margaret constantly juggled a hectic schedule to make time for them. She claimed never to need more than four or five hours' sleep.

By 1963, Macmillan stood on weak ground because of the Profumo Affair, involving his minister of war in a call girl scandal, and he resigned. His successor, Sir Alec Douglas-Home, called for elections in 1964. Thatcher kept her Finchley seat, but Britain gained a new prime minister, the Labour leader, Harold Wilson.

As their party head, the Conservatives chose Edward Heath. Since British opposition leaders set up a shadow government to follow the fortunes of the ruling party, he became shadow prime minister. Although notoriously uncomfortable with women in politics, he gave Thatcher the number two post at the shadow treasury in 1966, later moving her to the shadow ministry of fuel and power, then to shadow transport, and finally to shadow education.

Concerned about the deteriorating economy and the influence of the powerful trade unions, Britain elected a Conservative majority in 1970, and the aloof Heath became prime minister. Thatcher moved up from her shadow post to become secretary of education. Because Heath planned to slash governmental spending, Thatcher abruptly canceled the free milk allowance for schoolchildren aged 7 to 11, her rationale being that most parents could pay for the milk. The outcry stunned her. At one public meeting, a rock hit her on her chest. Much of the press made her out a villain. Newspapers blasted her as "Thatcher the Milk Snatcher."

She was unpopular, not only with the public, but in the cabinet and Commons, whose members disliked her driving ambition and often strident manner. These qualities belied her physical attractiveness, bolstered y an English rose complexion, regular features, trim figure, and model legs. But, recognizing her talent, hard work, and impressive command of statistics, Heath did not drop her. Meanwhile she confused her critics, who had vilified the milk bill, by spending freely in the education department to rebuild and replace schools and improve technical and vocational training.

As he marked two years in office, Heath found himself struggling with economic problems, caused for the most part by the rapid rise in oil prices determined by the Organization of Petroleum Exporting Countries (OPEC). Worry over worsening unemployment made him slowly reintroduce state control over the marketplace and industry, according to the Labour pattern. For the time being, Margaret Thatcher went along with his moves, but later his turnaround would be called the reason she launched her revolution in 1979.

Because of a coal miners' strike, Heath called for elections for early 1975, then found himself returned to Downing Street by a paper-thin majority. Economic gloom sent voters to the polls again in October, and this time Labour gained a three-seat edge. Harold Wilson became prime minister again.

Heath was doomed as party chief and agreed to put the Tory leadership to a vote. Everyone expected his successor to be Sir Keith Joseph, who was popular in high Tory circles. But when Joseph blundered by publicly telling poor people not to breed, Margaret Thatcher, more than ever at odds with Heath, stepped into the breach. Helped by Airey Neave, a back-bencher and war hero whom she had known at Lincoln's Inn, and Gordon Reece, a television producer, Thatcher staged a brilliant series of operations and crushed Heath, who refused to serve in her shadow cabinet.

Now she had to prepare to become prime minister, first lord of the treasury, and minister for social service. More style, she concluded, was necessary. She acquired a bigger wardrobe, dyed her brown hair reddish blonde, and took lessons again to improve her voice and lower her pitch. It was also imperative to shed her insular outlook. Ignorant of foreign affairs, she decided to travel to Luxembourg, France, Germany, Romania, Canada, and the United States. But she found time to attend Carol's graduation from the university. Mark, known as something of a playboy, had not gone beyond public school. Racing cars were his current passion.

Also in 1975, the Russians gave Margaret Thatcher a title that she adopted with relish and that proved to be a campaign bonanza from then on. After she delivered a speech warning that the Soviet Union was bent on world dominion, the Soviet army newspaper dubbed her the Iron Lady, the Cold War warrior. Still, in 1976 she smilingly asked, "I stand here in my red chiffon gown, my face softly made up, my hair gently waved—the Iron Lady of the western world?"

To national surprise and shock, Harold Wilson suddenly resigned in 1976. Labour had lost several by-elections, but he gave no specific reason for leaving. Rather than schedule a new election, he asked the party to choose the foreign secretary, James Callaghan, popularly known as Sunny Jim, as his successor.

With Carol, who was studying law, Thatcher made a Far Eastern tour in 1977, indulging her taste for Chinese art and porcelain. When her daughter decided to remain in Australia for the next few years, Thatcher returned alone to London and the political wars. As party leader, she often made remarks that caused an uproar, such as her comments following a riot of black youths when she said on a television program that the government should halt all immigration.

Because of its unhealthy economy, Britain had been known for years as "the sick man of Europe." Journalists termed 1978–79 the "Winter of Discontent" after truckers, railroad workers, and public service employees staged the biggest general strike since 1926.

Certain that Callaghan would have to call an election, Thatcher began her energetic preparations and was furious when he made no move. What finally brought him down was the issue of devolution (limited home rule) for Scotland and Wales. Referenda were scheduled for March 1979 in the two countries. Only 11.9 percent of the Welsh voted for devolution. In Scotland, 30.85 percent said yes and 30.78 percent no. Sunny Jim was in a quandary. Opponents had already introduced into the devolution bill a clause stipulating a 40 percent yes vote. Finally, thinking he could save home rule for Scotland, Callaghan suggested all-party talks, thereby infuriating the Scottish Nationalist party and the Liberal party. Promptly a motion condemning the government for failing to implement the yes vote was offered in Parliament.

Thatcher now moved in for the kill, introducing a no-confidence motion that the Callaghan government lost by one vote, 311 to 310. The election was at hand, and she set herself a grueling pace. While swiping at the unions, she extolled thrift, individual enterprise, income tax cuts, privatization of industry, and spending cuts except for defense and the police. Whereas Callaghan stood for keeping the welfare state, she loudly proclaimed that she would halt the slide to socialism. While out speaking for the party candidates, Thatcher still had to win her own seat of Finchley, now called, Finchley, Barnet.

Election results on May 3 showed a solid win for the Tories. The next day, within half an hour of Callaghan's handing his resignation letter to Elizabeth II, Thatcher went to Buckingham Palace and stood before the queen, who asked her to form a new government. The two women were almost exact contemporaries, Thatcher older by eight months. Thatcher felt a deep reverence for the Crown and through her three terms of office would never try to upstage Elizabeth.

But perhaps fearing other rivalry for public attention, she presented no women in her own cabinet. She insisted that government was based on meritocracy. She would never endorse any form of preferment that did not turn on accomplishment. Birth and schooling were not enough.

By this time, Thatcher harbored an almost vitriolic hatred for the trade unions and blamed their excessive power for the country's economic ills. For the next 11 years she would push through laws designed to weaken the unions, but they failed to have the crippling effect she intended. Still, even her severest critics admitted that she forced the unions to modify some of their arrogant postures.

At the official opening of Parliament that spring of 1979, the queen read the speech prepared by the new prime minister, who promised to reduce income taxes, cut back on social services, and curb the government's role in economic and personal life. By June, Thatcher had slashed the highest tax rates on earned and unearned income, raised value-added taxes, reduced several subsidies, and begun selling off state-owned enterprises.

On her immediate agenda were two international summits, first in Strasbourg with members of the European Community and then in Tokyo, where seven Western powers were meeting to deal with the oil crisis. When Thatcher's plane made a refueling stop in Moscow on the way to Japan, Soviet Premier Alexei Kosygin waited on the tarmac to greet her. Not at all intimidated, she complained about the Kremlin's military buildup and its human rights abuses. Once she was in Tokyo, the Japanese press became fascinated by her blond hairdo, high heels, and standout position as the lone woman among the summit leaders, who admired her command of facts and figures. Like no other head of government, Thatcher could quote statistics.

In July she flew to Zambia for her first Commonwealth conference. One of the chief issues was Zimbabwe, formerly called Southern Rhodesia. Northern Rhodesia had turned into independent Zambia in 1964, but Southern Rhodesia had become a self-governing colony whose whites resisted any attempt to force a transfer to black majority rule. In 1965 a white minority government under Ian D. Smith unilaterally declared the British colony independent. The next year the United Nations imposed economic sanctions in an attempt to force a transition to black majority rule. When there was no progress by 1972, black nationalists mounted a guerrilla war.

In June 1979, a month before Thatcher arrived in Lusaka, a biracial government, headed by Bishop Abel Muzorewa, was installed, and Southern Rhodesia became Zimbabwe. But the two leading guerrilla groups, Joshua Nkomo's Zimbabwe African People's Union and Robert Mugabe's Zimbabwe African National Union, rejected the Muzorewa government and continued their violence.

The British head of government came to Africa supporting Muzorewa, but her foreign minister, Lord Carrington, argued persuasively that she must change her mind. Effectively she called for a cease-fire and a new constitution and offered British troops to oversee new elections. Carrington soon brought the warring parties to Lancaster House in London for a peace conference. By December they agreed to a cease-fire and a temporary resumption of British rule. In March 1980, Lord Christopher Soames, the interim governor, supervised preindependence elections that made Mugabe prime minister. Zimbabwe became independent in April 1980.

Thatcher's diplomacy brought her international prestige, but she had far less success with domestic problems. In spite of all her doughty praise of her policies, which were now coming to be called Thatcherism, the economy remained dismal. Unemployment rose ever higher. Then in April 1981 the worst race riot in Britain's history broke out in Brixton, a racially mixed section of south London. Most of the blacks involved were West Indians who were clamoring for more jobs and more money. The Brixton riot was put down, but within three months trouble had spread to other London neighborhoods and to the industrial cities of Birmingham, Liverpool, and Manchester.

More than ever, Thatcher seemed like a hectoring nanny as she lectured the rioters. Beyond her words she relied on a strict law-and-order approach. She would offer no compromise. In Liverpool, blacks were put down with tear gas, the first time it had ever been used for civil disorder in Britain. Soon after, the prime minister fired 40 regulars from their cabinet posts and replaced them with staunch loyalists.

Opinion polls, which she disdained, gave her the lowest rating in British history. At her nadir, an unexpected war thousands of miles away helped to rescue her. Few Britons knew anything about the Falkland Islands off the coast of Argentina. This rugged region had been British territory since 1833, but Argentina had continued to claim it. In March 1982, 40 Argentines, identifying themselvs as scrap dealers, invaded South Georgia Island, populated mostly by sheep and penguins. Their landing was part of beleaguered President General Leopoldo Fortunato Gultiere's plan to regain control before the 150th anniversary of British occupation.

British outrage led to Lord Carrington's resignation as foreign secretary and his replacement by Francis Pym, whom Thatcher disliked. Events were running on a double track. A military buildup proceeded as attempts were made to negotiate the crisis. To no avail, U.S. Secretary of State Alexander Haig tried to intervene in the peace process. Part of a British task force was already in place in the Falklands when Thatcher made a major decision. Except for some helicopter accidents, the facedown had been almost without casualties. Now she ordered the British submarine *Conqueror* to attack the Argentine warship, *General Belgrano,* which sank, drowning 368 sailors. The action alienated world opinion, but it made Thatcher the darling of the British military. Only two days later, the British destroyer *Sheffield* was hit by an Argentine-fired Exocet missile, and 21 British sailors were killed, many more injured. This time the Iron Lady wept.

Quickly the war escalated. Large troop carriers bore down on the Falklands, spilling out British soldiers. Three weeks of fighting followed till the British made their final assault on Port Stanley, and the Argentines surrendered. Victory had been achieved with 255 British deaths.

The Falklands triumph led to the overthrow of the Argentine junta and made Thatcher a national heroine. Euphoria was reinforced in July with royal magic, the wedding of Charles, Prince of Wales, to Lady Diana Spencer, hailed as the most televised ceremony in history.

It seemed an auspicious time for the prime minister to tour the Far East—Japan, Hong Kong, India, and Bahrain. In India she met again with Prime Minister Indira Gandhi, who had impressed her at a Commonwealth conference.

On her return, her aides greeted her with worrisome unemployment figures. Again London and Liverpool made daily headlines. Soon there were even more unwelcome newspaper stories about her son Mark, who was reported lost during a racing car rally through 1,000 miles of Baja, California. Fortunately he turned up quickly. It was the second time within a year that he had disappeared. In January the Sahara Desert had apparently swallowed him up during another rally, and Margaret and Denis Thatcher had agonized for six days until he was found.

Nationally, things seemed to be going her way. In 1983 the pound was still sliding, but inflation had dropped by half, and the trade figures showed a healthy balance. The Falklands victory remained fresh in the country's memory, and though elections were not scheduled until 1984, Thatcher's advisers believed that by calling an election in June 1983 she could secure a mandate. The North had borne most of the economic hardship and was pro-Labour; the South, much better off, supported the Tories so wholeheartedly that the party gained a 144-seat majority. Thatcher told aides that her challenger, Michael Foot, had been too weak.

With her solid win, she was determined to forge ahead with her program of "popular capitalism," which allowed private citizens to buy shares in giant nationalized concerns, such as Rolls-Royce, British Airways, and Telecon.

But she had to face her old enemies, the unions, which detested her with good reason. New laws held them responsible for their members' actions, demanded that leaders poll members before calling a strike, and prohibited sympathy strikes or closed shops. In March 1984, Thatcher decided to do battle with Arthur Scargill, the Marxist leader of the National Union of Mineworkers, who had called a violent coal strike. The strike lasted almost a year, but Thatcher, assisted by effective policing and high unemployment figures, refused to give in. Scargill finally called off the strike. The aftermath of his defeat was that union membership fell by almost 25 percent.

Although her opponents decried Thatcher's arrogance and obstinacy, they could not deny her courage. In 1984 she had appeared unnerved after the Irish Republican Army placed a bomb in her hotel at a Conservative party conference in Brighton. The explosion had occurred two minutes after she left her bathroom. But as much as she condemned IRA terrorism, which had claimed Airey Neave's life shortly after the 1979 election, she was sympathetic to allowing the Irish Republic a role in Northern Ireland's affairs and had to face down many Protestant objections.

The 1987 election was harder fought than that of 1983 because Thatcher had a strong opponent in Neil Kinnock, new leader of the Labour party. Particularly he scolded her for being unsympathetic to the poor. Thatcher icily told him that social services could be paid for only in an expanding economy, whose progress she would direct. The message caught hold with enough voters that the Tories gained a 102-seat majority, and Thatcher won an unprecedented third term. She said, "It is not that I believe no one else is fit. It is simply that people know the way I drive."

Many foreign leaders had long stood in awe of her. Only French President François Mitterand dared to remark that she had the lips of Marilyn Monroe and the eyes of Caligula. With President Ronald Reagan she had developed a special friendship, based on their aversion to too much government, their strong anti–Communist stands, and their genuine liking for each other. And with Mikhail S. Gorbachev, the secretary-general of the Soviet Communist party, she formed an unusual, close relationship. Gorbachev was a member of the Politburo when she had first met him in 1984 at Chequers, the prime minister's summer residence, and had declared, "This is a man we can do business with." She sympathized fully with his efforts to reform the Soviet economy. Resolved to open Britain's doors to the Soviets, the prime minister left for Moscow in April 1987 and linked arms control negotiations to progress in human rights. Labour spoke out for unilateral nuclear disarmament, but Thatcher advocated modernizing the nation's nuclear weapons so that Britain could keep its independent nuclear deterrent.

Only once did Margaret Thatcher use the royal "we" in public. Mark had become an auto executive in Dallas, Texas, and had married an American girl. When told of the birth of her first grandchild in March 1989, the prime minister announced, "We have become a grandmother."

Bad news on Britain's economic front continued to plague her, but she remained confident of her staying power until a cabinet crisis blew up that summer over her refusal to consider British participation in the European Community's proposed European Monetary System (EMS) to provide for a single currency by 1999. Because her foreign minister, Sir Geoffrey Howe, advocated it, she demoted him to the post of deputy foreign minister. Several other ministers were fired for taking Howe's stand. Chancellor of the Exchequer, Nigel Lawson, who had pushed for British membership, resigned, and was followed by Sir Alan Watkins, her economic adviser, who had bolstered her anti–EMS views.

One of Thatcher's pet principles was that everyone who used local services should pay something toward their cost. Thus in 1990 she imposed the Community Charge, popularly known as the poll tax, which amounted to a huge tax cut for large property owners, but higher taxes for lower- and middle-class homeowners. Eliciting a violent response, the Community Charge prompted riots across the country. In 1992 it would be abandoned.

Again her unbending stand caused some Tory stalwarts to wonder if it was not time for her to go. But most of all, it was her still-unbridled scorn for the EMS that led controversial Michael Heseltine, a former defense minister, to challenge her for the party leadership. The voting began in November 1990 while Thatcher was in Paris attending a European Community summit. When she returned to Downing Street, she learned that she faced a runoff with Heseltine. At first she said she would stay in the race. Then she stunned everyone by announcing she would resign as party leader in favor of two candidates she found more congenial than Heseltine: Foreign Secretary Douglas Hurd and Chancellor of the Exchequer John Major. The election of Major, who had no university education, fulfilled her ideal of meritocracy.

In her most gracious manner she resigned as prime minister on November 22, showing no bitterness as she said good-bye. She had decided to keep her seat in Parliament. But before long, no doubt urged by Denis to return to private life, she left the House of Commons, too. Her admirers firmly believed that after 11 and one half momentous years Britain's first woman prime minister actually departed in a blaze of glory.

Denis had been knighted because of her accomplishments. Soon it was reported that the queen might offer her the life title of countess of Finchley. But in June 1992 Thatcher became the Baroness Thatcher of Kesteven, entitled to sit in the House of Lords, a less exciting place than Commons. She had already begun a new role as elder stateswoman, more than willing to share with the world her convictions on issues that most concerned her.

Maria de Lourdes Pintasilgo

Prime Minister of Portugal
(1979)

As head of a caretaker government in 1979, Maria de Lourdes Pintasilgo functioned as a nonparty official, with backing from the Socialists and the Communists. "In the evolution of Portuguese politics," she later said, "it was rather important that I was not affiliated with a party. If I had been, the situation of prime minister would not have come up. I was not labeled immediately, and I could propose my own vision of society."

Portugal's first woman prime minister was born in Abrantes on January 18, 1930, the daughter of Jaime de Matos Pintasilgo and Amelia Ruivo da Silva. For 20 turbulent years, the former kingdom of Portugal had been a republic.

In 1908, on the streets of Lisbon, revolutionaries had assassinated King Carlos I and Crown Prince Luis. The new occupant of the throne was the king's second son, Manuel II, who was judged too young and inept to govern. After Manuel reigned for only two years, an uprising of soldiers and civilians forced him into exile, and a republic was then proclaimed. Until 1926 there were 18 revolutions.

When Maria was still a toddler in 1932, Portugal gained a new prime minister, who proved to be of towering importance. Antonio Oliveira de Salazar, an economics professor, had been serving as finance minister. Since World War I, the country's economy had been in great disorder, and he was given a free hand to solve the problems. The consequences were hardly expected. A new constitution, promulgated in 1933, made Salazar virtually a dictator. His Estado Novo (New Government), which was influenced by Italian fascism as practiced by Benito Mussolini, set up a police state, placed trade unions under government control, and abolished freedom of the press and political expression. Money matters were put on a firm basis, but at a tremendous cost to the Portuguese people, the poorest and least educated in Western Europe.

Maria was destined to live in the Salazar era for almost four decades. Although she was interested in studying piano and writing poetry, she decided to pursue a scientific education for two reasons. Deeply religious, she felt committed to workers' social causes and believed that she could better share their lives if she entered industry as an engineer. She had not yet begun to call herself a feminist, but she also wanted to demonstrate that Portuguese women could succeed as chemical engineers because too many women had lost heart in the beginning stages of their training. Maria was accepted at the Institute Superior Tecnico from where she received her degree in 1953. During her student days, a professor introduced her to Marcello Caetano, who would be chosen as Salazar's successor in 1968.

From 1953 to 1954 she worked in Lisbon as a researcher at the Nuclear Energy Commission and from 1954 to 1960, as head of projects in the research and development department of the Companhia Uniao Fabril (CUF), an industrial pool.

Meanwhile, from 1954 to 1958, she was a member of the board of directors of the Pax Romana International Movement for Catholic Students, an autonomous auxiliary of the Pax Romana International Catholic Movement for Intellectual and Cultural Affairs. This movement strove to broaden students' awareness of poverty, inequality, and oppression. Its activities included conducting protests, sending letters, and reporting human rights violations. Maria also affiliated herself with the International Grail Movement of Catholic Women (known as Graal in Portugal), working on educational, religious, social, and cultural issues, and was a board member from 1965 untl 1974.

A debilitating stroke in 1968 forced Salazar's resignation, and Caetano, his close associate, succeeded him as prime minister and continued the rightist posture. The old dictator died in 1970.

Under the Caetano regime, Pintasilgo agreed to be a member of an advisory group, the Department of Politics and General Administration, Corporative Chamber, which consisted of representatives of interest groups, even if leftist, and persons chosen by the prime minister. "It was extremely helpful to be in the second chamber," Pintasilgo recalled later, "because the system was that, whenever somebody was in the minority,

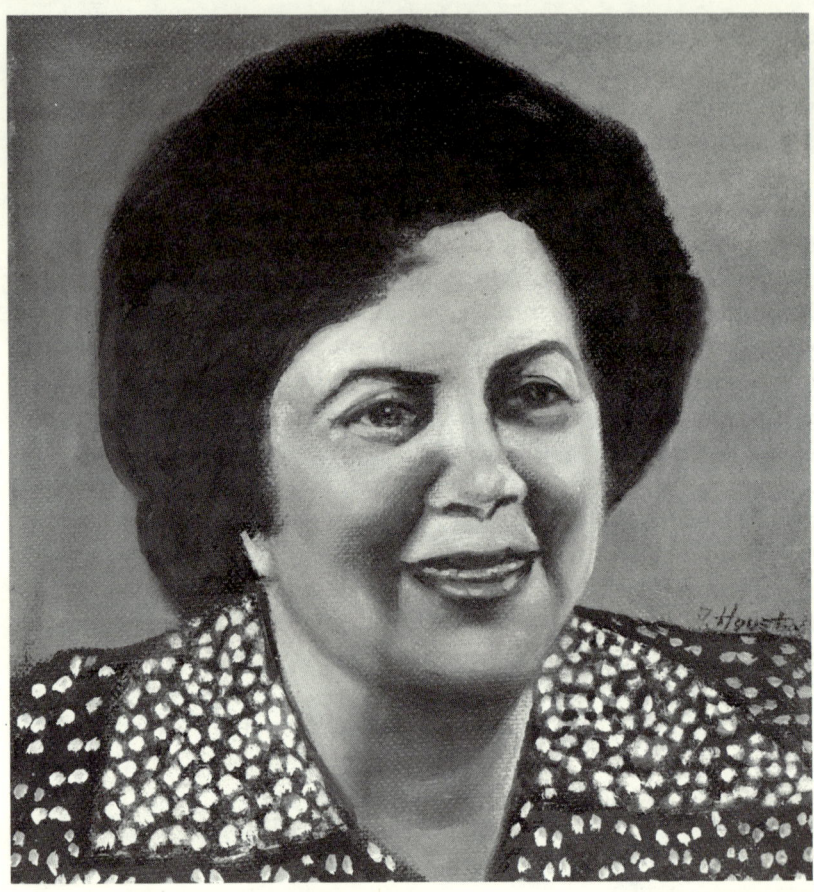

Maria de Lourdes Pintasilgo: oil portrait by John Houston.

he or she would be able to make a declaration, which I did every time — and a newspaper could publish it, regardless of censorship." She would remain on the commission until Caetano's fall in 1974. Concurrently, she became chair of the National Commission on the Status of Women, an office she held from 1970 to 1974. She had turned down suggestions to run for Parliament because it was made up of only the ruling party. For a year, 1971 to 1972, she had been a member of the Portuguese delegation to the United Nations.

With numerous insurrections in the African colonies and the loss of Portugal's enclave in India in the 1960s, the army grew restless over the futile warfare. In April 1974 in an almost bloodless coup at dawn, a group of army officers, calling themselves the Armed Forces Movement (AFM), overthrew Caetano and President Américo Thomaz, ending more than 40 years of civilian dictatorship. The revolution, which promised the return of democracy under a revolutionary junta, also brought independence for the colonies.

General Antonio de Spínola became provisional president, and Adelino de Palma Carlos, a right-of-center Democrat, became the prime minister. But within a few weeks, the regime ran into economic and political difficulties, and he resigned.

Under the next prime minister, leftist Vasco dos Santos Gonçalves, a veteran of African campaigns, Pintasilgo served as secretary of social affairs for a year. Saying that conditions made it impossible for Portugal to adopt true democracy, Spinola resigned that fall and was replaced by General Francisco da Costa Gomez, the armed forces chief of staff, who reappointed Gonçalves prime minister.

Pintasilgo arrived in Paris in 1976 as the Portuguese ambassador to the United Nations Educational, Scientific, and Cultural Organization (UNESCO), where she became one of 24 delegates to the executive board of the General Conference. The board supervised work on UNESCO programs and prepared the agenda for the General Conference, which determined UNESCO policies and programs. There was a broad palette. Since its landmark session in 1954, UNESCO had concentrated on problems related to illiteracy; primary education; racial, social, and international tensions; mutual appreciation of Eastern and Western cultures; and research on living conditions.

General Antonio dos Santos Ramalho Eanes, a nonparty candidate supported by the Socialists, popular Democrats, and Social Democrats, was elected president in 1976 for a five-year term, the first democratically elected head of state in 50 years. Dr. Mario Soares headed the minority Socialist government. But Ramalho Eanes dismissed his prime minister in 1977 for failing to persuade opposition parties in the National Assembly to agree to an economic austerity plan. A month later, Soares's Socialist-led coalition and the rightist Social Democratic Center (CDS) agreed to pass the austerity program, which had been demanded by the International Monetary Fund (IMF) and 13 industrial nations from which Portugal was seeking loans. Soares took office again, but in July 1978 was dismissed over disagreement with the CDS on agricultural and health policies. He had also refused to fire his controversial minister of agriculture.

Succeeding Soares was Alfredo Nobre da Costa, who formed a cabinet of nonpartisan technicians. But the Communists objected to him because he had headed large state and private companies under the right-wing dictatorships of Salazar and Caetano. After less than two months, Da Costa's government fell.

Ramalho Eanes then appointed law professor Carlos Alberto da Mota Pinto as prime minister. At once, his nonparty government faced continuing battles with political factions and trade unions. The Left was particularly angered by a proposed 56 percent tax on the traditional extra month's pay at Christmas. Negotiations to renew the IMF agreement began in January, but there was no consensus on how much Portugal should cut from its $920 million current account and how the economy should be stabilized. Portugal was asking for standby credit of $50 million. Mota Pinto lost a vote on the budget issue in March 1979. In June the Socialists and Communists introduced censure motions, and he resigned on June 7. The following month the Organization for Economic Cooperation and Development (OECD) criticized Portugal's inflation rate of 24 percent.

Then on July 18, a $300 million loan from a group of international banks eased the financial dilemma. The rescue came shortly before Ramalho Eanes asked Pintasilgo to form a government to stay in place until elections could be held. With her wide experience, Pintasilgo was a figure he could trust. On August 1 she was sworn in as head of the eighth government since 1974.

For five months, Pintasilgo presided over an all-male, 16-member cabinet described as mostly moderate. Only two women held government posts. She had invited several to participate, but had received only negative answers. She later commented, "Women who are very competent in their fields feel that political life is less pure, that they're going to have to make compromises on an intellectual or moral level." She also spoke of the Portuguese women's low self-esteem. They would say, "I am not competent."

Pintasilgo believed that during her brief exercise of power she should be concerned with speaking the truth frankly, even when people did not know all the implications. In general, simple people seemed to understand what she was saying. And it heartened her when women felt free to speak up at meetings. To her, their coming forward was more important than the passage of legislative measures. Even as prime minister, she continued to live in her modest apartment at the headquarters of Graal.

The General Alliance, a coalition of four Center-Right parties, won the elections for the National Assembly in December, and its leader, Social Democrat Francisco Sa Carneiro, was appointed prime minister in January 1980, replacing Pintasilgo. For a time she supported efforts to form a coalition of Center-Left groups to oppose the rightists who brought Sa Carneiro to power. The next year Sa Carneiro and his foreign minister were killed in an airplane crash.

Pintasilgo never married. In an interview she gave on leaving office, she revealed that when she was a young girl, groping for her "mission on earth," it had dawned on her that she could best fulfill her own existence by choosing a celibate life. "For me it has meant the possibility of relating to many different persons, and I have not been tied to one person."

Three of her books — *Sulcos do nosso querer comum (Furrows of Our Common Ground)*, *Imaginar a Igreja (To Imagine the Church)*, and *Les nouveaux feminismes: question pour les chretiens?* were published in 1980. From 1981, when Ramalho Eanes was reelected president, until 1986 she served as one of his advisers. Two more books were published in 1985: *Dimensoes da mundanca (Dimensions of Change)*, and *As minhas respostas (My Answer)*. She also had written countless articles on international affairs, development, and the status of women.

In addition to her continued involvement in Graal, Pintasilgo participated in religious groups at the local, national, and international levels.

Portugal entered the European Community in 1986 and thereby was entitled to send 24 members to the European Parliament. In July 1987, Pintasilgo was in the first group elected to the Parliament. But she stayed in Strasbourg, the site of the plenary sessions, only until 1989.

She remained on the advisory boards or councils of several organizations. But she had not forgotten her first loves, the piano and poetry. Just after she stepped down as prime minister, she said, "The whole realm of life, which I would call the poetic side of life, is very dear to me. Politics by itself is a highly dry thing.... In the Greek universe you need politicians and you need poets, and you put the two things together."

EUGENIA CHARLES
Prime Minister of Dominica
(1980–)

The prime minister of Dominica brought herself and her exotic island to world attention in October 1983, when, as chair of the Organization of Eastern Caribbean States (OECS), she persuaded President Ronald Reagan to intervene militarily in the nearby island of Grenada and remove its militant leftist regime. For all the success of this mission, it was not widely acclaimed, but Eugenia Charles, a veteran of receiving political barbs, never regretted her move.

Unlike the majority of Dominican blacks, she came from a well-to-do family. Born on May 15, 1919, in Pointe Michel and named Mary Eugenia, she was the first child of the enterprising John Baptiste (called JB) Charles and his wife, the former Josephine Delauney. After starting out as a mason, JB prospered as an investor, banker, and fruit exporter. Three sons and another daughter would complete the close-knit family. Long afterward, Eugenia Charles would tell an interviewer that her strong-minded mother was her primary influence.

When Eugenia was attending the Convent High School in Roseau and St. Joseph's Convent in St. George's, Grenada, she learned history lessons that began with French colonialism. In 1627 France raised its standard over Dominica, discovered and named by Christopher Columbus, when, having failed to find suitable anchorage, he sailed past it on Sunday, November 3, 1493. In the 16th century, Carib Indians drove back the Spaniards who came to explore a place Columbus had depicted to King Ferdinand and Queen Isabella as a crumpled-up piece of paper. Although the more successful French colonists imported Africans as a work force, they set a pattern of not deforesting the island, the most mountainous and rain swept in the Caribbean, and thus no large cane

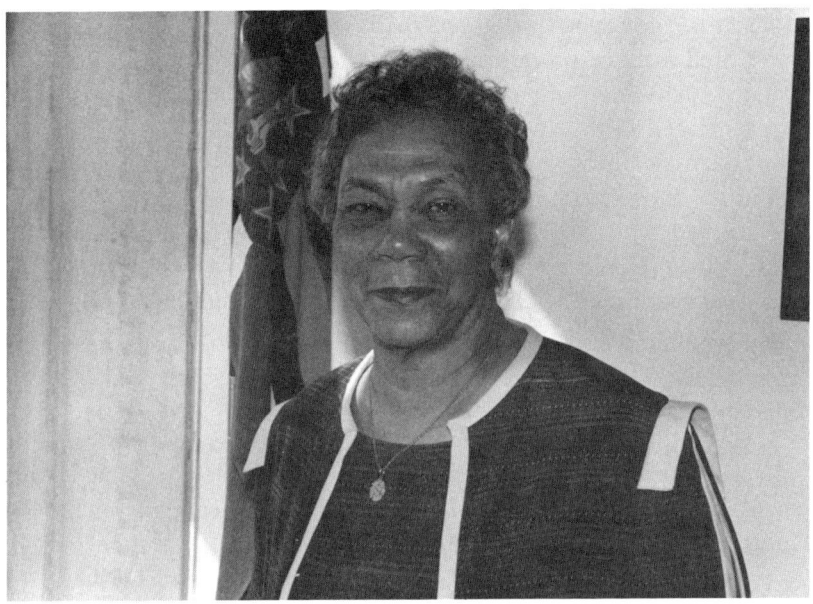

Eugenia Charles: courtesy Office of the Prime Minister, Roseau, Dominica.

plantations were established. Therefore, much of Dominica remained dark, secret, and unspoiled, dominated by a multilayered rain forest and swift-flowing streams.

The island belonged to the French king until the Seven Years War (1756–63), when the British occupied the island, which was ceded to them by the Treaty of Paris. During the American Revolution, the French regained Dominica and retained it until the war's end. Britain took permanent control in 1805.

Over the years, certain slaves bought their freedom with money saved from selling livestock and produce from small private gardens; some even became owners of small estates. On returning to the island, the British reestablished the two-chamber House of Assembly, but blacks were still barred from political participation. Finally in 1831 a bill allowed propertied free blacks to vote and seek office. By 1832 three were elected to the House of Assembly. In 1833 the British abolished slavery, and five years later a black majority held forth in the Assembly.

But gradually English absentee landlords lobbied so effectively that much of the representative government was whittled down, and in 1898 London instituted a Crown Colony government in Dominica. Under the new status, the blacks lost power, roads were built, and an agribusiness was started with the processing of lime juice. But progress was slow. The island, with its dominant agricultural pattern of small-scale peasant farming, remained in the depths of poverty.

So ran the history lessons Eugenia learned when she was in her teens, just at the time riots broke out all over the West Indies.

In 1940, when Eugenia Charles was 21, the Moyne Commission suddenly thrust Dominica into the modern world. After exposing the primitive conditions of all the British colonies in the Caribbean, it set forth a comprehensive economic development program that, together with British trade and investment, improved living standards, provided educational and medical facilities, and created jobs.

From 1942 to 1946, Eugenia studied at University College, the University of Toronto, where she received a bachelor's degree in law. Then she headed for postwar London and the Inner Temple, Inns of Court. She had dreamed of studying law ever since high school, when, as part of a secretarial course, she had practiced her shorthand by transcribing court proceedings.

She was called to the English bar in 1947 and promptly enrolled at the London School of Economics to specialize in laws related to juvenile delinquency. After completing her courses, she hoped to stay in England. But her parents came to London to urge her to return to Dominica, where, they said, she could enjoy the prestige of being the only woman lawyer on the island. Giving in to their wishes, Eugenia set up her office in Roseau. Soon she also handled cases in Barbados and other islands in the Leeward and Windward archipelagoes.

Without registering for any party, she became interested in politics and frequently wrote letters to the island newspapers. The political picture in Dominica was changing rapidly. Through the 1950s, demands intensified for better working conditions, higher farm prices, and more land for the poor. Such cries led to the formation of the Dominican Labour party (DLP). The party's leader, Edward Oliver Le Blanc, who claimed to represent "the little working man," became prime minister in 1961. For the first time, governmental leadership passed from the ruling elite in Roseau.

Le Blanc was also committed to obtaining freedom for the island. As a first step, Dominica became one of the six internally self-governing West Indies Associated States in 1967.

But the next year Charles rose in furious opposition when Le Blanc pushed through a sedition law to stifle dissent. She helped form a broad-based group called Freedom Fighters and became one of its most effective orators, appearing at countless political rallies. Before long, the Freedom Fighters organized themselves into the right-of-center Dominica Freedom party (DFP), associated with propertied interests. Her reputation for vigor and decisiveness made Charles a natural choice for party leader, a post she accepted somewhat reluctantly.

Women had been rare on the Dominican political scene. Before her, Elma Napier, a white, had settled on the island in the 1930s and become the first female elected to a West Indian legislative council. Another white, Phyllis Shand Allfrey, novelist and journalist, had served as minister of labour and social affairs in the short-lived Federal Government of the West Indies (1958–61).

These women were excellent role models. In 1970, after five DFP members were elected to the House of Assembly, Charles obtained an appointive seat for herself. When she was elected to represent Roseau in 1975, she became opposition leader.

Le Blanc had resigned in 1974 and had been succeeded by Patrick John, who made independence from Britain the cornerstone of his policy. Over the past seven years the West Indies Associated States had failed to agree on a plan for regional unity, and therefore at the end of 1975 each state decided to seek independence its own way. The DFP believed that Dominica was not yet fully prepared for independence, and Charles often warned of the consequences. Even so, she went to London in May 1977 as a delegate to a conference on independence.

The ties were broken the next year. Setting aside her earlier lack of enthusiasm, Charles joined the national celebration of independence in November, exactly 485 years since Columbus had sailed by the island. The large, brilliantly colored Sisserou parrot, unique to the island-state, was chosen as the national symbol. The bird and nation shared the gift of rare beauty and a brave struggle for survival. Dominica now became a member of the British Commonwealth and quickly joined the Organization of American States (OAS) and the United Nations.

But amid the outpouring of joy, scandals were brewing within the John administration. It was revealed that Rastafarians (called Dreads in Dominica), a religious sect based in Jamaica, controlled a prosperous marijuana trade involving government officials; that rich Dominican businessmen were making deals to avoid paying taxes; and that John himself was planning to construct an oil refinery to benefit South Africa.

Beyond this corruption towered the shadows of rampant inflation and unemployment.

Attacked from many sides, John pushed through legislation curbing freedom of the press and the rights of unions that supported the poorly paid tropical fruit workers and other menial laborers. In May 1979 he ordered his security forces to open fire on 15,000 protesters. The unions retaliated by calling a general strike. Several of John's legislative supporters now moved over to the DFP, and he resigned.

Charles acted as secretary of the Committee of National Salvation, which brought a peaceful end to the crisis. James Oliver Seraphine, the former minister of agriculture, was appointed interim prime minister, but Charles considered him worse than John. She refused to join his cabinet and remained on the opposition benches; she was, however, no longer its leader. Within a month of John's resignation, Hurricane David struck Dominica with relentless fury, almost destroying the banana crop, so important to the island's economy.

General elections took place in July 1980, and the DFP won 52.3 percent of the vote and 17 out of 21 parliamentary seats. The DFP exuded an aura of urban wealth, but Charles had also attracted poorer rural areas. As the new prime minister, she took on the portfolios of foreign affairs, finance and trade, and industry, decisively announcing that her government would be anti–Communist. Her immediate goals were to crack down on corruption and tax evasion. The DFP controlled all electronic media and was supported by the only newspaper, the weekly *New Chronicle*. Its Young Freedom Movement mobilized many youths.

The new year proved to be far more dramatic than Charles could have imagined. Enraged over government raids on their marijuana fields, Rastafarians kidnaped and killed the father of Lennox Honychurch, the press secretary. Charles responded by declaring a state of emergency, and the House of Assembly enacted a bill that authorized searches without warrants.

Before long, former Prime Minister John and two associates were placed under arrest and charged with conspiracy to stage a coup. A month later, FBI agents in New Orleans announced the arrest of ten mercenaries who were linked to the Ku Klux Klan and the neo–Nazi movement. Their van contained automatic weapons, handguns, and explosives. It was revealed that the mercenaries had been promised $150,000 to invade Dominica and restore John to power. There were also plans to establish a "free port" to allow gambling and the drug trade.

Immediately, John and his associates were thrown into the main prison in Roseau. Then, shortly before Christmas, other American mercenaries joined some discontented Dominican soldiers and Dreads to try to storm the prison and free John. They were unsuccessful.

Despite the stresses brought on by the conspiracies against her, the no-nonsense Charles moved energetically ahead. From the Reagan administration in Washington came a $355 million Caribbean Basin Initiative that made funds available for restoring Dominica's badly deteriorated road system. Plans were drawn up for new light industries and for rebuilding the banana, lime, and coconut industries. Consequently, the prime minister's critics complained that she thought more of business than of her people. Her supporters knew, however, that she was involved in many projects to help the aged and children. One of the most rewarding of these projects was obtaining proper quarters for several elderly people. In 1981 her government gave $400,000 to the housing fund established by Belgian organizations and private individuals after Belgian priests and nuns who resided in Dominica had made a compelling presentation of the need.

As inflation and the trade deficit fell, Dominica became a founding member of the OECS and joined the Caribbean Community and Common Market (CARICOM), established in 1973. CARICOM stressed the coordination of foreign policy and cooperation in science and technology, health, education, and culture.

Charles headed the OECS in October 1983 when extremists on Grenada overthrew the leftist prime minister, Maurice Bishop, and shot him. She said she had been informed that the Soviet Union and Cuba had promoted the coup because Bishop was planning to call new elections. The New Jewel government immediately took power, and Charles lost no time responding. Her first step was to gain the OECS's approval for her plan to ask President Reagan to send troops to Grenada.

With permission in hand, she flew to Washington and accompanied Reagan to a televised press conference, where he announced he was honoring the OECS's urgent request to restore order in Grenada. Three hundred soldiers from Dominica, Antigua, St. Lucia, St. Vincent, Barbados, and Jamaica then joined 1,000 U.S. troops and army rangers in restoring "democratic institutions." The White House claimed the American soldiers were also protecting 1,100 U.S. citizens, mostly medical students, and helping evacuate those who wanted to return home. Charles refused to call the successful action an "invasion," preferring to describe it as a preemptive strike. But she had to buck formidable criticism from the leaders of France, West Germany, Britain, and many of the Commonwealth nations. The action was further deplored by the United Nations and the OAS.

The DFP remained true to its promise of representing the propertied class. Charles confidently proceeded with her program of reducing unemployment and inflation and producing a surplus for the national budget. She was not afraid of the 1985 elections, although she was considered to have a tough opponent in Michael Douglas, a British-trained mechanical engineer and candidate of a powerful Labour party coalition, which had been put together by John, free from prison since 1982.

Charles accused Douglas of getting funds from Cuba, Guyana, North Korea, and Libya. He fired back by accusing her of mismanagement and toadying to the Reagan administration. Her charge seemed to bear more weight because Charles won with 59 percent of the vote. Sworn in for her second term, she kept her posts in foreign affairs and finance and added economic affairs and defense to her portfolio. One of her first tasks was to order John's trial on the 1981 conspiracy charges. Found guilty, he was sentenced to 12 years in prison.

Tall and grave, Charles has remained single, but likes being referred to as "mother of the people." She continues to live in her family's well-appointed home in Roseau, where her father died in 1982 at the age of 107. Her sister is a nun, and all three brothers are doctors. Leisure is rare, and Charles uses it for reading, travel, gardening, and cooking.

Although her personal prestige has grown with the years, she has had more than her share of enemies. In 1987 some of them alleged that the U.S. Central Intelligence Agency (CIA) had paid her $100,000 for her support of the Grenada invasion. This charge, however, was never proved, and no action was taken against her. She was also accused of gerrymandering so that the DFP could control the town council of Portsmouth, the island's second major urban center with a population of slightly more than 2,000.

In spite of her detestation of Communism, Charles is not averse to fostering social welfare programs and allowing government intervention in cases of overwhelming poverty. The election of May 1990 proved to be another victory. For her third five-year term, however, she was returned with a sharply reduced majority.

"We should give the people not luxury but a little comfort," she told an interviewer. Dominica will never be rich, but it can be self-reliant.

VIGDIS FINNBOGADÓTTIR

President of Iceland
(1980-   )

Since 1944, when Iceland regained its independence, each president has been removed from daily political affairs, serving as a cultural figurehead and symbol of national unity. Vigdis Finnbogadóttir is admirably fitted for such a role. With her sweeping victory in 1980, she became the world's first woman to be democratically elected head of state.

Icelandic women are commonly known by their first names because of the complex naming system, which adds "dóttir" to the father's first name to create a surname. So Vigdis Finnbogadóttir is referred to simply as President Vigdis.

She was born in Reykjavik, the capital, on April 15, 1930, to Finnbogi Rutur Thorvaldsen and Sigridur Eiriksdóttir. Her parents were both professionals. Finnbogi was a wealthy engineer and professor at the University of Iceland, and Sigridur was a nurse who would become the longtime chair of the Icelandic Nurses' Association.

At the time of Vigdis's birth, Iceland was united to Denmark under a common king, Christian X. Centuries before, it had been an independent republic. First settled by Norwegian sea rovers and outlaws, it was placed under Norwegian sway in 1262. When Norway and Denmark were united in 1380 under Danish control, Iceland received dominion status. After centuries of economic stagnation and rigid colonial rule, it achieved limited home rule in 1874, the 1,000th anniversary of its founding. The end of World War I gave it the status of a self-governing state within the Danish kingdom.

World War II was to bring more radical change. A week before Vigdis celebrated her tenth birthday, German troops occupied Denmark with scarcely a shot because the Danish government and king had realized they could not defend it. Thereupon British troops landed in Iceland to prevent its seizure for Nazi bases. American GIs replaced them in 1944 and remained on the island. But before the Americans arrived, Icelanders had voted to cut all political connections with Denmark. A month after an approving referendum, Iceland proclaimed itself a republic. Both Vigdis's parents had been educated abroad, and throughout the war the young girl worried that European countries might be destroyed before she would have a chance to see them.

When she matriculated from Menntaskolinn, a junior college in Reykjavik in 1949, she had difficulty choosing between staying at home and studying to be a doctor or seeking further cultural education in Europe. Memories of her childhood worries about the continent's possible destruction remained strong and influenced her decision to study the French language and French literature and dramaturgy at the University of Grenoble and at the Sorbonne in Paris. Later she pursued theater history in Denmark and French linguistics in Sweden. Her foreign experiences ended, she rounded out her education with classes in English literature and education at the University of Iceland.

Her first teaching job was as a French instructor at her old school, Menntaskollin, which she left in order to build up the French teaching department at Menntaskollin vid Hamrahlid, a new experimental junior college. Teaching occupied her winters. Summers she acted as a guide for the Icelandic Tourist Bureau, accompanying journalists and writers to research sites. She was proud to show them her "land of fire and ice," with its startling contrasts of glaciers and ice fields and hot springs and volcanoes. Later she became head of guide training. A sabbatical year brought her back to France to explore the cultural relationship between that country and Iceland in the 19th century.

Vigdis moved on to the University of Iceland as an instructor in French drama. At the same time, she entered Icelandic homes through the state television network, giving French lessons and introducing the theater in a popular series. Tall and slim, with sculptured features and shining blond hair, she was a natural for the television screen.

Next she produced an Icelandic version of *A Flea in Her Ear* by the French playwright Feydeau; it became a national success and inaugurated a theatrical career for her. She also joined Gima, the first experimental theater group in Iceland, but never wanted to appear on stage. Here again her Nordic good looks would have been especially appropriate. She pursued her consuming interest in avant-garde theater when she was ap-

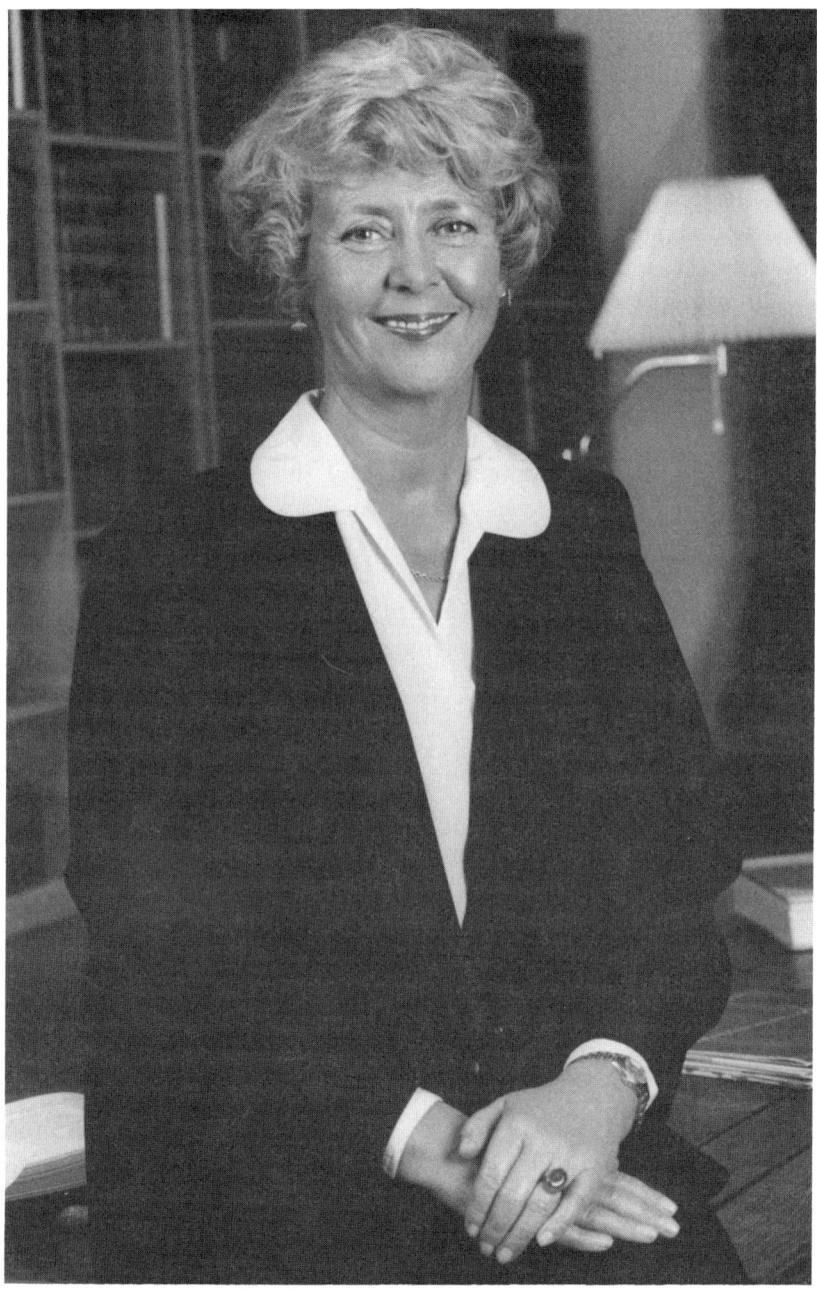

Vigdis Finnbogadóttir: courtesy Embassy of Iceland, Washington, D.C.

pointed director of the Reykjavik Theater Company in 1972. From the outset, she said she wanted to encourage Iceland's young playwrights.

In frequent lectures, both at home and abroad, she managed to change many European perceptions as she dwelt on her native culture, particularly the rich literary heritage. Icelandic literature ran from the sagas and eddas of the Middle Ages to the novels of Halldór Kiljan Laxness, who won the Nobel Prize for literature in 1955 without having wide readership outside Iceland.

In addition to keeping a managerial eye on her theater group, Vigdis became a member of the Alliance Française and later its chair. She was also named chair of the Advisory Committee on Cultural Affairs in the Nordic Countries.

Other than participating in a demonstration against the U.S. naval base at Keflavik, an important outpost of the North Atlantic Treaty Organization (NATO), she stayed away from the Icelandic political scene, which was so turbulent that only coalition governments could be formed. But by 1980 she was such a well-known television personality and cultural expert that friends persuaded her to run for president. It was time, they said, to prove that a woman could hold that office.

Three men also declared their candidacy for the nonpartisan post. Some of Vigdis's supporters feared that part of her personal history might alienate certain voters. She had always refused to discuss the circumstances of her marriage at 23 and her divorce nine years later. At 41 she had adopted a daughter, Astridur. A single parent was highly unusual in Iceland, but as things turned out, instead of being critical, the voters applauded the courage she had shown. During a strenuous, four-month campaign, "jumping into airplanes and like an ogress covering the country in three steps," to use her picturesque phrase, she talked about cultural identity, history, and ecology and pointed with pride to Iceland as being one of the least polluted countries in the world.

Nonetheless she warned: "We have to be very much on our guard today. Iceland is less green than it was. There is erosion from wind and water and volcanic eruptions, so we are involved in reforestation programs, in sowing grass in the highlands. We need every green blade of grass to be able to feed humanity. It is a matter of not only protecting our own country, but also the countries of the world."

Icelanders elected her president in June 1980, with 33.8 percent of the vote. She attributed the relatively low tally to the fact that many women, reflecting low self-esteem, had not cast ballots. Yet enough voters obviously thought that the sex of the candidate was immaterial.

President Vigdis was inaugurated in August 1980 for a four-year term. Despite her politically passive role, she had to sign all bills passed by the Althing, the oldest parliament in Europe. She had the right of veto, but never exercised it. As a campaigner, she had particularly enjoyed meeting people, and as president she continued to be friendly and accessible. Her office door was open to whoever wanted to talk to her. She could not always help her visitors, but she could lend a sympathetic ear.

She especially enjoyed her position as Iceland's cultural ambassador. In 1982 she met with Prime Minister Margaret Thatcher and demonstrated her enthusiasm for British theater. To this visit there was a political overtone. Her charm and easy command of English helped warm relations with Britain, which only a few years before had been waging a cod war with Iceland.

That fall she flew to the United States to promote a 15-month-long exhibit of Scandinavian culture, "Scandinavia Today," in Washington, D.C., Minneapolis, New York and Seattle. During her keynote address at the Kennedy Center, she spoke of the "golden ring," her term for cooperation among the Nordic countries—Denmark, Finland, Iceland, Norway, and Sweden.

In 1983, after Prime Minister Gunnar Thorodssen asked for the dissolution of the Althing and announced he would not be a candidate for reelection, no new coalition seemed to be forthcoming. President Vigdis threatened to name a nonparty administration, but Steingrímur Hermannsson of the Progressive party succeeded in forming a coalition with the Independence party.

In 1984 Vigdis decided to run for reelection. This time she had no opponents. Icelanders called her the best ambassador their country had ever had.

The next year she became involved in a controversy. In the fall of 1975 the Icelandic Women's Liberation Movement had staged a strike, asking thousands of women to walk off their jobs or refuse to do housework as a protest against unequal wages and various forms of discrimination. That strike had brought too few reforms, and on its tenth anniversary, the women struck again.

The president intended to stay out of her office, too. On the day of the strike, the Althing hurriedly passed a bill forbidding the female flight attendants on Icelandic Air to join the protest. When Vigdis refused to sign the bill, Hermannsson put great pressure on her, arguing that if air traffic was disrupted, Iceland would suffer economically. Vigdis signed, then quickly went home. Silently she applauded when the flight attendants joined the strike after all. No immediate reforms were forthcoming because of the walkout, but Icelandic women received an extra dose of self-esteem.

In her international speechmaking, Vigdis praised the small nations for giving "flavor to the world" and said that they could best set a pace for global initiatives. Graciously she played hostess at the 1986 summit in Reykjavik between President Ronald Reagan and Soviet leader Mikhail S. Gorbachev. "Something extremely important came out of the summit," she later said. "There was a thaw. The door was opened just a little bit." If the summit did not resolve East-West differences, it had the effect of encouraging tourism as an alternative to Iceland's almost total dependence on fishing as a source of foreign exchange.

In 1987, Hermannsson and his Center-Left coalition lost the general election. The Women's Alliance gained 10 percent of the vote, doubled its seats in the Althing to six, and held the balance of power in forming a new coalition. Hermannsson resigned, but President Vigdis invited him to stay on in a caretaker capacity. The Women's Alliance leadership, however, refused to enter the government unless their pay was made more equal with the men's. They did not gain their point. In the end, Hermannsson assumed the post of minister of foreign affairs in the government of Thorsteinn Pálsson of the Independence party.

An opponent presented himself for the 1988 presidential election, but Vigdis again proved her enduring popularity and was reelected. More than ever, she enjoyed her duties, which she could perform, for the most part, without pomp. Never could she be just a ceremonial marionette. She could drive her car through the streets of Reykjavik, and she could go shopping without a security force tagging behind.

Before the scheduled presidential election in 1992, as in 1984, no challenger appeared. Vigdis Finnbogadóttir began her twelfth year in office, as enthusiastic as ever about her cultural, unifying role.

GRO HARLEM BRUNDTLAND

*Prime Minister of Norway
(1981, 1986–89, 1990–   )*

Norwegian newspapers described her political rise as meteoric because only six years after she entered the Norwegian cabinet, Gro Harlem Brundtland became prime minister. That term lasted only eight months, but in 1986 and again in 1990, still in her energetic prime, she returned to office.

She was born in Baerum, an Oslo suburb, on April 20, 1939, to young but politically aware parents. Her father, Gudmund Harlem, then a medical student, would twice serve in cabinet posts and act as personal physician to all the prime ministers of the social-democratic Labor party. Her mother, Inga Brynolf Harlem, later became a secretary in the party's parliamentary group.

Gro was just short of her first birthday when the Nazis invaded Norway. Her father went to fight with the resistance forces in the north, and her pregnant mother deposited her in Stockholm with her Swedish grandmother. Inga Harlem then joined her husband in Tromsö, where a son Lars was born. A few months later the family was reunited in Oslo and lived there through the Nazi occupation.

At the age of seven, Gro joined a junior group, Framlag, affiliated with the Labor party and dedicated to outdoor life, especially camping and backpacking. The whole Harlem family was equally enthusiastic about getting out into nature. Expert cross-country skiers, they owned a cabin in the mountains.

In 1949, Gudmund Harlem received a scholarship at Harvard and took his family, which now included a second son, to the United States. Trygve Bratteli, a future Norwegian prime minister, who was then studying English and American history in Cambridge, was much impressed by the Harlems' clever ten-year-old daughter. When the family returned to Oslo, Gro also impressed her schoolmates, and she took a leadership role in many groups. One friend later said that she had to disengage herself from the somewhat autocratic Gro to feel independent.

When Gro was at Hedehaugen Gymnasium, she was elected deputy chair of the Upper Secondary School Socialist Union. Meanwhile her father was entering a decade of public service (1955–65), first as minister of social affairs and then as minister of defense.

For all the political discussions at home, Gro did not consider politics as a career. Rather, her mind was set on becoming a physician like her father. She enrolled at Oslo University Medical School, but kept alive her interest in the Labor party. As deputy chair of its newly formed student union, she gained prominence as a skilled debater.

In the midst of her studies, though, she had found time for romance. In 1960 she married Arne Olav Brundtland, a handsome young political science student. Love had overcome their political differences; he was then a dedicated conservative and has remained so. As Gro expected, Gudmund Harlem received him stiffly at first, but was gradually won over.

Gro and her mother were pregnant at the same time, Inga with her fourth child, a daughter, Helle. The Brundtlands' son Knud was born in 1961. During rest breaks from classes, Gro usually could not relax with fellow students over coffee and cigarettes, but had to dash off to a child care center to nurse her son. A daughter Kari arrived in 1963, the year Gro completed her medical studies. She felt comfortable with her decision to enter the field of social medicine, since a government post would allow her to be home in the evenings.

Except for the war years, the Labor party, Norway's largest since 1927, had held the majority from 1935 until 1963, when power between it and coalitions of socialist parties began to shift. All, however, supported the concept of welfare security and basically agreed on foreign policy.

Taking their young family with them, the Brundtlands settled in Cambridge, Massachusetts, while Gro pursued a master's degree in public health from Harvard and Arne Olav was a visiting scholar at Harvard's Center for International Affairs. Gro's studies sparked her special interest in family planning, sex education, and the issue of abortion. In 1965, the year she obtained her degree, a second son, Ivar, was born. A third son, Jørgen, arrived in 1967.

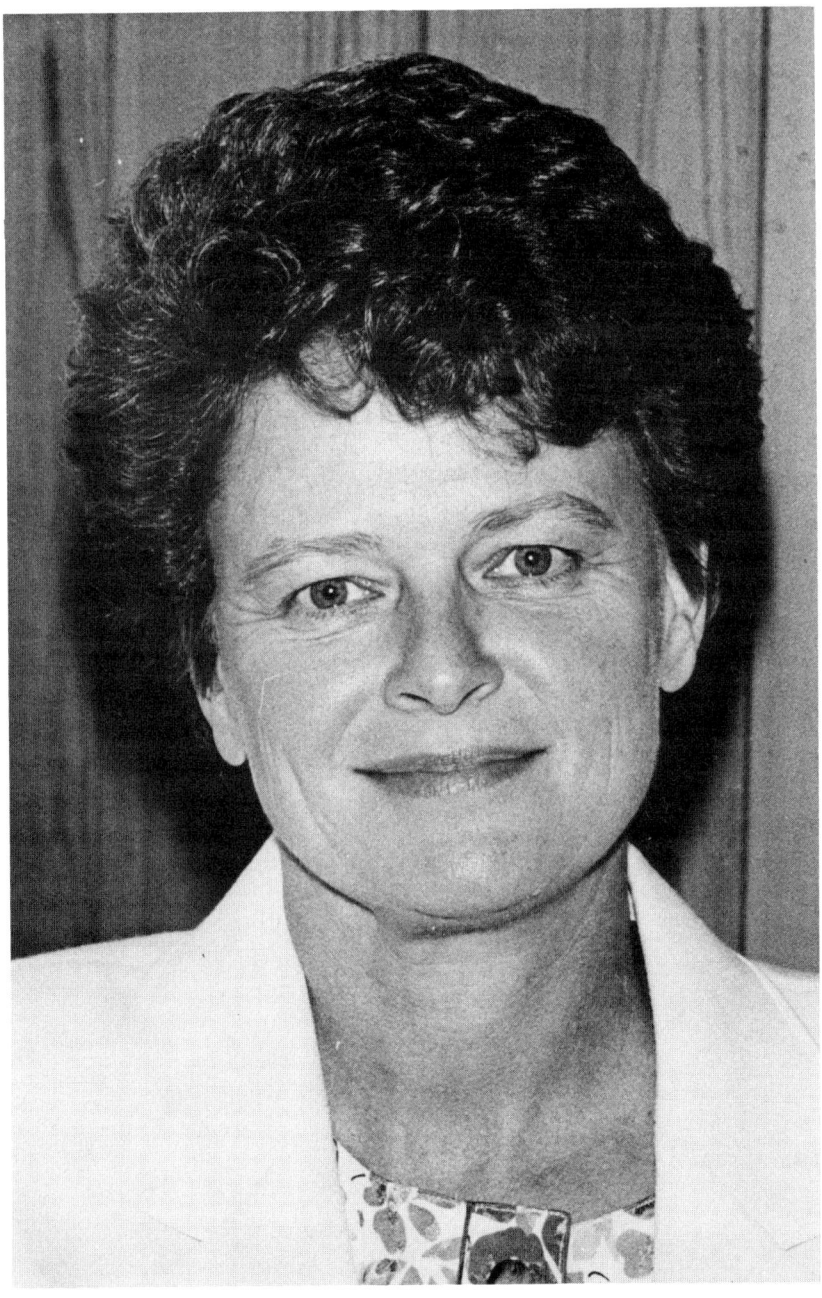

Gro Harlem Brundtland: courtesy Ministry of Foreign Affairs, Oslo.

The attractive physician with her charming smile and springy step found her first job as a consultant to the ministry of health and social affairs. Then in 1966 she was given the post of junior medical officer in the hygiene department of the Norwegian Directorate of Health. From 1969 to 1974, Gro served as assistant medical director of the Oslo Board of Health. In 1969 she assumed more duties as deputy director of the city's school health service and as a physician with the children's department at Oslo's Ulleval Hospital. Her superiors praised her for her personal commitment and deep respect for medical theory. Meanwhile, Arne Olav Brundtland again became a visiting scholar, at the University of Helsinki in 1968 and at the Soviet Academy of Sciences in 1970. From 1977 to 1989 he would serve as editor-in-chief of *International Politik*, the scholarly journal of the Norwegian Institute of International Affairs.

As a professional, as a woman, and as a politically active person, Gro became infuriated by the antiabortion activities of the Conservative party in the 1970s and launched a press campaign that made her name well known.

Husband and wife shared domestic responsibilities in their fine villa on the Bygdøy peninsula. Like the Harlems, the Brundtlands had a holiday cabin in the mountains and enjoyed skiing together. They were good sailors, too. Gro maintains a warm relationship with her daughter and sons, but as prime minister she would say that she wished she could have spent more time with them.

At Harvard, Gro had studied pollution problems and became interested in environmental protection. As a medical doctor, she continued to show deep concern for the environment. Appreciating her commitment, the prime minister, her father's old friend Bratteli, appointed her to his cabinet as minister of the environment. As expected, the choice raised some eyebrows because she was inexperienced at holding political office. But she stayed in her post when Odvar Nordli succeeded Bratteli in 1976. The year before, she had been elected deputy leader of the Labor party. To an interviewer, Brundtland later said, "There is a very close connection between being a physician and being a politician. The doctor first tries to prevent illness, then tries to treat it if it comes. It is exactly the same as what you try to do as a politician, but with regard to society."

Arne Olav Brundtland had urged her to accept the cabinet post. He would take care of the home front, he said, but on his terms. Husband and wife laughed about a sign he hung in the downstairs hall of their four-bedroom home: "A house must be clean enough to be healthy and dirty enough to be happy." In time, the Brundtland children would go into diplomacy, law, and engineering.

Immediately, in 1974, the new minister of the environment began doing things that angered industrialists. She established nature preserves and pleaded for the protection of the Norwegian landscape environment from the North Sea oil that had recently been discovered off the coast. In April 1977 a blowout of the Bravo 14 well in the Ekofisk oil field in the North Sea thrust Brundtland into a crisis. The spill cost the country $17 million in lost taxes and royalties before the well could be sealed. Decisively she directed all moves. Offshore oil and gas drilling were indefinitely postponed. By now she had become internationally well known as a speaker on environmental issues. Her travels took her to the Soviet Union, North and South America, and Africa. It was noted that no matter where she went, at home or abroad, the short, stocky Gro Brundtland always appeared in high heels, even when inspecting sites.

Also in 1977 she ran as a representative from Oslo for the Storting (Parliament) and won, but had a proxy hold her seat while she stayed on as minister of the environment. Then in 1979, because the Labor party had suffered losses in local elections, she decided it was her duty as deputy leader to revitalize it. She resigned from the cabinet and took her seat in the Storting, where she served on the finance committee and then as chair of the committees on foreign affairs and the constitution. Colleagues said she had a will of steel, but was also a volcano of emotions. Often she lost her temper; often she was moved to tears.

Suddenly, on January 30, 1981, Odvar Nordli announced he was stepping down as prime minister for reasons of health. Observers of the political scene maintained that his colleagues had asked him to resign because he had failed to show decisive leadership.

Decisive was an adjective that well fitted Brundtland, who was also competent, aggressive, and self-assured. Despite her academic background and residence in exclusive Bygdøy, she had good contacts with the party's grass roots. The whole country called her by her first name, pronounced "Grew." On February 3 the Labor party's central committee unanimously elected her to succeed Nordli. The next day at the Royal Palace, King Olav V installed Norway's first woman prime minister and its youngest. Brundtland kept most of the Nordli cabinet. It was inevitable that she also undertook leadership of the Labor party. On hand to greet the new prime minister was a female delegation of the Samis, an indigenous people from the north. The Samis had long been critical of the past degradation of their language and cultural traditions. Brundtland promised to help them gain greater representation and obtain new cultural institutions.

She believed that her first task was to strengthen the party for the fall elections. Despite her personal popularity, discontent was rising, especially over inflation. In August the government announced a price freeze and warned that the conservative opposition might try to dismantle the state system of social welfare. Norwegian industrial workers had had accident insurance since 1894 and health insurance since 1909. Unemployment insurance was available to all who lost their jobs, and the blind, the disabled, and persons over age 70 were eligible for pensions. Except for the first born, mothers received government allowances for children under age 16. Consequently a large part of governmental funds was spent for social services.

Labor lost the October elections, however, and Kåre Willoch, the Conservative party leader, with coalition help, moved into Brundtland's office. Brundtland remained in the Storting and kept her roles as leader of the Labor party's parliamentary group, chair of the committee on foreign relations and constitutional affairs, and member of other committees. Though more than busy, she accepted Swedish Prime Minister Olaf Palme's invitation to join the Independent Commission on Disarmament and Security, which issued its report, *On Security,* in 1982. She formed a close friendship with Palme, matching him in moral commitment and humanitarianism and would grieve over his assassination in 1986.

She also worked on the United Nations World Commission on Environment and Development with members from 22 countries. At the commission's organizational session in the spring of 1984, she offered a ringing statement: "There is an urgent need to fashion a long-term, integrated global strategy for survival on this planet. We need a strategy for common survival and common security, a strategy for a common future." This theme became constant in Brundtland's thinking. Before long, UN Secretary-General Javier Pérez de Cuellar asked her to chair the commission. The commission, for which Brundtland served as such a confident and charming spokesperson, broke new ground when its meetings spread over five continents. It held public hearings in which expert environmentalists had their say, along with politicians and ordinary people.

Gro and Arne Olav Brundtland respected their different political credos. While criticizing the Labor party itself, he always bolstered her with absolute devotion. After she left the prime minister's office, husband and wife grew even closer through a dramatic experience. One day when they were sailing their boat along the Sørland coast, stormy weather suddenly blew up. As Arne tried to take in the mainsail, he fell overboard. Fortunately he was attached to a lifeline. Gro thought she could pull him back into the boat, but the wind proved too powerful. For two agonizing hours she steered the boat through heavy seas until it reached land.

Gro was pleased to note a national upsurge in environmental concern even though Willoch did not share it. He was busy grappling with economic problems. Norwegians had not accepted his austerity measures, the so-called Easter package, one of whose most unpopular features was an increased gasoline tax. Willoch lost the elections of April 1986, and Brundtland came back to power, again as head of a minority government. Her supporters saw her as possessing more confidence and verve than ever before, keenly intellectual, and indefatigable despite a heady pace on both the national and international scenes. Her capacity for work, like Margaret Thatcher's, seemed unlimited. "The greater the demand," she said, "the more important are commitment and a sense of honor." Her detractors, however, pointed to an easily aroused temper, self-important air, and often aggressive style.

The Labor party had long been building toward equality of the sexes within its ranks, and therefore it was no surprise that Brundtland formed the world's first gender-balanced government. Into her 18-member cabinet she brought seven other women, placing them in key administrative and public service posts. As she told the press, "A natural balance of men and women makes prejudiced decisions less likely and gives the greatest possible breadth of experience."

Although Norway was the first country to grant women the right to vote, in 1913, women had been slow to enter government. The first woman was elected to the Storting in 1921, and a second woman was elected in 1927. Throughout the 1930s there were only two or three women representatives. But World War II brought dramatic changes. From 1945 until 1957, women members constituted 6 percent of the Storting, increasing to 10 percent in 1960, 20 percent in 1970, and 34 percent in 1985. Representation in the cabinets followed a similar pattern. Kirsten Honsteen was the first woman cabinet minister in 1945. Thereafter, until 1965, one woman had been appointed in each administration. Then came two women. In 1970 there were three, and in 1976, four.

Brundtland still faced the economic problems that had defeated Willoch. Offshore drilling in the North Sea had long since been resumed, but the price of Norway's oil was tumbling fast because of a glutted world oil market. The Brundtland government agreed to cooperate with the countries in the Organization of Petroleum Exporting Countries (OPEC) to cut the output of oil. However, the annual inflation rate remained at 8 percent, and there was still a foreign trade deficit. To restore Norway's export market, the prime minister put a cap on wages, devalued the *krone,* and bore down on consumer credits. Abiding by her campaign pledges, she also shortened the workweek to 37 and a half hours and extended paid maternity leave to six months.

Her foreign policy continued Norway's support of the North Atlantic Treaty Organization (NATO), although she openly criticized United States policy in Nicaragua and President Ronald Reagan's plans to build a strategic defense system. She had special sympathy for Third World countries, and right-wingers complained that she had set up one of the highest per capita foreign aid budgets in the world.

For her, environmental issues were not peripheral to mainstream politics, but belonged at the top of the political agenda. Her government duties did not keep her from her role as chair of the UN World Commission on Environment and Development. Its report, *Our Common Future* (also known as the Brundtland Report) completed in 1987, attracted more attention than any other document initiated by the United Nations. It resulted from three years of hard work based on the best scientific advice and on public hearings throughout the world; Brundtland well knew that ordinary people responded to its warnings about the destruction of the environment. Her theme never wavered: "We must learn to think globally and in a long-term perspective. No single region or nation can isolate itself from the rest of the world." Passionately she believed that her crusade was the greatest challenge she would ever face. It involved exhausting rounds of diplomatic shuttling and public appearances, which often were recognized with numerous awards. To sustain the momentum generated by the Brundtland Report and to extend the global debate on "sustainable development," the Centre for Our Common Future, a small, independent, charitable organization, was established in Geneva in 1988.

For all Gro's international popularity, discontent was becoming widespread at home. By September 1989 she could not stem record unemployment, and the Labor party suffered its worst election setback since World War II, dropping 6.5 percent. She said she would fight to stay on, but a few days later a no-confidence vote defeated her. Jan Syse of the Conservative Party formed a coalition government with the Christian Democrats and the Center party.

Arne Olav Brundtland, now a research fellow in strategic studies at the Norwegian Institute of International Affairs, never allowed his conservative bent to lessen his support for his wife. She, in turn, showed a vital interest in his special field: East-West relations and their particular relevance for the Nordic states.

In 1990, fears were being expressed about "black gold," Norway's oil riches in the North Sea. The traditionalists worried that oil drilling could destroy long-established, small-scale industry and debase the simple values of rural life. Brundtland had made peace with drilling because it augmented national resources, and in the Storting she argued that it would help slow down unemployment, always a vexing problem; assist developing countries; and actually improve the quality of life.

Tensions heightened in the fall of 1990 over Norway's membership in the European Community (EC). Actually, it was a longtime divisive issue. In a 1972 referendum the Norwegians, fiercely protective of their traditional life-style of close-knit agricultural and fishing communities and their 12-mile fishing limits, had voted down membership. Norway had joined the European Free Trade Association (EFTA) in 1959.

In 1990, Syse favored EC membership, but the Center party, a coalition partner, was stubbornly opposed. Representing farming interests, it refused to back the government's request for a change in negotiating position and brought down Syse at the end of October. But debate about the EC would be ongoing.

Five days later, on November 3, after Crown Prince Regent Harald installed Gro Harlem Brundtland at the Royal Palace, she became prime minister for the third time.

Her cabinet of nine women and ten men included two celebrities. Thorvald Stoltenberg, former UN High Commissioner of Refugees, became the minister of foreign affairs, and Åse Kleveland, one of Norway's most popular singers, was appointed minister of cultural affairs.

With deliberate recruitment of women in all three of her cabinets, Brundtland set the tone for amazing change. In 1991, commentators would refer to "modern history's political matriarchy in Norway." Three women led the parties, which commanded the allegiance of about 70 percent of the electorate: Brundtland, head of the Labor party; Kaci Kullman Five, elected leader of the Conservative party in 1990; and Anne Engen Lahnstein, chosen by the Center party in 1991.

Brundtland was in favor of Norway's participation in the EC, but the Labor party had not reached a consensus. Quickly she began to establish links between the 12-member EC and the seven-member EFTA. Stoltenberg told the Storting that negotiating over a European Economic Area (EEA) was a cornerstone of Norway's foreign policy. By October 1991 an EEA agreement was reached in Luxembourg, seeking to form a 19-nation, free-trade bloc. It awaits ratification by the various national parliaments and endorsement by the European Parliament. Brundtland sees Norway's acceptance of the EEA pact as a step toward joining the EC.

Norwegians were delighted when this enthusiast for winter sports succeeded in winning the 1994 Winter Olympics for Norway, with Lillehammer as the site. Stories were told that she wrested the honor away from Sweden by practicing her well-known punctuality. At a breakfast for the president of the Olympic Committee, she arrived on time, whereas Swedish King Carl Gustav was tardy.

Late in 1991 there was expectation in some quarters that because of her international profile, Brundtland might be chosen to succeed the retiring Perez de Cuellar. But Egypt's deputy prime minister, Boutros Boutros-Ghali, was selected UN secretary-general. Brundtland, who had not campaigned for the post, was happy to remain Norway's prime minister. Her name seems certain to come up again.

Within another United Nations context, she was soon prominent again. *Our Common Future* called on the General Assembly to convene an international conference "to review progress made and promote follow-up arrangements to set benchmarks and maintain human progress within the guidelines of human needs and natural laws." The result was the Earth Summit, held in Rio de Janeiro for two weeks in June 1992 with representatives from 178 nations.

Still chair of the World Commission on Environment and Development, Brundtland warned in an opening statement, "There are less than 400 weeks left of the twentieth century. Time is short for us to rectify the present unsustainable patterns of human development. We must eradicate poverty. We must achieve greater equality within and between nations. We must reconcile human activities and human numbers within the laws of nature."

She went on,

> A sharp reduction in the arms race and the expected peace dividend can be used to finance today's most urgent form of collective security—

environmental security.... We should not be surprised that developing nations are approaching the Rio summit with open economic demands. For them, it is essentially a conference about development and justice.... Sustainable development can be advanced only by an international trading system which enlarges freedom of market access, especially for developing countries and which incorporates environmental values.

She concluded by declaring that within the UN system, the General Assembly should act as the supreme policy-making forum for sustainable development.

Addressing the Earth Summit toward its conclusion on June 15, Brundtland was frank about what had been achieved. "Progress in many fields, too little progress in most fields, and no progress at all in some fields." She felt grateful that two important conventions, on biological diversity and global warming, had been opened for signature, but asked that they be made more effective by having all major countries sign, ratify, and implement them. The United States did not sign the biological diversity accord.

Brundtland expressed particular disappointment over the lack of adequate financial commitments. Proudly she pointed out that Norway provides 1.1 percent of its gross national product for official development assistance, well over the 0.7 target.

Her assessment was: "When we arrive at our final consensus here in Rio, we will have taken neither a small step, nor a giant leap. But the direction of where we are heading will have been set."

That fall Gro and Arne Olav Brundtland faced tragedy. Their youngest son, Jørgen, who had been suffering from depression, took his life. In early November, citing "personal reasons," Gro stepped down as head of the Labor party, thus breaking Norway's "political matriarchy." Her supporters understood that she needed extra time to be with her family as they came to grips with their loss. Thorbjørn Jagland succeeded her.

But she did not resign as prime minister. Within two weeks Norway applied for membership in the EC, scheduled to become an enormous, single market on January 1, 1993. She was needed to follow through on the application and to watch over the consequences.

MILKA PLANINC

*Prime Minister of Yugoslavia
(1982–86)*

By becoming prime minister of Yugoslavia in 1982, Milka Planinc reached the top of a political ladder she had been climbing for 30 years. She was the first woman head of government in the Communist world.

At the time she was born on November 21, 1924, in the village of Drns in the rugged Dalmatian hinterland of Croatia, her parents were living in a patchwork kingdom. Created in 1918, it included Croatia, Serbia, Slovenia, Bosnia-Herzegovina, Montenegro, and part of Macedonia. When Milka was five, King Alexander I, troubled by unrest coming principally from Croatia, changed the name of the Kingdom of the Serbs, Croats, and Slovenians to Yugoslavia, land of the south Slavs. Simultaneously he imposed a dictatorial rule with a censored press and a ban on political parties.

The Croats, however, remained a disaffected minority under a regime dominated by the Serbs. In 1934, while visiting Marseilles, France, Alexander was assassinated by a Macedonian in the pay of a Croatian nationalist group. Since his son Peter, the heir to the throne, was only 11, three regents were delegated to rule until the boy came of age. The most powerful was Prince Paul, the late king's cousin, who proved to be highly unpopular. Among the many opposition groups confronting the regency, the Communists attracted the most followers.

World War II interrupted Milka's schooling. She joined the Communist Youth League in 1941, a year that brought dramatic changes to her country. Prince Paul, pressured by Adolf Hitler, decided in April to throw in his lot with the Axis powers. Angry Serbian military and air force officers lost no time in deposing him and taking over in young King Peter's name. An enraged Hitler thereupon invaded Yugoslavia, whose army capitulated after ten days. To set up a government in exile, King Peter fled with his advisers to London.

The country was divided among German, Italian, Hungarian, and Bulgarian occupying authorities. Milka's native Croatia, created an independent state, and was expected to become a separate kingdom. But it lacked a king, and for practical purposes fell under German and Italian control. Much of Dalmatia remained outside the puppet state, but was still under Axis rule.

Events moved ever faster. When the Nazis invaded the Soviet Union in June, its dictator, Joseph Stalin, appealed for guerrilla activity in Yugoslavia behind the German lines. The general secretary of the Yugoslav Communist party, a onetime locksmith named Josip Broz, who called himself Tito, responded immediately. At first, the National Liberation Army that he cobbled together was without uniforms and arms. Known as the Partisans, his patriot soldiers functioned best by taking to mountain hideouts to harass the enemy. Many Croats sympathized with the Germans, but Milka waited impatiently for the time she would be old enough to join the Partisans.

To provide them with a useful political base, Tito met with representatives of the democratic and antifascist parties in 1942. At his bidding they proclaimed themselves the Anti-Fascist Council for the National Liberation of Yugoslavia.

The Partisans were not the only resistance group. Before they were organized, men from the defeated royalist army had gathered together a guerrilla force called the Chetniks, led by Draza Mihailovic, a Serbian colonel. Besides the Axis invaders, the Chetniks had to contend with Catholic Croatian separatists, who, under the command of a local führer, were massacring Orthodox Serbs.

At the age of 19, Milka joined the Partisans in 1943 and became fiercely devoted to Tito, whose guerrillas were surviving with great difficulty. By summer, however, Italy's surrender changed their fortunes, enabling them to seize war materiel left behind by the retreating troops. After the Italian capitulation, Dalmatia was theoretically reintegrated into Croatia, although Partisans controlled most of its territory.

Meanwhile the Chetniks, unwilling to surrender to the Germans, but reluctant to fight them, began attacking the Communist-led Partisans. The Allies were not impressed by this performance and threw their support to Tito's warriors. Toward the end of 1943, a second Anti-Fascist Council congress set up a kind of provisional government, the Council

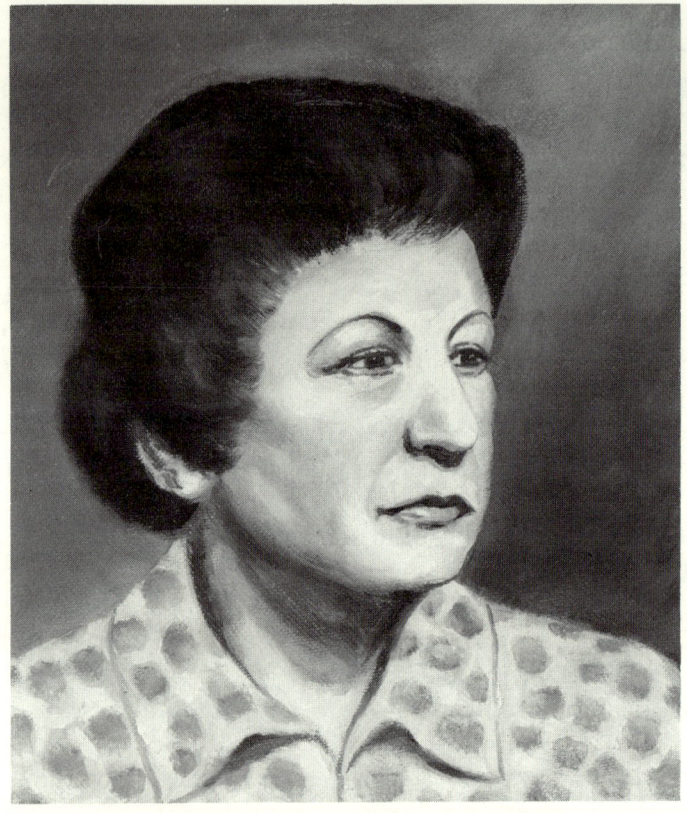

Milka Planinc: oil portrait by John Houston.

of National Liberation, with Tito as prime minister. It also gave Tito the military rank of marshal.

The next year, 1944, Milka joined the Communist party. She became county commissar of the 11th Dalmatian Shock Brigade, teaching party principles and policies and ensuring party loyalty. Her hero Tito now commanded so much British respect that, from London, King Peter sent his prime minister, Ivan Subovic, to meet with the Partisan chief in June 1944 and to sign an agreement for the creation of a new and democratic Yugoslavia. Another regency was to be in place until a referendum would define the fate of the monarchy. In September, Partisan units met up with Soviet troops moving in from Romania, and Tito flew to Moscow to confer with Stalin. Within a month, Soviet troops drove the Germans out of Belgrade.

The new provisional government was formed in March 1945 with Tito as prime minister and Subovic as foreign minister. After the Chetniks surrendered, Mihailovic was captured, tried, and eventually shot.

VE Day came in May. Milka was now 21 and a seasoned Partisan veteran. Over 1.7 million Yugoslavs, most of them her contemporaries, fighting either the Axis soldiers or each other, had been killed. Many cities lay in ruins.

Some 40 years later when a newspaper interviewer asked Milka Planinc about her service with the Partisans, she said, "Those were dangerous times; I vividly recall very hard, very dramatic moments that left deep scars." But she would not discuss them specifically. She then told her questioner, "Fortunately it is inborn that people hold on to memories that are nice, that are pleasant, rather than the atrocities they underwent. What left the deepest imprint was the feeling of what people as a group and as individuals can do when they experience a unity of stance and of courage."

Soon after the Allied victory, Tito was in full control. First, the members of his government who were representataives of the five democratic parties were forced to resign; in October, Subovic departed.

Tito had no wish to antagonize his Western allies, who were sensitive to the term *Communist* so, for the time being, he called his party the National Liberation Front. Later he spoke openly of the Communist party. Elections were scheduled for October 1945. Under a political movement known as the People's Front, the Communists waged an effective campaign for a republican, federal, democratic government. They won overwhelmingly.

Within a few weeks, a constituent assembly sat in session. After abolishing the monarchy, it approved a new constitution, clearly modeled on that of the Soviet Union. The constitution established six republics, following the traditional divisions: Serbia, Croatia, Slovenia, Bosnia-Herzegovina, Montenegro, and Macedonia. Included under Serbia were an autonomous province, Vojvodina, and an autonomous region, Kosovo. The power of the republics, however, was subservient to that of the central government in all important matters.

The national assembly, which consisted of the Federal Chamber and the Chamber of the Republics, elected the Federal Executive Council, or cabinet, for four-year terms to operate the federal government. Tito became the council head, or prime minister. The six republics and two provinces all had League of Communists parties, assemblies, and executive councils of their own, elected by delegates from subsidiary political units. The basic unit of administration was the *opstima,* or commune.

In the midst of all this governmental restructuring, Milka, who had set her sights on gaining party prominence, enrolled at the Higher School of Administration in Zagreb. The war had cut short her education, and finally it was time to study.

Further emulating the Soviet Union, Tito began a five-year plan that emphasized heavy industry. Half the land was kept for state farms and forests, and half was given to peasants. But, after using the Soviet Union as a role model, Tito broke with Stalin in 1948, stunning the international community. Some of the antagonism between the two men dated back to wartime disagreements. The more recent ill feeling resulted from resentment on both sides. Tito thought that Stalin had not given Yugoslavia enough economic help for postwar reconstruction and objected to being asked to carry out the Kremlin's directives in too many areas. For its part, the Kremlin often was irritated by Tito's independent initiatives in Balkan affairs.

At a Communist Information Bureau (Comintern) meeting, which Tito refused to attend, Yugoslavia was expelled from the Communist bloc and subsequently suffered a political and economic blockade by the Soviet Union and its East European allies. Like Tito's other fervid supporters, Milka stayed loyal to him. Fortunately for Tito, Western arms and economic support helped keep him on his independent path, his "road to socialism," which Milka thoroughly endorsed. It was based on decentralization and less government control over the economy, with workers' councils participating in the management of industry.

In 1953 the ever-popular Tito became president under a new constitution, but remained head of the Federal Executive Council. That same year Stalin died, and to suggest an ideological leadership that was less authoritative than in the Soviet Union, Tito changed the name of the Communist party of Yugoslavia to the League of Communists of Yugoslavia (LCY). Each republic had a smaller league. Nonetheless, with Stalin's death that year, Tito's relations with Moscow began to improve.

Service with the Partisans automatically made one a member of the political elite, and now Milka, the wife of an engineer named Planinc and the mother of a son and a daughter, started to pursue a full-time career within the League of Communists of Croatia (LCC), in which she specialized in education and agitation and propaganda. In 1959 she was elected to the Croatian Central Committee, the executive body.

For Planinc there would be other party posts in Zagreb: as an official in the Secretariat for Education and Culture of the Zagreb City Assembly, as secretary of the Zagreb City League of Communists Committee, and then as republican secretary for education. Greater party prominence came with her election to the Presidium of the LCC in 1966 and to its executive committee in 1968. The Presidium ruled on all questions of policy. For a time Planinc also served as chair of the republican Chamber of the Croatian Assembly.

Her career had been helped even more by a new constitution in 1963, which attempted to draw the people into economic and administrative decision making at all levels. Each year brought more liberalization, more stepping up of decentralization. Workers' councils became ever freer of government control.

Planinc's interests lay within the economic sphere, but she applauded Tito's joining India's Prime Minister Jawaharlal Nehru and Egypt's President Gamal Abdel Nasser in a nonaligned movement for countries that did not want to link themselves politically with either the Western or the Eastern blocs.

Tito served as president and prime minister until 1963, when Peter Stambolic, a Serb, became head of the cabinet. While relinquishing one of his offices, Tito guaranteed power sharing among the diverse nationalities by reorganizing the leadership structure of the LCY.

Even so, the ethnic problems could not be solved. In 1971 Croatian students staged an uprising to support more economic and political autonomy for their republic. Tito responded by making a wholesale purge of the Croatian party apparatus except for Milka Planinc, who supported him wholeheartedly. As a reward for her support, Planinc became president of the Central Committee of the LCC. But many Croats showed their intense dislike of her actions. In her first speech as president she pledged to work for party unity and to carry out Tito's policy of eliminating chauvinism and "counterrevolutionary activity."

That year Tito was 79, and amid worry over his successor, he proposed a unique plan. He would remain president and party leader for life. After his death there would be a collective presidency, giving representation to all the major nationalities. Each of the eight members would preside in annual rotation. A new constitution of 1974 confirmed and simplified the system. In what would become a problem for Planinc and future prime ministers, it transferred a great deal of economic power to the republics.

Croatian nationalists, still demanding a separate state, were active in the next few years. Tito always took severe measures against them, but Planinc never objected, despite his blackened record on civil liberties and freedom of expression. When Tito died in 1980, disruptions were feared, but as he had envisioned, the collective presidency functioned smoothly.

On April 29, 1982, the Federal Conference of the Socialist Alliance of the Working People of Yugoslavia approved a list of ministers submitted by Planinc, the outgoing president of the Croatian Central Committee. On May 15 a joint session of the National Assembly's two houses named her head of the Federal Executive Council, the cabinet. Thus she became prime minister.

She kept her family life intensely private. It was known only that she left Belgrade every weekend for Zagreb. There in her villa she refused to receive politicians, friends, or even accredited foreign diplomats. She soon acquired the reputation of being inaccessible. Some critics called her dour. Friends, however, said she had a ready chuckle.

Under Tito an agrarian nation had been transformed into an industrial one. And yet growth was accompanied by high inflation, hazardous pollution, and balance-of-payments problems. Tito had borrowed heavily from Western banks and suppliers since the mid-1970s, and the foreign debt was almost $20 billion.

Planinc called for radical measures to put the economy back on its feet. "People need a determined and courageous person," she said, "and I am courageous and determined." But the 1974 constitution, giving so much power to the republics, had left the federal authority weakened. It was further crippled by economic nationalism and investment undertaken at the behest of local politicians and regional interests. The prime minister knew she would have to move slowly and patiently to restore federal authority over the economy.

She faced problems in the international sphere as well. The Soviets were angry because of Yugoslav criticism of their intervention in Afghanistan. Albanian nationalists in Kosovo rioted for two years in a row and were put down, straining relations with Albania.

To obtain some foreign assistance from Britain, Planinc decided on a trip to London in 1983. When she met with Margaret Thatcher, reporters called her another Iron Lady, but Planinc quickly rejected the title.

Back in Belgrade, she spent hours in exhaustive debate with her colleagues, finally deciding on an austerity stabilization program to pull Yugoslavia out from an economic crisis that had only worsened. Inflation was now approaching 50 percent. Tough new laws had to be passed.

Planinc scheduled visits to both Washington and Moscow in 1985. Just before she left on her first visit to the United States, a public opinion poll listed her as the most popular personality in Yugoslavia. She brushed off the rating: "I am not the type that welcomes a superficial and comforting sense of popularity. I experience this more as a burden or responsibility. It is a result more of a belief that a single man or woman can do more than they really can accomplish."

In Washington she declared that the economic problems could best be solved on a long-term basis. Explaining how a woman felt performing a duty "considered as that of a man," Planinc said, "The late Indira Gandhi gave the best answer during her visit to Yugoslavia. She asked, 'Are not we women human beings too? Don't we belong to the same species?' And really, why should we be viewed differently? The people elected me themselves. I did not impose myself on them. I had been politically active for a very long time, since the liberation movement. On my way up to the post of prime minister I was often the only woman at various levels of leadership. I feel completely at ease in this respect." Also asked if the system's leadership tied her hands, she answered, "Our system is democratic. Can other presidents make important decisions on their own? Only dictators could do that, and I am not one."

Whereas she left Washington with promises of economic support from the government and leading American businessmen, she departed from Moscow, as one report put it, with "nothing lost, nothing gained."

Planinc's term ended in May 1986. Before long, she became a member of the LCY Central Committee.

By 1990, with the disappearance of the Berlin Wall and the downfall of communism in Eastern Europe, the artificial unity Tito had imposed was fraying badly. Through the sheer force of his personality, he had held together 18 ethnic groups, six nationalities, and three religions. But ancient cultural frictions persisted, and freedom was in the air. Strong movements for secession developed. That year the LCY gave up its political monopoly. Croatia and Slovenia elected non–Communist governments and then declared independence in June 1991. But the Serbian minority in Croatia pitched the republic into civil war. Dominated by Serbs, the federal army entered battles there and in Slovenia.

When Bosnia-Herzegovina and Macedonia declared independence at the beginning of 1992, unprecedented bloodletting terrorized the civilian population. Serb minorities, abetted by the federal army, led the attacks, aimed especially at resident Muslims. The European Community and the

United Nations seemed powerless to mediate or to deploy peacekeeping troops. Cease-fires were signed, only to be broken. Foreign powers debated military intervention.

At the height of the carnage, Serbia and Montenegro formed a new federation, roughly half the size of the one Tito had created and Milka Planinc had fervently supported throughout her political life. The former prime minister was living through bitter days of war.

MARIA LIBERIA-PETERS

*Prime Minister of the Netherlands Antilles
(1984–86, 1988–   )*

After Maria Liberia-Peters became prime minister (minister-president) of the Netherlands Antilles, she decided she did not always have to follow protocol. Eleven months into office in August 1985, the tall, smiling woman in a pink and green lamé costume danced exuberantly through a hail of confetti as the streets of Willemstad, Curaçao, reverberated with the joyous, raucous sounds of carnival. When announcing her intention to participate as usual in the annual parade, she had been warned that to do so would be inappropriate for a head of government. But she shrugged off the admonishment. "In the first place I'm Maria," she said, "and in the second place I'm prime minister. So I'm going."

She was born Maria Philomena Peters on May 20, 1941, in Willemstad. Her father came from the island of Saint Martin (Dutch portion called Sint Maarten), her mother from Saba. With its gable-roofed buildings on the Punda side of the city, Willemstad had a Dutch look, but the colors were distinctively Caribbean: lilac, purple, violet, aquamarine, terracotta, plum, and apricot. It had a famous landmark, the Queen Emma pontoon bridge, the largest in the world.

Before Maria was a year old, German submarines tried to sink tankers that carried petroleum supplies to Curaçao, where the Royal Dutch Shell Company had established one of the world's largest refineries, and to nearby Aruba, site of the Standard Oil refinery. Curaçao and Aruba had no crude oil of their own, but they lay close to huge oil fields in Venezuela and had excellent natural harbors. Accordingly, U.S. Army troops were stationed on Curaçao from 1941 to 1947, and their presence kept the island from suffering wartime shortages.

Dutch was the language Maria learned in school. But she also was taught English and Spanish. Papiamento, the lingua franca, was a mixture of Dutch, English, Spanish, and Portuguese.

Maria was 13 when momentous changes shaped the area known as the Dutch West Indies, or Netherland Antilles. Aruba, Bonaire, and her native Curaçao, the largest of the six-island group, belonged to the Leeward, or southern, islands, and Saint Martin's, Saint Eustatius, and Saba belonged to the Windward, or northern, islands. The Leewards and Sint Maarten, Sint Eustatius, Windwards lay approximately 500 miles apart. In 1954 they were incorporated as a federation and, together with Surinam, granted constitutional equality as an autonomous component of the Kingdom of the Netherlands.

Like Aruba and Bonaire, Curaçao had first been settled by the Spanish and then been taken by the Dutch in 1634 during the long war of Dutch independence against Spain. The Dutch made it a naval base and the hub of the slave trade. After a brief occupation by the British during the Napoleonic wars, Curaçao was returned to the Netherlands in 1816 and had remained a Dutch dependency.

When Maria was playing center on the girls' basketball team of Wilhelmina School in Willemstad, she met Niels Liberia, known throughout the Antilles as a crack center. He was assisting the coach, and 17-year-old Maria was instantly impressed by his hook shots.

Because she planned to become a teacher, she soon left for Emmen in the Netherlands to enter the Normal Training School for the Teaching of Children. By 1962 she had earned two diplomas, one for teaching and one for administration. Returning to Curaçao, she became principal of the Maria Goretti School in Stedrijk. Two years later, she was named head of the Johan Maurits School, keeping that post until 1967. She was also appointed inspector of the department of education and services. In 1970 she began teaching methodology and didactics at the Pedagogic Academy in Willemstad.

Meanwhile she had joined a women's basketball team affiliated with a Roman Catholic school. On the court she again met with Niels Liberia, who played on the men's team.

In 1971 she came to New York to attend a parent-teacher workshop in Harlem. She was so pleased with the experience that the next year she spent four months at Ohio State University taking a special course sponsored by the Council of International Programs for Youth and Social Leaders.

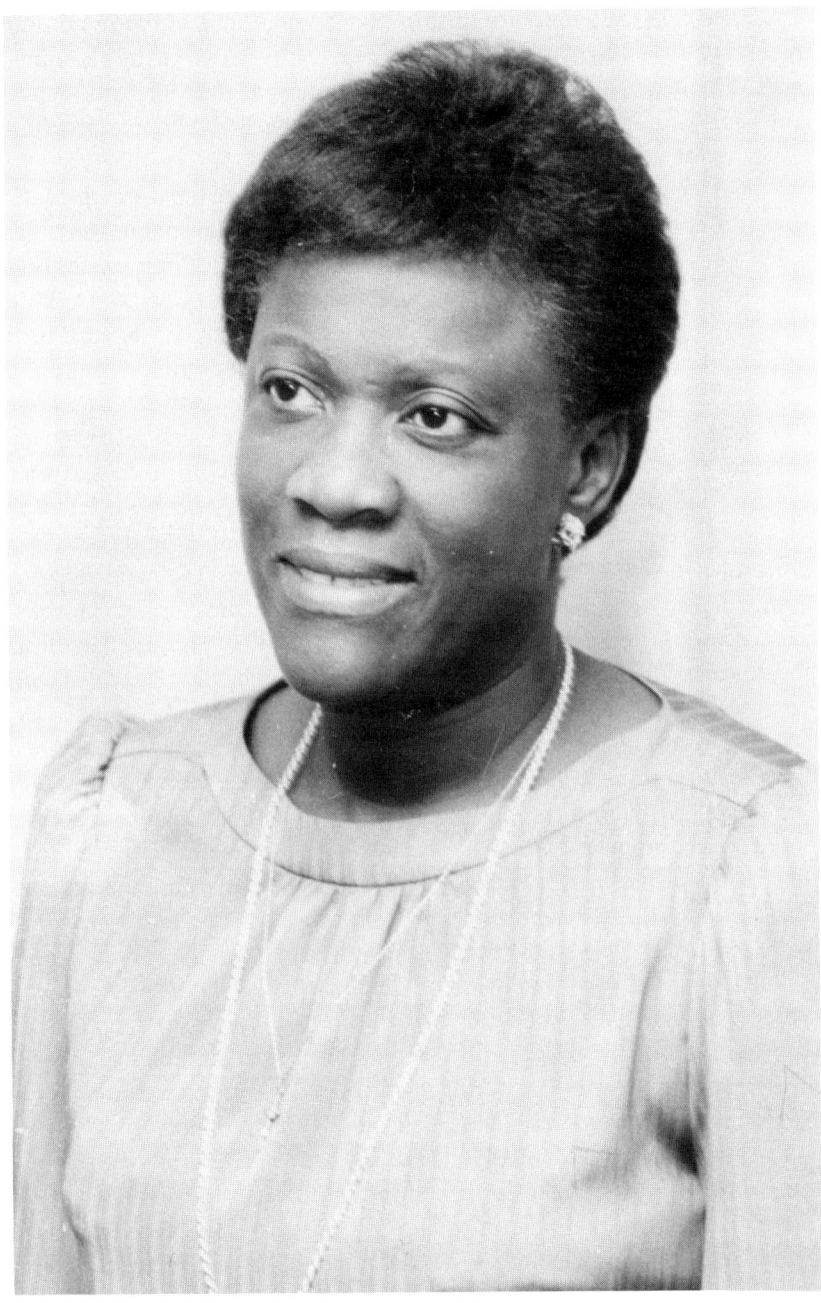

Maria Liberia-Peters: courtesy Office of the Prime Minister, Willemstad, Curaçao.

The basketball court friendship had ripened into romance, and at the end of 1973 Maria married Niels Liberia, 15 years after they had first met. When the couple decided to adopt children, they obtained a boy and a girl from the Catholic archdiocese in New York. Niels worked as a civil servant.

As a school administrator, Maria Liberia-Peters had organized parents' groups for political and social action and had joined the conservative National People's party (NVP). So it was a natural step for her to run for a seat on the 21-member Council of the Island Territory of Curaçao in 1975. That same year Surinam became independent, leaving the Netherlands Antilles the sole co-partner of the Netherlands kingdom.

Two months after Liberia-Peters entered the council, it named her a deputy of the island Executive Council, which sat with a lieutenant governor appointed by the queen—a position she held until 1980. A year later she was reelected to the island council. In 1982 she was elected to a four-year term in the Staten (legislature) of the Netherlands Antilles, which met in Willemstad. Of the Staten's 22 deputies, the majority were from Curaçao because it was the largest island. At the close of the year, Liberia-Peters became minister of economic affairs in the coalition government of Prime Minister Dominico F. Martina, leader of the Curaçao-based Netherlands Antilles Movement (NAM).

Federation politics had entered a turbulent period. Following decades of prosperity, Curaçao and Aruba were in economic trouble. Unhappy over having to share financial support of the other islands, Aruba had proposed separation; the big Exxon refinery, which provided about 50 percent of the island's income, had closed in the spring. In Curaçao, the Shell refinery was threatening to shut its gates unless the government promised to buy two-thirds of the failing businesses.

The Martina government, which had reached agreement on Aruban status aparte in 1983, was weakened by the withdrawal of the NVP in August and finally collapsed in June 1984. That September, Maria Liberia-Peters, the top vote getter in the NVP, was asked to form a five-party coalition government. She took office in September.

As titular head of the Netherlands Antilles, Queen Beatrix was represented by a governor. Control of foreign affairs and defense lay with The Hague, but the prime minister and a Council of Ministers, approved by the Staten, had charge of the domestic scene. Liberia-Peters was complimented for her ability to reach consensus among the ministers.

But in November 1985, three months after she had danced in the carnival celebration, she was defeated in an election held in preparation for Aruba's departure from the federation, and Martina formed a new administration. A colorful figure in her vivid gowns, turbans, and dangling earrings, Maria stepped down to become leader of the opposition and chairman of the NVP delegation.

Aruba's leaving the federation was scheduled for January 1, 1986, with full independence promised for 1996. Sint Maarten was also clamoring for independence, and Claude Wathey, leader of the Democratic party of Sint Maarten (DPSM), resigned from the government over that issue. When two other DPSM members left as well, Martina held a legislative majority of only one.

Martina resigned in March 1988 after the Workers' Liberation Front withdrew its support over a proposed layoff of public-sector employees. It was Liberia-Peters's turn again, and she came back as head of a new coalition that was supported by 13 Staten members, more than half. She appointed herself minister of internal affairs.

Meanwhile a "rescue package" had been arranged for the Shell refinery of Curaçao. With the cooperation of the Netherlands and Venezuela, the Netherlands Antilles government was permitted to purchase the installation at a token price to lease it at $11 million a year to the Venezuelan state oil company through 1990.

Even before Liberia-Peters returned as prime minister, Wathey appeared to draw back from his demands for full independence for Sint Maarten, and she asserted, "The central structure imposed from above must be reduced to a minimum so that even Sint Maarten can feel at home within it."

Her second term began on a high note of popularity. More than ever, she showed her engaging personality. She laughed easily; when she spoke English, she peppered it with Spanish exclamations. She reached out, having more meetings with business and community leaders than had any previous prime minister. Since there were 240,000 people to communicate with, she used newspapers, radio, and television with more flair than any of her predecessors. She also traveled widely.

In the spring of 1990 the Dutch government published a draft constitution, "Outline for a Commonwealth Constitution for the Kingdom of the Netherlands," aimed at perpetuating ties between the Netherlands and the last remains of its colonial empire. Intended as a discussion paper, it was sent to each of the island governments. The Hague had given in to pressure to consider splitting the Netherlands Antilles into two separate administrative parts, the Windward (Curaçao and Bonaire) and the Leeward (Sint Maarten, Sint Eustatius, and Saba) islands.

Despite the high degree of autonomy, the draft declared that the Antilles would remain Dutch territory with Queen Beatrix as sovereign, with foreign and defense policies conducted from The Hague, and with several thousand Dutch navy and air force troops stationed on their soil. As the islands were being asked to review the draft, they were also invited to submit their proposals for constitutional restructuring. Their ultimate choice was to be between federation and commonwealth.

Still head of a coalition government, Liberia-Peters was reported to go along with Antillean Affairs Minister Ernst Hirsch's declaration that the commonwealth formula was the most effective guarantee for "the democratic character, the rule of law, and fundamental human rights." Five parties competed in local elections in April 1991, which gave the NVP ten seats on the island council, again assuring her of her popularity, which spilled over to the whole federation.

CORAZON AQUINO

President of the Philippines
(1986–92)

Small, shy Corazon Aquino was propelled to prominence by the murder of her husband, Benigno Aquino, Jr., who had been widely expected to become president of the Philippines, succeeding Ferdinand E. Marcos. The family was in self-imposed exile in Newton, Massachusetts, on August 21, 1983, when the eldest daughter Ballsey answered the telephone, wholly unprepared for the message she heard. From half a world away, a voice crackled that her father had been gunned down at Manila Airport, where he had just arrived.

There was no time to recover from the shock. Suddenly a public figure, Corazon Aquino had to bring her family, four daughters and a son, back to Manila for the funeral. After that, in the full wake of her grief, she wanted to confront Marcos, the dictator; she believed that he had ordered his archfoe and rival shot. She had no idea that within 2 and a half years, following an almost bloodless "people's revolution," she would be president.

The Philippines is a nation sharply divided between rich and poor. It was Maria Corazon Cojuangco's good fortune to be born into a powerful landowning family on January 25, 1933, in the town of Paniqui in Tarlac Province. She was the sixth of eight children of Jose Cojuangco and Demetria Sumulong, a graduate in pharmacy. Jose Cojuangco owned a sugar plantation that spread over 15,000 acres.

By the year of Corazon's birth, the Philippines had been under American rule for 32 years. Spain ceded the islands to the United States in 1898 at the end of the Spanish-American War, which had been fought over Cuba's struggle for independence from Spain. During the war, Admiral George Dewey sailed the U.S. fleet into Manila Bay to destroy the

Spanish fleet. At the time, Philippine rebels, also fighting for independence from Spain, were close to victory, and their leader, Emil Aguinaldo, felt betrayed by the Spanish-American peace treaty. He declared a republic in 1899 and set his troops to fighting the Americans. Final peace was declared with Aguinaldo's capture in 1901.

Although the U.S. Senate adopted a resolution stating that the Philippines would be free some day, President William McKinley felt the time was not yet ripe for independence. Therefore, he appointed a civilian commission, headed by William Howard Taft, who became governor.

Philippine representatives were permitted to form a lower house in 1907; the governor and his commission formed the upper. Finally, in 1916, Filipinos were elected to replace the commission.

Through the 1920s the Philippines slowly progressed toward independence. When Corazon, called Cory, was a year old, the U.S. Senate promised independence as soon as a constitution had been drawn up and ratified. It further provided for the Commonwealth of the Philippines to be established in 1935. Cory's maternal grandfather, Juan Sumulong, a brilliant jurist, served on the committee paving the way for Commonwealth status. He and his son both took seats in the Senate.

Under its president, Manuel Luis Quezon, the new commonwealth governed itself almost completely. The constitution was finished in 1936, and Cory's family spoke excitedly about complete independence within ten years. Her father Jose was elected a congressman.

During Cory's early childhood, the Philippines bustled with enterprise as Americans constructed roads, railroads, public buildings, and schools. They also introduced important health measures to reduce deaths from malaria and yellow fever.

The Cojuangco children were raised in Manila, but spent summers and weekends at the big house in Paniqui. They considered their father relaxed and flexible; to them, their mother was the strict disciplinarian with ironclad rules of right and wrong. Since the family belonged to the Philippine elite, Cory attended the elementary school of Manila's prestigious Saint Scholastica College, where German nuns emphasized religion. Obedient, well mannered, and well behaved, she excelled in every subject.

She was eight when the Japanese bombed Pearl Harbor. Like Hawaii, the Philippines were in for some high drama. Two days later, after a declaration of war by the U.S. Congress, the Japanese invaded

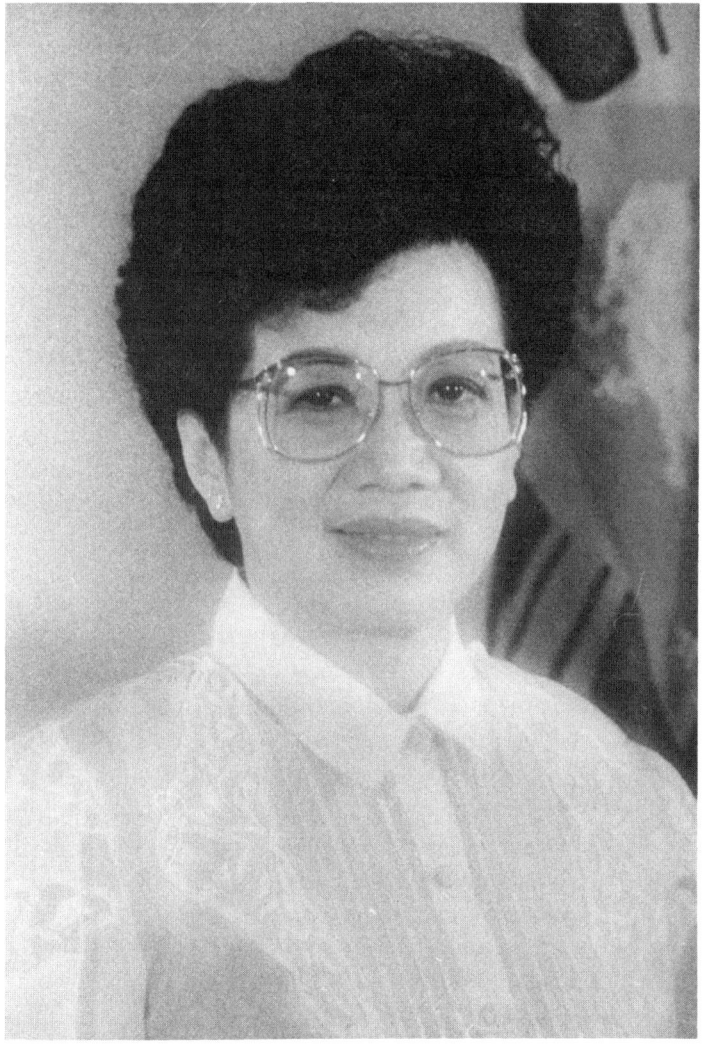

Corazon Aquino: courtesy Embassy of the Philippines, Washington, D.C.

Luzon Island. General Douglas MacArthur, who had acted as military adviser in the Philippines since 1935, promptly concentrated his outnumbered troops on Bataan Peninsula with a fallback to fortified Corregidor Island at the entrance to Manila Bay. He then fled to Australia to secure his command in a safe place. General Jonathan Wainwright, who had tried to defend Bataan, was forced to surrender by spring. His troops were marched under blazing sun to concentration camps 40 miles away. Fifteen thousand soldiers succumbed to heat or exhaustion during the Bataan Death March. However grim the news, classes at Saint Scholastica continued during the Japanese occupation.

But U.S. bombing raids intensified, and the Cojuangcos, survivors of one attack that had left their house in shambles, changed residences frequently. At last in October 1944, MacArthur made good on his promise to return. American troops landed at Leyte after the Battle of Leyte Gulf, one of the greatest struggles in the Pacific theater, and then moved on to the other islands. Manila was recaptured in February 1945.

With family and classmates, Cory celebrated the end of the war in August. That fall she enrolled as a freshman at Assumption Convent, also in Manila. The war had caused tremendous devastation, but American-assisted rebuilding came with the Japanese surrender, and the city slowly began to normalize. The next year, the United States granted independence to the Philippines on July 4.

A special academic adventure lay immediately ahead for slight, pretty Cory. Jose Cojuangco needed to take care of banking interests in the United States, and he and Demetria brought their children along.

Accompanied by her sister Teresita, Cory registered as a sophomore at Ravenhill Academy in Philadelphia, and for her junior and senior years, she went to Notre Dame Convent School in New York. In 1949 she came to Mount St. Vincent College, also in New York. The other students found her delicate and refined, though sometimes impish.

During a summer vacation in Manila after she finished her junior year, she came across Benigno Aquino, Jr. (Ninoy), who was studying at the Alteneo, a Jesuit school in Manila. He, too, belonged to a landowning family in Tarlac Province. They were the same age and had once met at a children's birthday party, where Ninoy had irritated her by bragging that he was ahead of her in school. Grown up, he was far more charming and already a young celebrity. At 18 he had been awarded the Philippine Legion of Honor for his coverage for the *Manila Times* of the Philippine Expeditionary Force during the Korean War. He had gone on to become the foreign correspondent and then the foreign news editor of the paper.

Like Cory's family, the Aquinos were prominent in the independence movement, but during the occupation Benigno Aquino, senior, who had sat in the cabinet of Commonwealth President Quezon, became part of the Japanese puppet government because he believed Tokyo's promise of giving quick independence to the islands. Under the republic, he had been jailed on charges of treason, but had been released. His family defended him, saying that he had actually worked for counter-Japanese intelligence, but he died a broken man two years later. Ninoy would suffer many disturbing thoughts about his father's performance.

That summer of 1952, Cory was attracted to Ninoy's involvement with journalism and politics and he, to her unmistakable air of refinement. When she returned to Mount St. Vincent, letters flew back and forth. After graduating in 1953 with a major in French and a minor in mathematics, she went home and began studying law at the Far Eastern University, but only as a mental discipline because she did not intend to become a lawyer. Ninoy's courtship took on more urgency, and she dropped out of law school to prepare for their marriage in October 1954.

Ninoy had caught the eye of President Ramon Magsaysay. A few months before the wedding ceremony, the president sent him to a rural area still controlled by the Huks (Hukbalahaps), a Communist guerrilla group that had been formed to fight the Japanese and had continued to do battle with the government. Ordered to arrange the surrender of Luis Taruc, the Huk leader, Ninoy was able to hand Taruc over to the authorities. But he grew bitter when Taruc, who had been assured of amnesty, was put in prison. Still, he did not break his ties to Magsaysay, who attended Ninoy and Cory's wedding. The young couple spent their honeymoon in the United States because Magsaysay had asked Ninoy to observe the training methods of U.S. intelligence schools.

When they returned in February 1955, Ninoy gave up his law studies and journalistic career and bought land near his home town Concepcion. While he was managing his farm and cutting back forests and jungle, a pregnant Cory lived with her mother-in-law, Doña Aurora, in Manila until Maria Elena was born. Before long, the new mother moved back to Concepcion with her baby, who had acquired the nickname Ballsey.

Benigno took Magsaysay's suggestion to run for mayor of Concepcion and won. But his election was declared illegal because he fell just short of being the required age of 23. Nonetheless he took office. After Magsaysay was killed in an airplane crash in 1957, the political climate changed immediately, and the Supreme Court declared that Benigno Aquino held power outside the law.

The ousted mayor then became manager of the Hacienda Luisita and Tarlac Development Corporation, a 17,000-acre sugar plantation bought by Corazon's family. He quickly converted it to a highly mechanized agribusiness but was deeply sensitive to the farm workers' discontent, encouraging unions and giving his employees improved houses, food, and schools.

In 1959, as leader of the Nacionalista party, he was elected vice-governor of Tarlac, the youngest man ever to hold that post. Three years later, he was appointed provisional governor and then was elected governor the same year.

Corazon had borne another daughter, Aurora Corazon (Pinky), and a son, Benigno III (Noynoy). So that the children could have proper schooling, she moved back to Manila. Benigno commuted constantly, for he was also acting as special counselor to President Diosbado Macapagal, and in that capacity he accompanied Macapagal on state visits to Cambodia and Indonesia.

The year 1965 introduced a commanding new figure to the political scene. Ferdinand Marcos was an ambitious lawyer who had switched from the Liberal to the Nacionalista party in 1963 at the same time that Benigno had done just the reverse out of loyalty to Macapagal, who belonged to the Liberals. Marcos had a glamorous wife, Imelda, a former beauty queen, and with her considerable help he easily won the presidential election.

Benigno ran for the Senate in 1967, and his wife and mother Doña Aurora joined his campaign. He was the only opposition candidate to win and was considered the politician most likely to succeed Marcos. Again, he fell a little short of the required age of 35, but the Supreme Court allowed him to keep his seat.

Marcos was reelected in 1969. But many voters felt disenchanted with Imelda's lavish spending and the president's seeming tolerance of corruption and graft and failure to halt rising inflation. By 1971 Benigno had become his archcritic, accusing Marcos of encouraging insurgencies to justify new authoritarian measures. Calling themselves the New People's Army (NPA), Mao-Marxist terrorists operated as an offshoot of the Huks. A rebellion was also in full swing on Mindanao, where the Moros, or Muslim tribesmen, wanted independence.

All the while, Corazon had stayed more or less in the background, content to be a supportive wife and devoted mother. The family had been completed with two more daughters, Victoria Elisa (Viel) and Kristina Bernadette (Kris).

On September 22, 1972, the attempted assassination of Juan Ponce Enrile, secretary of national defense, spelled dramatic changes for the Aquino household. The next day Marcos declared martial law, citing

Communist subversion, bombings, and anti-U.S. demonstrations. But at the same time he promised social reforms.

Hours before the declaration was made public, Benigno was arrested and detained. During an agonizing period for his family, he disappeared, and Corazon went from camp to camp looking for him. Finally she discovered that he had been flown from Fort Bonifacio to a dungeon camp up north, where he was kept in solitary confinement. Fairly soon he was returned to the fort, where Corazon was allowed to visit him once a week. She had become the family anchor, both father and mother to the five children. Meanwhile, during the bittersweet moments with Ninoy in his jail cell, she was acquiring a deeper political education.

Four months later, a military tribunal formally charged Benigno with subversion and illegal possession of firearms. In April 1975, he was brought to trial before a military commission. Calling the proceedings a sham, he refused to participate. When a military order forced him to attend the sessions, he staged a protest hunger strike that lasted 40 days. Corazon kept him alive with vitamin pills.

The tribunal found him guilty in November 1975. Corazon reacted in horror when he was sentenced to death by a firing squad. But then he suffered a heart attack, and worldwide pressure caused the death order to be rescinded.

With the new year, Marcos called an election for an interim National Assembly. Still in prison, Benigno declared himself a candidate of the Laban People's Power party, and Corazon became his manager. Her diametric opposite, Imelda Marcos, headed the New Society Movement's ticket, which won all 21 seats. Soon Marcos took the additional post of prime minister. As president, he retained his power of ruling by martial law decree.

Less than a year later, Benigno suffered a second heart attack. Trusting that he and his family would remain in exile, Imelda Marcos visited him in prison and told him that her husband had granted him permission to fly to the United States for heart bypass surgery.

After a successful operation at Baylor Medical Center in Dallas, Texas, Benigno settled his family in a Georgian-style brick house in Newton, Massachusetts. Corazon again was prepared to lead an unobtrusive life while he began as a research fellow at Harvard's Center for International Affairs and at the Massachusetts Institute of Technology.

The Newton house and their summer house at Brookfield became centers for the Filipino community in the Boston area, and Benigno held countless meetings to discuss how Marcos could be toppled. By 1983 he was itching to return to Manila, even mentioning the possibility that he might be able to talk to Marcos about restoring rights and freedoms. Although he and Corazon were both aware of the danger that might lie in wait, she would not stand in his way. They agreed that he would go by a circuitous route through Taipei, Taiwan, and that she and the family would follow in due course.

As Benigno Aquino stepped out of his China Airlines plane at the Manila International Airport on August 21, 1983, he was shot in the head and died instantly. When soldiers surrounding the plane fired more shots, the body of a stranger, the so-called hit man, joined Aquino's blood-stained corpse on the tarmac. A few hours after the shocking news had been relayed to Newton by telephone, Corazon regained her composure and appeared on television newscasts, showing a steely stoicism.

Back in Manila within a week, her small figure clad in black, she marched at the head of the procession bringing Benigno's body to the Santo Domingo Church, where it lay in state. Ten days later, she led an 11-hour march to Benigno's grave in Paranaque, impressing everyone with her self-possession. The "simple housewife," as she described herself, had become a symbol of the opposition to the Marcos regime, a fighter in the struggle for the restoration of liberty.

Over the next months, bright and strong spirited, she directed rallies and began working for opposition candidates. The murder remained an all-too-vivid national memory, and advisers and the Catholic prelate Cardinal Jaime Sin told Marcos that without an investigation, confidence in the regime would be destroyed. Alarmed by Sin's warning, Marcos appointed a commission that determined that high-ranking military officials had planned the assassination. To popular disgust, the armed forces chief of staff, General Fabian Ver, and 25 other alleged participants were eventually acquitted.

One piece of good news from the congressional elections in May 1984 was that 56 of the candidates for whom Corazon had worked gained office. Corazon continued to say that she herself had no political ambitions. Still, in October 1985, former publisher Joaquin (Chino) Roces began a Cory Aquino for President movement, which campaigned for signatures asking her to run. Corazon set two conditions for accepting the challenge: Marcos, aging and ailing, must call quick presidential elections, and she must see 1 million signatures endorsing her candidacy.

After being pressured by Washington, Marcos announced elections.

The signatures materialized in November 1985, and Corazon Aquino filed her candidacy, identifying herself as a housewife. Quickly UNIDO, the dominant opposition party, held a big rally to proclaim her as its choice. Now she had to engage in some difficult negotiations with Salvador Laurel, who himself wanted to be president. Finally Laurel agreed to be her running mate.

The 45-day campaign went nonstop. Corazon traveled all over the country, making several speeches a day. At first, the speeches were written by her advisers, but when they fell flat, she took charge of her scripts, often speaking in parables, which caught on with her audiences. Despite his ambitious wife, Marcos appealed to a macho-oriented society and repeatedly declared that a woman's place was in the bedroom. More invidiously, he taunted Cory with being a Communist and being totally inexperienced. Invariably, her answer was: "Sure, I don't know anything about stealing or cheating, and definitely I don't know anything about killing my opponents." What she offered was a triad of security, honesty, and leadership.

On August 21, 1983, Benigno's supporters at the airport had waved yellow banners, draped buses and cars in yellow, and loudly sung "Tie a Yellow Ribbon Around the Old Oak Tree," an American ballad about a young woman who used the ribbon to demonstrate her love and support for her prisoner sweetheart. During her campaign, wearing little makeup or jewelry, Corazon always appeared in yellow cotton dresses. Volunteers handed out yellow posters, stickers, and even T-shirts.

The polls opened on February 7, 1986. Almost at once, charges of stolen ballots and intimidation surfaced. Counting was a slow process; tallies from CONELEC, the president's commission on elections, and NAMFREL, a watchdog committee, gave the lead now to Marcos, now to Aquino. Every day both candidates claimed victory. Neither camp would hear of concession. Then on February 16 the National Assembly declared Marcos the winner.

Six days later, Juan Ponce Enrile, the defense minister, and Lieutenant General Fidel Ramos, the deputy chief of staff of the armed forces, barricaded themselves inside the defense ministry headquarters at Camp Aguinaldo and then at the constabulary headquarters at Camp Crame and announced they had defected to the Aquino side. Enrile also disclosed that the assassination threat of 1972 had been a trumped-up charge giving Marcos an excuse to declare martial law.

On February 23 Marcos sent his troops toward the garrison. It was no easy passage. Thousands of Aquino's followers surrounded the tanks, handing flowers to the mystified soldiers. Unwilling to fire on their countrymen and women, who were reciting rosaries, the armed forces retreated before this human barricade. The people also besieged Malacañang Palace. As Marcos continued to warn the rebel camps, his soldiers began defecting in large numbers. A warning came from President Ronald Reagan in Washington not to fire on the rebels.

On the same day, February 25, Marcos and Aquino held rival inaugurations. Before nightfall, however, the U.S. government persuaded Marcos to leave, and he flew to Clark Air Base with Imelda, the first step on the way to Hawaii. Celebrations engulfed the streets everywhere to extol "people power" and the end of 20 years of dictatorship that had left a ravaged economy, a crippling foreign debt, and long-term insurgencies by the Moro separatists on Mindanao and the Communist NPA.

Firmly Corazon Aquino declared that she would not live in Malacañang Palace, which had become a symbol of the indulgent expenditures and autocracy of the Marcos regime. Instead, she threw open the rooms to public view, and thousands came to gape at Imelda's vast shoe collection and the egregious bad taste of her furnishings.

Aquino placed overriding importance on her fixed conviction that the people must relearn the principles of democracy. Not wanting to rule through Marcos's institutions, she declared a transitional government on March 25 and gave herself the right to rule by decree until a new constitution could be promulgated. At the end of May she would appoint a commission to produce the new constitution within three months. Thus she honored a campaign pledge.

At once she formed a presidential commission on good government to try to reclaim the billions of dollars the Marcos government had concealed in foreign real estate and secret bank accounts. She settled into a busy work routine in a small office, knowing that in spite of her increasing popularity she faced enormous problems. Out of gratitude she included Enrile and Ramos in her 17-member cabinet, made up of businessmen and professionals. But she angered them when as a gesture of reconciliation she freed four Communist leaders. Determined to show her independence of the military, Aquino simply stayed her course. Meanwhile, on her demand the Marcos-appointed Supreme Court justices resigned, together with several allegedly corrupt generals.

Another of her pledges had been to call a cease-fire with the Communist insurgents. By summer she succeeded in getting the leaders to the negotiating table, but their demands were hard. They refused to surrender unless she promised genuine land reform and forced the United States to relinquish its military bases. But Aquino could not come to terms with them. Marcos had boasted that he had stopped the rebellion of the Moro separatists, but it was not over. Aquino took first steps in negotiating with them. After some truce agreements, however, she realized that lasting peace was far off.

Marcos had sought asylum in Hawaii, where he kept in constant communication with his supporters in Manila. To forestall any coup attempt, Aquino placed the armed forces on alert in August when she visited Indonesia and Singapore in connection with attending the conference of the six-member Association of South East Asian nations.

The soldiers were likewise on alert when she left again in September for a trip to the United States that included a meeting with President Reagan. She assured him that her government would support a five-year agreement allowing the United States to keep the bases it had long held. She also addressed Congress and the United Nations General Assembly. Congress, captivated by her grace and dignity, soon offered $200 million in additional aid. On her return to Manila, Aquino told her people: "Let us not hold our breaths for total answers coming from anywhere but our own efforts by which we won our freedom. The main effort is ours to do, so that the greater honor will be ours again."

The new constitution she had called for was ready in October, and in February 1987, a few days short of the first anniversary of the people's revolution, Filipinos, in a landslide vote, ratified the charter, which guaranteed the primacy of human rights.

Before another year had passed, elections were held for members of the legislature and provincial and city officials. Laurel, the vice-president, who had pitted himself resolutely against Aquino, announced the formation of a new opposition party. He wanted to change the government to a parliamentary system dominated by a prime minister. But he posed no special threat. Meanwhile the Aquino government set about strengthening the judiciary according to democratic principles. Corazon felt more confident about her support and went abroad for the first time since 1986, visiting China and Hong Kong.

Despite her popularity, she was continually beset by cries of economic injustice. The landowners were still firmly entrenched in Congress, where several members of her family sat and regularly gutted any attempts to bring about land reform and relief for the peasants who were living under medieval conditions. Aquino herself never made specific recommendations, although she pledged to include Hacienda Luisita in any reform program.

She could never be certain of the loyalties of the military, enraged because she would not use force against the NPA. Several unsuccessful coups were led by Enrile, who had presidential ambitions. Another coup attempt in 1990, the seventh, would result in over 100 deaths.

Her Catholic faith gave Aquino the serenity and increasing assurance she showed in public. Family warmth also helped. By 1989 her two eldest daughters were married, and she had four grandchildren. The two youngest daughters and Noynoy lived with her in a house near Malacañang Palace. As a television actress and model, Kris had become something of a celebrity herself. At home, the president of the Philippines savored those rare moments when she could putter in the kitchen making pâté or her specialty, Peking duck.

Always the Marcoses were on her mind. A New York grand jury indicted them for fraud and stealing, but trials were postponed because the former dictator was suffering from a variety of ailments. Several times he begged to be allowed to come home to die. But Aquino was deaf to his pleas even though his followers staged several demonstrations in his behalf and were often involved with the military in attempted coups. After Marcos died in 1989, Imelda pleaded many times to bury him in his native soil. Aquino's answer always was that she might consider giving her consent if all the millions of dollars the Marcoses had looted from her country were returned.

The 1986 pledge of economic recovery had been hard to fulfill. Poverty was rampant. A special millstone around the government's neck was the foreign debt accumulated during the Marcos years. Foreign investors were nervous about setting up new companies in a climate of instability. Fighting the insurgents was also expensive. By 1991 public discontent was at its height because of double-digit inflation and belt-tightening measures.

At this time, Aquino was engaged in her major foreign policy initiative, renegotiating the leases of the U.S. bases, particularly Clark Air Field and Subic Bay. These bases, particularly objectionable to the Communists, were a long-standing source of friction. In 1947, following Philippine independence, Washington and Manila had signed a Military Bases Agreement, which covered 27 facilities in 13 regions. These bases became crucial to U.S. action in the Vietnam War. In 1965 the size and number of bases were reduced, and in 1966 the leases for the bases were shortened to 25 years. Subsequently more bases were closed.

In 1991, when there were only six bases left, the United States insisted that a new treaty on the two largest and most important, Clark Air Base and Subic Bay Naval Base, be ratified by the Philippine Senate. Fearing the impact of withdrawal on the fragile economy, Aquino favored the treaty, but many Filipinos saw the bases as an incursion on national sovereignty.

Clark Air Base lies close to the Mount Pinatubo volcano. In June 1991 the volcano suddenly erupted, sending smoke and ashes for miles and pouring hot lava down the mountain at 60 miles an hour. Villages were shrouded, 100,000 persons were homeless, and 200 were left dead in the subsequent fallout. The air base was rendered useless and had to be evacuated; the American flag would be lowered in November. From June to September the four smaller bases were returned to the Philippine government.

To exert pressure on the Senate to approve the treaty, which now concerned only Subic Bay, Aquino determinedly led a "people's power" march in the rain. All the same, in September, the Senate voted 12 to 11 to turn down the treaty. Aquino felt the rejection as a stinging blow. Her own brother-in-law, Agopito Aquino, was one of the naysayers. He called the treaty lopsided in favor of the United States.

Aquino then gave assurance to the United States that its forces would be permitted to remain at Subic Bay for at least another year while a joint commission of U.S. and Philippine officials discussed how to return Subic to the Manila administration. Later, after consultation with the Senate, she offered a three-year deadline. In late 1991, however, negotiations collapsed, and Aquino gave notice that Subic must be evacuated in 1992.

She had already announced that she would not run for a second term in May 1992. No doubt her decision encouraged Imelda Marcos to come home in October 1991. The president was adamant, however, that Mrs. Marcos would have to face charges. The excitement over the exile's return was dampened by two violent hurricanes that took thousands of lives. Aquino informed her that after the election she could bury her husband in his home province, but Imelda Marcos insisted that it would be only a temporary grave until the body could be moved to Manila.

There were seven presidential candidates, among them the former first lady, who had pleaded not guilty to a fresh batch of corruption charges. Aquino endorsed retired General Ramos, who had given her so much support in 1986. A third prominent candidate was ex-Judge Miriam Defensor Santiago.

It was a huge election with over 17,000 posts at stake, and after a tedious and convoluted vote count, the Philippine Congress proclaimed Ramos president. Imelda Marcos, who faced more court appearances, had come in seventh. On June 30, Corazon Aquino proudly watched her country's first peaceful transfer of power in 26 years.

Aquino watchers called her well intentioned but indecisive. They praised her because she had completed six years in office despite numerous coup attempts, but they faulted her for being a weak administrator who lacked the decisiveness to get the economy back on track and who allowed too much cronyism and corruption within her cabinet. Frequently they quoted one of her administrative aides, who characterized her term as "being somewhere between a disappointment and a disaster."

No one, however, disputed her place in Philippine history.

BENAZIR BHUTTO

Prime Minister of Pakistan
(1990–91)

"Shaheed" — martyr — is the term Benazir Bhutto uses for her father, the defining presence in her life. Their relationship inspired the title of her autobiography, *Daughter of Destiny*. Before Zulfikar Ali Bhutto was hanged in 1979, she had already been held under house arrest for speaking out against his jailing. After his death she was detained over and over again until she became prime minister. As a political heir, she paid a heavy price.

Benazir Bhutto was born on June 21, 1953, in Karachi, West Pakistan. Just six years earlier, the British had partitioned the subcontinent of India along religious lines, Hindu and Muslim. The Muslim state, a British dominion, was Pakistan, with a West Wing and an East Wing (East Bengal), separated by 1,000 miles of India. Its founder, Mohammed Ali Jinnah of the Muslim League, became its first governor-general.

Benazir was always called Pinkie by her family because of her rosy complexion at birth. She was the eldest child of Zulfikar Ali Bhutto, a Western-educated lawyer, and his beautiful second wife, Nusrat Ispahni, daughter of an Iranian merchant in Bombay, India. Three more children followed Pinkie — a son, Mir Murtaza; another daughter, Sanam (Sunny); and a second son, Shah Nawaz.

The Bhutto family had owned large estates in the Sind region and had dominated local politics for years. Although Zulfikar's father had started to break away from the feudal role, the son still lived in luxury at Al-Murtaza, his home near the town of Larkana.

In 1956, Pakistan became a republic. Under the new constitution it was divided into two provinces, West Pakistan and East Pakistan, the former West and East wings. East and West had equal partnership in the

National Assembly. The first president was Major General Iskander Mirza, ousted in 1958 by General Mohammed Ayub Khan, defense minister. Zulfikar Bhutto, who had been a university lecturer, began a rapid political rise under President Ayub Khan and established his wife and children in a house at 70 Clifton Road in Karachi. But they always returned to Al-Murtaza for winter vacations, his birthday, and family weddings. First named as a United Nations delegate, Zulfikar became, in turn, commerce minister, energy minister, foreign minister, and then leader of the UN delegation. Nusrat usually accompanied her husband on his trips abroad, leaving the children with an English governess and the household staff. As the eldest, Pinkie took on added responsibilities.

Zulfikar Bhutto belonged to the Sunni branch of Islam, and Nusrat, to the Shiite branch, but they harbored no great differences over religion. It was common practice for Sunnis and Shiites to intermarry. Husband and wife agreed that their children should attend Roman Catholic convent schools for the best instruction. No conversion was required.

Islamabad had replaced Karachi as the capital in 1960 when plans were already being made for a new seat of government in Rawalpindi. In spite of his frequent absences from home, Zulfikar was able to give his children a first-class political education, filling their heads with history lessons; tales of past Muslim glories; and, most of all, pride of country. He and Benazir were especially close.

When Benazir was 12, a pupil at a convent school at Murree in the Himalayas, she was deeply disturbed over Pakistan's tragic, all-out war with India over Kashmir. So much responsibility lay on the shoulders of her father, the foreign minister. For years Pakistan had been calling for a UN plebiscite in predominantly Muslim Kashmir to determine its status. Originally acquiescing, India now declared that the UN preconditions had not been fulfilled and lost no time in moving to assimilate Kashmir more completely. In response, Pakistani guerrillas crossed into Kashmir in hopes of igniting a popular rising. Indian Prime Minister Lal Bahadur Shastri, fearing a Vietnam-type war, ordered his troops to wipe out the bases where the infiltrations had begun. In turn, Pakistan resorted to tank warfare. All-out war developed by September. India opened a second front in the Punjab region, making Lahore the principal target. Soon the United Nations brought about a cease-fire that was not too rigidly observed. It was a war without victors. The day after he signed a peace accord in Tashkent in January 1966, Shastri died of a heart attack and was replaced by Indira Gandhi.

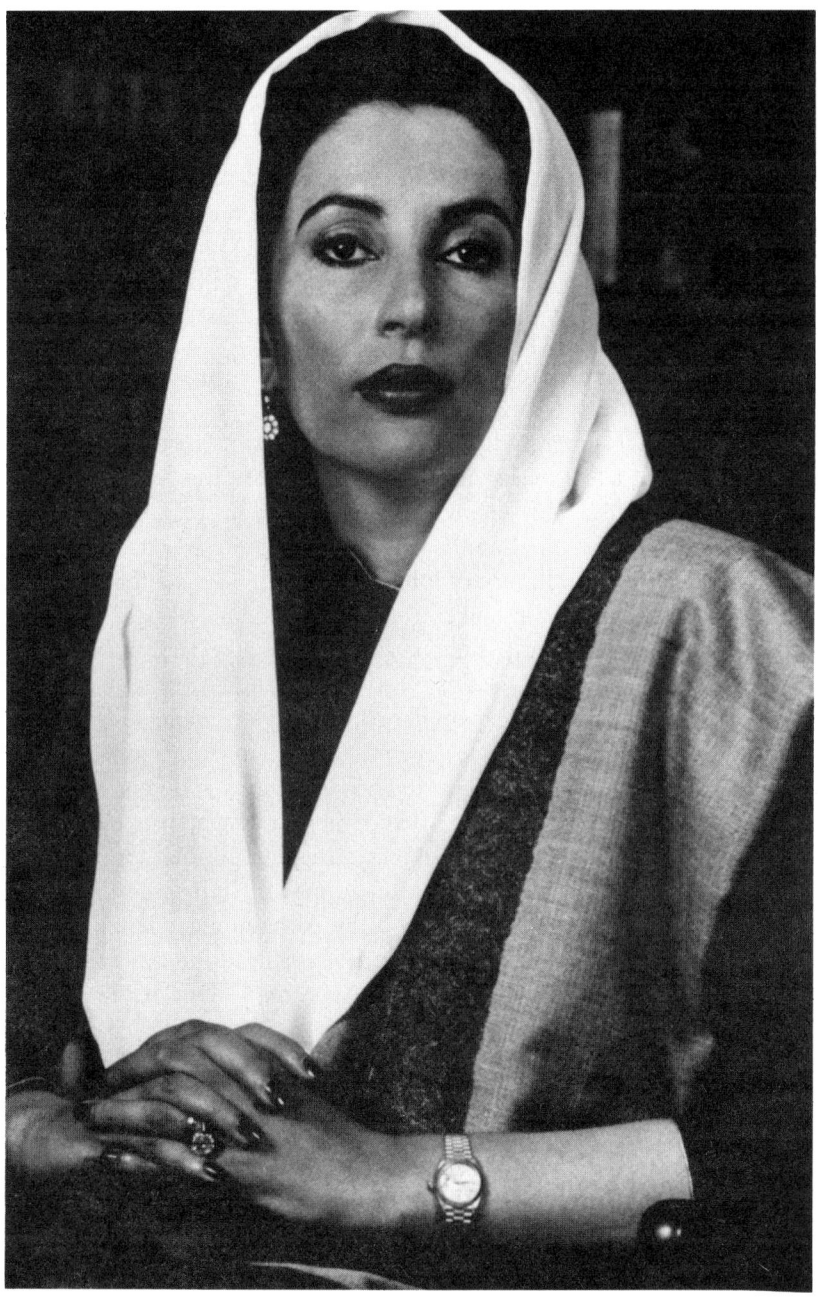

Benazir Bhutto: courtesy Embassy of Pakistan, Washington, D.C.

Zulfikar resigned his post as foreign minister in 1966 and the next year formed a new political party, the Pakistan People's party (PPP), which promised "Bread, Clothing, Shelter" to the millions who lived in extreme poverty. The Bhutto house at 70 Clifton Road became a branch office of the party, and Benazir and her sister joined the ranks and helped sign up new recruits.

Eleven months later, President Ayub Khan, smarting under criticism of the unpopular Kashmir war, arrested Zulfikar for dissent. But the prisoner was released within three months.

Because he had obtained degrees from the University of California at Berkeley and from Oxford, Zulfikar expected his children to enjoy an elite education similar to his. In 1969 he sent Benazir off to Radcliffe College, the women's undergraduate adjunct of Harvard. Nusrat stayed with her daughter for a few weeks and then left after assuring herself that the Bhuttos' old friends, John Kenneth Galbraith and his wife, would act as "parents in residence." Galbraith, an economics professor, had served as U.S. ambassador to India under John F. Kennedy. For all the kindness of the Galbraiths and their son Peter, the pampered 16-year-old girl from Karachi had to make many difficult adjustments like serving herself at table, walking miles to classes, and enduring the bitter cold of Massachusetts winters. The experience, she said later, made her grow up. Soon the student of comparative government exchanged her saris for blue jeans and sweatshirts and took part in anti–Vietnam war demonstrations.

With mounting excitement, Benazir read newspaper stories about Pakistan, where Ayub Khan, grown increasingly unpopular for his tight-fisted rule, resigned in March 1969 after an orgy of violence, strikes, and riots and handed power over to the army commander, General Agha Muhammad Yahya Khan. For Benazir the best headline was printed in December 1970: "Zulfikar Bhutto's PPP Captures 72 Out of 138 Assembly Seats."

She had not imagined that war again lay just over the horizon. East Pakistan had long felt misgoverned, neglected, and exploited. More stridently than ever, Mujib-ur Rahman of the Awami League and other Bengali leaders were demanding autonomy. In March 1971, West Pakistan cracked down on the rebellious Bengalis, and a nine-months-long war of independence followed. Then in December because refugees were streaming across its border, India intervened with a three-pronged pincer attack on Dacca and achieved victory after 12 days. East Pakistan became the independent nation of Bangladesh.

Following the fall of Dacca (its spelling was soon changed to Dhaka), Yahya Khan stepped down, and Zulfikar Bhutto, leader of the largest parliamentary group, became president of Pakistan. The capital was now Rawalpindi. At Radcliffe, Benazir enjoyed her new status as the daughter of a head of state. Home for summer vacation in 1972, she accompanied her father to a summit with Indira Gandhi, whom she described as tiny but elegant. In turn, Gandhi must have been struck by the willowy, dark beauty of the young woman who often had the Pakistani president's ear.

As a student of international affairs, Benazir was tempted to remain in Pakistan to participate in the fast-changing political arena. But her parents were determined that she finish at Radcliffe and continue at Oxford. Soon after she received a degree in government in 1973, Pakistan adopted a new constitution, and Zulfikar, who had pushed it through, gave up the presidency and became prime minister.

Following her father's wishes, Benazir left for Lady Margaret's Hall at Oxford to study political philosophy and economics. After she was graduated with honors in 1976, Zulfikar urged her to stay at Oxford for another year to take a foreign service course.

The next spring she became the first foreign woman ever to be elected president of the Oxford Union, the famous debating society that develops many political leaders. Her term lasted three months.

During his years in office, Zulfikar had instituted many reforms, including the redistribution of land, electrification, nationalization of monopoly industries, a literacy program, and a fixed minimum wage for laborers. He opened the civil service and police force to women, and Nusrat went to Mexico City to head Pakistan's delegation at the International Conference of Women. She also stood for election in the National Assembly and won. Benazir was proud of both parents.

In mid-1977, she flew to Rawalpindi to join her family amid a troubled political atmosphere. Since March, when the PPP again had won a sweeping victory in parliamentary elections, demonstrations and riots intensified as the opposition protested that elections had been rigged. The death toll reached the hundreds.

A few days after Benazir's arrival, Mohammed Zia ul-Haq, the army chief of staff, took the leaders of all parties under "protective custody." Zulfikar Bhutto was brought to the prime minister's rest house in Murree. After three weeks the detainees were released. Fourteen days later, Zulfikar Bhutto was charged with conspiracy to murder the father of a former party colleague, turned opponent, who had been killed in an ambush. On the same day the summons came, Zia declared martial law. Before a month had passed, Benazir was arrested for speaking out against her father's jailing and was held under house detention until January.

Just before Zulfikar's trial began in October 1977, Zia canceled new elections. He was now a dictator for real. Meanwhile he had heaped more charges against the prisoner: corruption and misappropriation of funds.

In March 1978 the Lahore High Court sentenced Zulfikar Bhutto to death. To no avail, world leaders appealed for clemency. Benazir was arrested again in October for making "objectionable speeches" against the verdict.

She was still under detention when her father was hanged in April 1979, and she was not allowed to attend his burial in Larkana. Only at the end of May was she released. She would later say that wherever she was detained, jail rules always applied.

On her husband's imprisonment, Nusrat Bhutto had become nominal head of the PPP, but it was always understood that Benazir would take over. Some days after Zulfikar's funeral, his grieving daughter laid rose petals on his grave and said, "I feel a part of me has died." Nor could she contain her anger. She was again arrested in October on charges of holding a protest meeting, unauthorized under the ever-expanding martial law, and was kept in confinement for six months.

Nusrat cautioned her about provoking Zia's anger. Benazir was left alone until early 1981, when the Bhutto brothers' exploits made their mother and sister terribly insecure. Mir Murtaza, schooled in the United States and England, and Shah Nawaz, educated in Switzerland, had stayed abroad after Zulfikar's "judicial murder," as Benazir called their father's death. With sympathizers they formed an antigovernment group, named Al-Zulfikar, that became the core of a coalition of several parties, the Movement to Restore Democracy (MRD), based in Afghanistan. When the group hijacked a Pakistani International Airlines plane en route to Syria, Zia was forced to exchange some imprisoned Bhutto supporters for the hostages.

To get revenge on the Bhutto family and to stop a ground swell of support for the MRD, Zia imprisoned both Benazir and Nusrat Bhutto. Nusrat was held at Karachi central jail. At first, Benazir was placed in solitary confinement at Sukkur jail. When she lost weight rapidly, her keepers became alarmed. Then doctors decided she must have an exploratory operation for uterine cancer. No cancer was discovered, but Benazir was tired and anemic for months afterward.

Because Nusrat had been throwing up blood, she was freed from jail, but soon afterward, another door banged shut against Benazir, who was transferred to the Karachi central jail until December. One bright note in her bleak existence was her temporary release to attend her sister Sanam's wedding in September. Another was her knowledge that, in the United States, Senator Claiborne Pell of Rhode Island and her old friend Peter Galbraith were raising the issue of human rights abuses and Benazir Bhutto's detention at a time when Zia was seeking restored aid from Washington.

As 1981 ended, Benazir was locked up in Al-Murtaza for a year. A prison staff came daily to oversee what she was doing, and paramilitary forces were posted inside the walls of the compound. Few visitors were allowed, and she felt she was once more in solitary confinement. Teaching herself to cook proved one way to pass the time. Mostly she worried about her mother, who, it was feared had lung cancer. Nusrat was allowed to go to West Germany for medical treatment in November 1982, and fortunately the cancer was arrested.

As young as Benazir was, the years of confinement had taken their toll. She felt her memory fading and her ability to converse deteriorating. She had experienced ear problems before, but her middle ear and mastoid infection in 1983 was far more severe than any of her previous illnesses. Finally in January 1984, after numerous foreign leaders pleaded with Zia, she was allowed to fly to London for microscopic surgery.

After her recovery she was determined to make London the seat of political activity for the PPP in exile. The goal was to expose Zia's brutal treatment of the 40,000 political prisoners he had jailed. Benazir and her helpers gathered "reams of material" on them.

In March she was invited to speak at the meeting of the Carnegie Endowment for International Peace in Washington. She used the podium to expose Zia, whom the Western press and much of the Washington establishment had been portraying as a "benign dictator." She had found sympathetic ears in Congress, where some members had been demanding tough antinuclear requirements for American aid. But the Reagan administration exerted intense pressure for the passage of a new amendment allowing assistance to Pakistan to continue if Zia certified that his country did not have a nuclear bomb. Benazir received this disheartening news as she prepared to return to London.

From her Barbican flat, letters, reports, and photographs poured out to organizations and governments all over the world. But she worried that she and her volunteers were losing the race. Whenever news came that a prisoner had been hanged, she suffered intensely.

To remove herself temporarily from the sad stories she heard every day, she went to Cannes in July for a vacation with her mother and her brothers, who had never returned to Pakistan. It became a true family reunion when Sanam and her family arrived, too. Then tragedy struck the Bhuttos once more. One morning Shah Nawaz, Benazir's younger brother, was found dead at his apartment. Police hinted that the handsome, 25-year-old, one-time guerrilla had been poisoned. At first they arrested and then released his Afghan-born wife Rehana; the marriage had been in trouble. Mir Murtaza had wed her sister Fauzia, but they were in no way involved. Benazir's suspicions centered on Zia, whom she believed had ordered Shah Nawaz killed in fear that guerrilla activities would be resumed.

The Zia regime, dreading a public emotional outburst, reluctantly gave permission for the dead man to be buried in Larkana. Just as Benazir left Zurich Airport, the prime minister of Pakistan announced that martial law would be lifted in December. Benazir flew home with her brother's body and arranged for his burial beside that of their father, "Shaheed, the martyr." To impress Zia, she staged a funeral procession with thousands of mourners. Zia had assured the press that she would not be arrested when she brought her brother back to Pakistan, but within a few days she was detained again at 70 Clifton Road.

Back in Cannes, an inquiry was scheduled to be held about the circumstances of Shah Nawaz's death. Benazir was released from confinement to fly to France to give a deposition. She claimed her brother had been killed by unknown persons. The widow, who had maintained that his death was a suicide, suddenly told police that he had not died instantaneously. Rehana Bhutto then received an arrest warrant for having failed to assist a person in danger. But her trial was indefinitely postponed, and she left for the United States. The turmoil also destroyed Mir Murtaza's marriage to Fauzia, who sided with her sister.

For once true to his word, Zia lifted martial law in December. A civilian prime minister, Mohammed Khan Junejo, was said to be in charge of the administration. It was common knowledge, however, that Zia as president was still in command. The powers of a newly elected national assembly were only advisory. Political parties would not be allowed to participate in elections, and many prominent politicians would not be permitted to run for office. Zia wanted to hold off elections until 1992.

And yet, in London, Benazir could read of some reform. Military courts could not rule on civilian affairs, the press was no longer under censorship, and protest rallies met little harassment.

So Benazir Bhutto told her PPP activists in London that she was going home, and some of them agreed to accompany her. First she went to Washington to shore up support from her congressional friends. She later wrote:

> Members of the American press were intrigued by the similarities between my upcoming battle with Zia and Corazon Aquino's challenge to Ferdinand Marcos. Their views of the similarities between Mrs. Aquino and me were a bit romantic, however. Yes, we were both women from well-known landowning families who had been educated in the United States. Both of us had lost loved members of our families to dictators, Mrs. Aquino, her husband, and I, my father and brother. Mrs. Aquino had fought Marcos with "people power" to orchestrate a peaceful revolution just as I was hoping to do. But the similarities between us ended there.
> ... Corazon Aquino had enjoyed the support of both the military and the church.... I had neither. The generals opposed me because I threatened the corrupt system by which they received discounts on land, free cars, and exemptions in customs duties. And while some of the religious establishment was with me, the fundamentalist mullahs supported Zia's dictatorship.
> Most important of all, the Americans had served notice on Marcos, even providing transportation out of the country for him, his family, and entourage. The Reagan Administration was solidly behind Zia. I could expect little real help from America, save for the good wishes and moral support of various members of the U.S. government and the press.

No flight was available from Europe to Lahore, where Benazir wanted to land. So she went by way of Dhahran in Saudi Arabia. She smiled when just before the plane taxied to a stop, the pilot said, "We welcome Miss Benazir Bhutto to Pakistan." At the airport, adoring crowds waited for her. Speaking enthusiastically to them, she called for Zia's ouster and immediate national elections. Buoyed by the joyous welcome, she went on an extensive lecture tour. The tour was marred, however, by several death threats and news that certain PPP supporters had been killed. Meanwhile she and Nusrat were elected cochairs of the PPP.

To observe July 9, the ninth anniversary of Zia's coup, the PPP planned "Black Day" demonstrations in all the district headquarters. For August 14, Pakistan's Independence Day, it wanted a big rally in Lahore, where the Zia regime had also announced its intentions to celebrate. The PPP now was joined by the MRD, which had stood behind the airplane hijacking in 1981. But all too soon Bhutto felt that the MRD was forcing her into dangerously provocative positions. She opposed the Lahore rally, which ended in bloodshed.

At 70 Clifton Road she was again arrested and placed in solitary confinement in a prison for juveniles near Karachi. Before her case came up for trial, however, the jail superintendent announced that she was free.

The goal was to rebuild the PPP as a political institution. A million members joined the party in the next four months. In January she narrowly escaped an assassination attempt, but she kept on tirelessly.

In spite of her beauty, Benazir had had no time for romance. Her family believed that at 34 she should be married and told her that wedded status would help her in politics. So in July 1987 she agreed to an arranged marriage. The candidate was Asif Zardari, a personable young member of a landowning family. Nusrat Bhutto assured her daughter that love would come later.

By May 1988, Benazir was pregnant, and Zia suddenly announced fall elections, scheduling them for November 16 after his agents calculated that the Zardari baby would be due on that day. In July, fearing a PPP sweep, he announced that party-based elections violated the spirit of Islam and that no parties would be on the ballot. In anger, Benazir and her allies turned to the courts.

A fiery airplane crash in August prevented Zia from carrying out his design. He and his party of 30, returning from a visit to a military base, were killed in a never-explained accident. But there was no change in the government, since the interim president, Ghulam Izhaq Khan, retained all Zia's cronies. Benazir persisted in shoring up support, but on her doctor's orders, she had to spend some days in bed and then schedule daily rest periods. She was going to stand for two seats, one from Larkana and one from Chitral, and had asked her mother to come home from abroad to campaign for her during her confinement. She had kept secret the mid-October date and had smiled when Zia miscalculated.

But as she said, "The baby outmaneuvered them all." A boy, Bilawal, was born five weeks early, giving her a month to regain her strength before campaigning began in mid-October. She encouraged Nusrat to run for a seat, too.

To stack the odds against the PPP, the acting president suddenly announced that for the first time voters had to show national identity cards. Bhutto and her followers took the matter to the Lahore High Court, which struck down the requirement, saying it invited voting fraud. In answer, the government appealed to the Supreme Court, which stayed the decision.

Despite the ruling, which disenfranchised more than half the voting population, Benazir and Nusrat led the PPP to a narrow victory, 92 of the 205 seats. A series of alliances between the PPP and a number of smaller parties, notably the Mohiujar National Movement, brought Bhutto to the office of prime minister.

Initially her access to power inspired great enthusiasm. Pakistanis talked about the grit and persistence she had shown for a decade. Possessed of an elite education, she was expected to show political intelligence and social vision. But quickly she appointed her mother as her senior minister, a position so powerful it allowed Nusrat to take the reins of government during her daughter's frequent absences. Next Bhutto rewarded her father-in-law, Hakim Ali Zardari, with the chairmanship of the National Assembly's key public accounting committee. As she continued to place members of wealthy feudal families in her government, she was accused of reducing government to mere patronage. Many former supporters said they felt alienated by her haughtiness and aristocratic bent. Within the still-powerful Zia circle she had her share of enemies. In addition, Islamic fundamentalists, who had supported Zia for his Koranic bans and punishments, felt disturbed by a woman's political prominence. They also suspected the PPP of leftist leanings.

Only six months in office, and newly pregnant again, Bhutto flew to Washington to meet with President George Bush. The two were in complete accord on the civil war in Afghanistan. The United States and Pakistan were the biggest suppliers of aid to the rebels. Besides, Bhutto had 3.5 million Afghan refugees in her country. To ease one of Bush's worries, she assured him that Pakistan's nuclear program was committed to peaceful purposes. Following her White House talks, Bhutto gave the commencement speech at Harvard and spoke to the United Nations General Assembly.

That fall she saw Pakistan rejoin the British Commonwealth 17 years after it had resigned in protest over the Commonwealth's recognition of Bangladesh. Meanwhile, stories multiplied about her granting political favors, but she was complimented for restoring civil liberties and championing the poor. She was, however, engaged in a constant power struggle with Ghulam Izhaq Khan and the opposition in Rawalpindi and the provinces. But the greatest danger came from the military, which never trusted her.

Benazir gave birth to a daughter in January 1990. During the confinement, her mother Nusrat had acted as prime minister. A new baby, however, did not dampen criticism. By spring the military was totally disenchanted with her failure to restore law and order in her native Sind. Sindhi-speaking natives were engaged in a civil war with Urdu-speaking Indian immigrants (muhajirs), who formed the backbone of a growing middle class.

In the last two weeks of May, fighting between the Sind natives and the Muhajirs left over 300 dead, a toll made higher because the constabulary had fired on demonstrators. Izhaq Khan severely criticized the action and ordered an inquiry. Stubbornly Bhutto refused to accede to the demands of the head of the armed forces for special emergency powers in Sind.

Ethnic hatred was only one aspect of the violence sweeping Karachi, which was filled with international drug syndicates and local bandit mafias. It was the hub of heroin exports leaving the frontier between Afghanistan and Pakistan and for arms supplied by the U.S. Central Intelligence Agency to Afghan guerrillas.

According to the constitution, removing a prime minister was a presidential prerogative. On August 6, 1990, Izhaq Khan dismissed Bhutto, charging corruption and nepotism. She declared that her ouster was "quasi-military intervention." The same day, the military took charge of the national television system and the telephone exchange.

Since she had tried to secularize the Pakistani judicial process during her 20 months in office, she reacted in dismay to the president's August 15 order directing the criminal code to conform to the "injunctions of Islam." Under the religious codes, a woman could be sent to prison for adultery and had to have four male adults support her charges of having been raped.

September saw five of Bhutto's ministers accused of official corruption. She herself was formally charged, with few specifics given. When thousands of her supporters stormed the courtroom, the hearings were postponed.

In October, Benazir's husband, Asif, was arrested, accused of involvement in the kidnapping of a Pakistani-born British businessman.

People had been calling him "Mr. Ten Percent," alluding to his eagerness to gain commissions from business deals.

The guilt or innocence of Benazir Bhutto and her family became the central issue of the forthcoming campaign. In the October election, the PPP was decisively defeated, but Bhutto, Nusrat, and Asif, who had campaigned from jail, won their seats. The PPP's total was less than half its total in the 1989 election. Naraz Sharif, a Zia protégé, was named to the post of prime minister.

In 1992, Rehana Bhutto remained a fugitive from a trial that had finally begun in Cannes. Asif was still in jail, but at least the Karachi High Court acquitted him of charges that he had used political influence in pressuring a bank to grant a huge loan without sufficient collateral. Nonetheless he faced trial on other charges.

Most important, Benazir and Nusrat remained in the National Assembly, Benazir as the leader of the opposition.

Unceasingly she accused the Sharif regime of corruption, repression, and rigging elections. She and her top advisers staged a huge rally in Rawalpindi in November 1992 and called for the overthrow of the government, threatening that 100,000 marchers would storm the National Assembly building. But before any march could begin, police barricaded the route, fired tear gas into the crowd, and beat unruly dissidents.

Two hundred officers surrounded Bhutto and her party leaders and pushed her into a plane bound for Karachi. Government sources said she would be under house arrest for an indefinite period.

Ertha Pascal-Trouillot

President of Haiti
(1990–91)

She was the first woman ever promoted to the bench in Haiti. As a Supreme Court justice, Ertha Pascal-Trouillot expected to have a distinguished career, but dramatic events in the spring of 1990 whisked her into a short-term presidency and ultimately house arrest.

Born on August 13, 1943, Ertha Pascal was the ninth of ten children of Thimocles Pascal, a worker in ornamental iron, and his wife, Louise Damanoy. The family lived in the affluent suburb of Pétionville, high in the hills above the steamy, hot capital of Port-au-Prince. But they did not rank among the wealthy residents because Thimocles died when Ertha was young, and his widow earned a living as a seamstress and embroiderer and, according to some reports, a laundress.

Like 95 percent of Haitians, the Pascals were black. The other 5 percent were mulattos, who adopted their education, religion, and way of life from France. This mulatto minority elite had long dominated the economic and political environment. Ertha, who attended schools in Pétionville, is remembered as thin, studious, and aloof, even then. She wanted to become a writer or a doctor, unusual goals for a poor girl in a country with a 90 percent illiteracy rate.

When she was 14, François Duvalier, a black country doctor with a professional goal of dislodging the mulatto elite, was elected president. His chief instrument of power was the Haitian army, a legacy from the American occupation of 1915–34, which was ordered to protect American economic interests through years of political turmoil. In a poverty-stricken and superstitious country, where voodoo held sway, Duvalier, known as Papa Doc, easily assumed dictatorial powers. Cleverly he blended populism and mysticism and carefully cultivated the image of a frock-

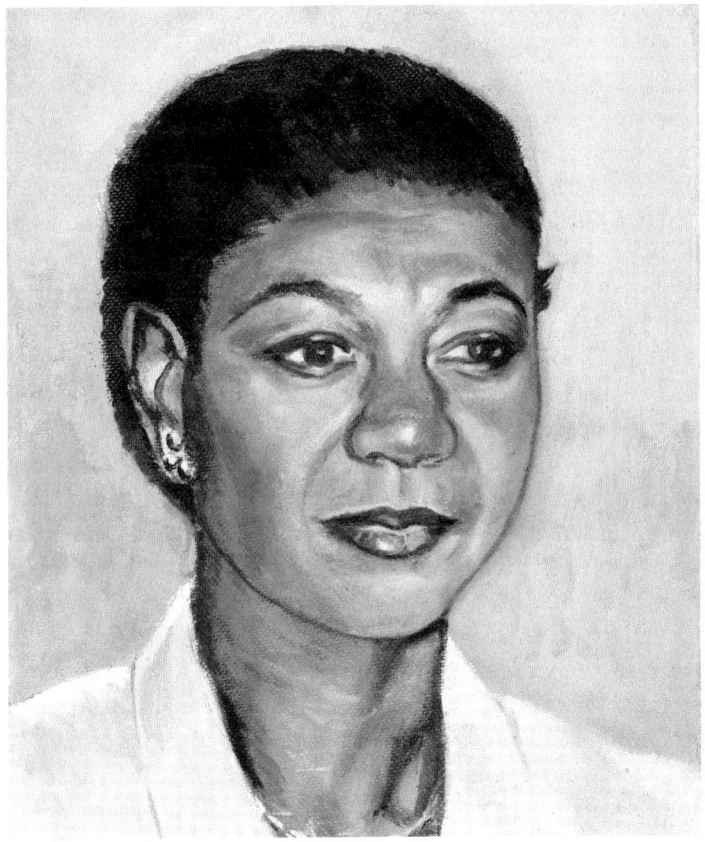

Ertha Pascal-Trouillot: oil portrait by John Houston.

coated voodoo priest. In 1964, calling himself "renovator" of the nation, he became president for life.

Ertha and her family lived through hurricanes Cleo and Flora in 1964 and 1965 and saw economic conditions worsen after these disasters. The National Palace, where the Duvaliers resided in luxury, rose like a fairytale castle over the shantytowns of Port-au-Prince. The most frequent guests, disgorged from Rolls-Royces, were men in gold military braid. Although there were sporadic attempts to oust a brutal and corrupt regime that was lining its pockets, Duvalier remained in full control with the help of a secret army, a gang of thugs known as the Tontons Macoutes (Creole for bogeyman) militia. The merest hint of dissent was not permitted. Uncounted thousands of Haitians ended up in exile or in Fort

Dimanche, a notorious prison, never to emerge. The Pascal family felt the weight of the Tontons Macoutes' terror when one of Ertha's brothers, a high school student, was shot in a cabaret and permanently paralyzed from the waist down.

In a social science class, Ertha caught the eye of her teacher, Ernst Trouillot, a journalist and lawyer, 22 years her senior. With his encouragement she studied law at the École de Droit de Gondaieves in the port city of Gondaieves. It was a historic spot, the site of the slaves' proclamation of the independence of the French colony of Saint-Domingue in 1804 after 13 years of continual civil war. There the name Haiti was bestowed on the first slave nation to become free.

Trouillot, who had thrived professionally under Papa Doc, was president of the Bar Association when he watched his protégée being sworn in at the bar in 1971. Reportedly, he was so overcome with emotion that he swooned. Four months later, he married her.

That spring Papa Doc died after having survived several attempted coups and invasions in the previous 14 years. His record was dismal. State terrorism had killed 30,000 to 60,000 persons. Haiti had become the poorest country in the western hemisphere. Too-swift deforestation and urbanization, dangerous population growth, and official pilfering had never ceased. Earlier, Papa Doc had made sure that the Chamber of Deputies approved constitutional amendments allowing his 20-year-old son, the obese and allegedly dim-witted Jean-Claude (Baby Doc), to succeed him. The heir also was named president for life. To general surprise, Baby Doc made some promising moves toward democratization. But national stability was soon threatened by a behind-the-scenes power struggle between two factions, one led by the new president's sister Denise and her husband, Colonel Max Dominique, and one by his mulatto mother Simone and the interior and defense minister, Lieutenant Colonel Luckner Combone. Jean-Claude gave in eventually to his mother, who feared rapid liberalization.

And yet the atmosphere of intimidation seemed to be lifting. The Tontons Macoutes almost vanished for a time. Jean-Claude even commuted the sentences of several men who had been convicted of plotting the elder Duvalier's assassination in 1970. But he was said to be so depressed by the misery in the streets that he seldom left the palace.

Meanwhile Ertha had joined her husband's commercial and family law practice. She was co-author with him of several law books; *The Judicial Status of the Haitian Woman in Social Legislation* was considered the best. Motherhood came, too, with the birth of a daughter Yantha in 1975.

Trouillot had swept his wife into Haitian high society, much of it revolving around Baby Doc's glamorous mulatto wife, Michele. Without any notion of competing, Ertha Pascal-Trouillot almost matched her in chic. Her sense of style seemed natural, and she achieved it without the reckless spending of Mme. Duvalier.

Travel gave the young lawyer further polish. In 1980 she came to the United States to observe the legal system and on her return wrote *On the Grand Boulevard of Liberty*, which was full of praise for the American Supreme Court. Travel also brought out her courage and determination. During a visit to Paris with her husband, she confronted two thieves who had snatched her purse and insisted so firmly on its return that they threw it back to her.

But few travelers came to Haiti after the early 1980s, when the AIDS panic struck worldwide, and the country was falsely stigmatized as its source. The tourist trade on which Haiti depended so heavily disappeared, and with it thousands of jobs. As the country floundered in an even greater economic mess, hundreds of unemployed Haitians desperately climbed aboard rickety, overloaded boats to escape to Florida, and massive public demonstrations broke out in the streets. Helpless to do anything, Jean-Claude Duvalier fled the country aboard a U.S. Air Force jet in February 1986. A military coalition, headed by General Henri Namphy, one of his favorites, assumed control. Soon after Duvalier's departure, Ertha served on a commission to revise the civil and penal codes.

François Latortue, the minister of justice, appointed her to the Supreme Court that year. In spite of her husband's connections to Duvalier, she was considered well qualified, even brilliant.

The next year, Ernst Trouillot died of a heart attack as they sat and conversed at home. In her grief Ertha shrugged off rumors that as general counsel of a bank used by the Duvaliers, he had benefited financially. She was grateful she could be more than busy. When not involved with her court duties, she began to compile a biographical dictionary of well-known Haitians. Her leisure hours were devoted to reading Voltaire and Racine and listening to classical music, particularly Beethoven.

Namphy was no improvement on his old boss. He scheduled elections for 1987, but 34 voters were killed by thugs protected by soldiers, and the polls were shut down. Another election in 1988 brought in a university professor, Leslie Manigat, as president. When he attempted to arrest Namphy, the general turned around and threw him out. Namphy's second occupation of the presidential palace lasted only four months.

Charging bribery and corruption, General Prosper Avril, who had close ties to the Duvaliers, headed a coup that pushed Namphy out of office. Avril also proved unpopular, especially when, throughout 1989, he followed the Duvalier policy of ordering the arrest and exile of prominent members of the opposition. Protests multiplied, and after a week of bloody violence, the American ambassador, Alvin P. Adams, Jr., persuaded Avril to leave; the Bush administration sent in a plane to fly him out of the country in March 1990.

With Avril gone, the task was to prepare for new elections. A provisional president had to be appointed. Unity Assembly, an opposition coalition of 12 prodemocracy parties, which had been instrumental in Avril's downfall, faced the challenge of finding a suitable candidate. From long tradition, the concurrence of the army would be necessary. Unity Assembly did not like the army's first choice, Supreme Court Justice Gilbert Austin, who was deemed to have been too close to the Avril regime.

Three other justices refused the job. The nod finally fell on Pascal-Trouillot, who said she accepted the "heavy task" in the name of Haitian women. Her job would be to steer the country toward early elections. She would have to work with a 19-member Council of State, which had veto power over her. But it was confidently expected that in dealing with the council she would use the same tact, finesse, and patience she had shown in court. At a ceremony at army headquarters, Unity Assembly leaders gave the army high command a letter nominating Pascal-Trouillot as provisional president. The army accepted her, and she resigned from the Supreme Court.

Tall and elegant in her trademark white suit, Pascal-Trouillot was inaugurated on March 13, 1990, at the Palace of Justice. During her early weeks in office, she spoke of taking power from the police and investigating the 1987 massacre at the polls. She also appointed Irene Ridore, wife of a jailed opposition leader, Evans Paul, mayor of Port-au-Prince. With a bit of snobbery she had at first declined to do so, complaining that Ridore did not have a university education. Other appointments included several of Pascal-Trouillot's relatives and friends, and charges of nepotism began to be raised against her. The man with the greatest influence was her brother-in-law, Dr. Belland St. Louis.

The all-too-sudden resignation of her finance minister presented

Pascal-Trouillot with new problems and made her long to have Ernst by her side. Without asking for the approval of the Council of State, she appointed Violène Leganeur, who came from the inner circles of both Duvaliers, to the vacant finance post. The council was furious, but Pascal-Trouillot, with her customary firmness, would not budge. Suddenly critics spread rumors that because of her husband's business connections she, too, was incriminated in the Duvalier wrongdoings.

Article 291 of a new 1987 constitution had banned political participation for a decade by any "architect" of the Duvalier dictatorships. In June, just before the president opened a council meeting, Serge Villard, the author of Article 291, was assassinated. No specific evidence implicated Pascal-Trouillot, but the president was widely held responsible for encouraging the murder. She kept her job, however, because there seemed to be no alternative.

As the preparations for the December election began to move ahead, one presidential candidate caught everybody's attention. Jean-Bertrand Aristide was a diminutive, homely slum priest, who vowed, with socialist fervor, to clean up all the pockets of power and privilege. Wild street youngsters flocked to his protection as he went about preaching his message.

During the summer, Dr. Roger Lafontant, Baby Doc's former interior minister and the reputed head of the revived Tontons Macoutes, returned from exile in the Dominican Republic, which shares the island of Hispaniola with Haiti. Promptly he declared himself a presidential candidate, but was declared ineligible because of his link to the Duvalier dynasty. He bided his time for revenge.

Over the months, Pascal-Trouillot seemed curiously passive and withdrawn. Nobody knew where she stood politically. She was compared unfavorably to the blunt Mayor Ridore, an activist, who at once had begun to clean out City Hall.

That December, Aristide won the election with 66 percent of the vote, and Haiti's long-brutalized, diseased, and dirt-poor millions were ecstatic. But suddenly terror struck. Early in the new year, Lafontant, who had vowed to keep Aristide from taking office, ordered his supporters to seize Pascal-Trouillot at her three-story house. They held her hostage for 12 hours in the palace while the usurper forced her resignation and proclaimed himself president. But, as thousands of Aristide's supporters began coursing through the streets, the army assaulted the palace and arrested Lafontant. Pascal-Trouillot then appeared on national television to announce that she would continue in office until Aristide took his oath.

For his inauguration, on February 7, 1991, the fifth anniversary of Baby Doc's departure, the gritty streets of Port-au-Prince were cleaned as they never had been cleaned before, and wave after wave of exuberant Haitians danced in them.

For Pascal-Trouillot, however, the inauguration of Father Aristide brought no pleasure. Popularly labeled a Duvalierist, with little evidence for the charges, she found herself under house arrest. A month later she was released, but forbidden to leave the country. There was no further publicity about her.

By fall, the military hierarchy, tied to the economic elite, was clearly disgusted with the messianic Aristide. A coup toppled him, and Pascal-Trouillot's old enemy Lafontant was killed in the fighting that erupted afterward. A despairing Aristide fled to Venezuela, where the Organization of American States (OAS) took up his cause and imposed strict economic sanctions against Haiti.

The new government, mostly Duvalierist, was only a front for the army. Aristide's supporters were vulnerable to attacks by the soldiers and remnants of the Tontons Macoutes. From his exile, the little priest and the OAS tried to arrange various compromises by which he could return to power, but they all failed. Meanwhile he seemed to lose international support because of a campaign of disinformation about his human rights record.

But in the summer of 1992, the United States was reported trying to arrange for the deployment of an international peacekeeping force and the return of Haiti's first freely and fairly elected president. The military would be allowed to pick a prime minister. Pascal-Trouillot, however, was completely out of the political picture.

KAZIMIERA PRUNSKIENE

*Prime Minister of Lithuania
(1990–91)*

Kazimiera Prunskiene stood in the forefront of Lithuania's struggle for independence, but did not endure as a leader. Both her economic views and her moderate stance on all aspects of relations with the Soviet Union paved the way for her downfall after only nine months as prime minister.

In the midst of World War II, Kazimiera Danute Stankeviciute was born on February 26, 1943, in the village of Vasiuliskiai. Lithuania had been under German occupation since 1941. But the Soviet Union, which had annexed the republic in 1940, returned victorious in 1944 and reannexed the country.

Kazimiera's father, Pranas Stankevicius, owned several hectares of land and worked as a forest ranger. He was well known as a jovial musician, who played the concertina, fiddle, guitar, and a pipe of his own making at country weddings. Others considered him a ruthless enemy of peasants.

When Kazimiera was two, her father was killed in a gunfight in the Labanor Forest. There are no details of her upbringing. During her childhood, a partisan war was fought against the Soviets, and 30,000 to 40,000 Lithuanians were killed.

She received a degree in economics from the University of Vilnius in 1965. In the late 1980s she would earn a doctorate in the same subject. The new graduate stayed on at the university, first as an instructor and then as a senior associate in the industrial economics department. Meanwhile she had married and changed her name to Prunskiene. Between 1963 and 1971 she bore a son, Vaidotos, and two daughters, Raisa and Dayvita.

Gradually Kazimiera moved from university to government circles. She joined the Lithuanian Communist party in 1980. In 1986 she began as deputy director for the Lithuanian Soviet Socialist Republic's Agricultural Economics Research Institute. Two years later she was appointed rector of the Institute for Improving the Qualifications of Economic Specialists and Managers.

Lithuania, like the two other Baltic states, Estonia and Latvia, had long dreamed of gaining independence from Russian domination, such as they had enjoyed from 1918 to 1940. In Lithuania, however, democracy had lasted only until the end of 1925, when a dictatorship evolved under Antanas Smetona, the first president. During World War II, Estonia and Latvia, like Lithuania, had been occupied by Soviet, then German, and again Soviet troops and had become republics within the Soviet Union.

Freedom fervor exploded in the 1980s after Soviet President Mikhail S. Gorbachev set forth his doctrine of *perestroika,* which encouraged rapid change throughout the countries behind the Iron Curtain. In 1988, at age 45, Kazimiera Prunskiene was one of the founding members of the grass-roots Lithuanian Restructuring Movement, Sajudis, which would grow into the leading proindependence group. Another founder was Vitautis Landsbergis, a noted musicologist and an ardent patriot. Four months later, the personable, articulate economist, who prided herself on her stylish dress, was elected to the Sajudis national assembly and then to its ruling executive council. Sajudis ran a campaign to restore Lithuanian as the official language and to legalize old national symbols.

The following summer, in July 1989, Prunskiene became the first member of Sajudis to enter the Soviet-controlled Lithuanian government, accepting the portfolio of deputy chair for economics in the Council of Ministers of the Lithuanian Soviet Socialist Republic (LSSR). She was elected the same year to the Union of Soviet Socialist Republics Congress of People's Deputies and the USSR Supreme Soviet. But both in Sajudis circles and in the government, Prunskiene attracted attention as the most visible and vocal advocate of economic independence for her country. Energetic and forceful, she was a skilled debater.

In eastern Europe, 1989 was a year of dramatic upheaval. The Berlin Wall was torn down, and Communist governments were crumbling. Through a parliamentary vote in December, Lithuania became the first Soviet republic to permit a multiparty system. Then the proindependence Lithuanian Communist party split from the USSR Communist party.

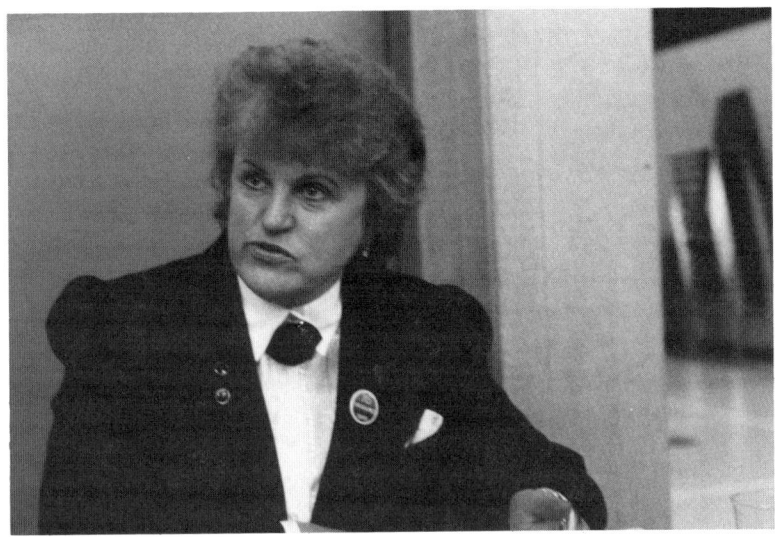

Kazimiera Prunskiene: photograph by Saulius Girnius.

Moscow reacted to the moves by calling them illegitimate. On January 11, 1990, Gorbachev arrived in Vilnius to try to persuade the Lithuanian Communist party to rescind its break. The same day, 250,000 persons demonstrated in the city streets, but Gorbachev stoutly insisted that independence was a dead end. The Soviet Union could not afford to lose the Baltic republics.

Elections for the Supreme Council (Parliament) were scheduled for February 25. The two major factions were Sajudis and the Lithuanian Communist party. In the first round, candidates backed by Sajudis were elected in 72 of 90 districts, but Prunskiene did not gain one of the 141 seats until the second round of voting shortly thereafter.

On March 11, the Supreme Council voted 124 to 0, with six abstentions, for independence. It dropped the name Lithuanian Soviet Socialist Republic in favor of Republic of Lithuania and adopted a new constitution that deleted all mention of the word *Socialist* although it still followed the Soviet model. Landsbergis, the chairman of Sajudis, was immediately elected chairman of the Supreme Council, defeating Algirdas Brazauskas, the chairman of the Lithuanian Communist party. His post was tantamount to the presidency. The United States, however, declined to recognize the new state. Again Gorbachev warned of illegitimate and invalid actions.

On March 17, the Supreme Council appointed Prunskiene prime minister. At once she resigned from the Communist party, but named Brazauskas one of her two deputies. The same day Soviet forces began maneuvers in Lithuania. The new government ignored Gorbachev's demand that it rescind its declaration of independence. His patience at an end, the Soviet leader ordered Lithuanians to surrender all their arms to Soviet officials and banned all sales of new weapons in the country.

Prunskiene's first days in office put her at a dangerous juncture, but she remained cool and collected and brushed away fears. "Gorbachev is always saying that he and I are such good friends," she confided, with a smile, "so I may write a letter to my dear friend saying, 'Mikhail Sergeievich, will you attend your dear Kazimiera Prunskiene with tanks?'"

But he did just that. A military convoy entered Vilnius on March 23, and Western diplomats were ordered to leave. In a couple of days the order was extended to all foreigners. Next the Kremlin seized the headquarters and other property of the Lithuanian Communist party. Then Lithuanian deserters from the Soviet army were rounded up, and 21 young men seeking refuge in a Red Cross hospital were dragged away. Thereupon Soviet troops swooped down on the state prosecutor's office and the printing plant of a proindependence newspaper. On the last day of March, Gorbachev warned Prunskiene's government of "grave consequences" if the declaration of independence were not rescinded. Reporters wrote about a war of telephone calls and telegrams with Landsbergis saying that the date the Lithuanian declaration of independence would go into effect was open for discussion.

On April 18, Gorbachev countered with an economic embargo, halting shipments of oil and natural gas and barring the delivery by rail of many other goods. The USSR was Lithuania's primary source of raw materials and its principal export center. Prunskiene and Landsbergis had hoped for a quick rebuke from the United States, but the Bush administration refused to enflame the situation. Just as the embargo began, Prunskiene set out in search of support, going to Denmark, Norway, Sweden, and Canada in April.

The Lithuanian government still wanted talks with the Kremlin, and at the beginning of May, Landsbergis announced that proindependence laws passed by the Supreme Council might be suspended if the Kremlin would open a dialogue.

Prunskiene flew to Washington on May 4, her trip and expenses paid for by Lithuanians in the United States. After a whirlwind day meeting with the members of the House Foreign Affairs Committee, the Senate Foreign Relations Committee, and the joint congressional committee on the Helsinki Commission (human rights), she headed for the White House, where she knew she would have to be received as a private citizen. She was not prepared, however, to have her Lincoln sedan stopped outside the White House gates and to be obliged to walk to her appointment with President George Bush. Her brother Rimantas, who had hoped to sit in on the meeting, was denied access to the grounds and sat unhappily on a bench in Lafayette Square. Later a red-faced protocol officer explained that a gate mechanism had broken down.

To the American president, Prunskiene explained her government's hopes for negotiations with Moscow. It would be willing, she said, to stop implementation of some of the new laws if only talks could be arranged. There was no change, however, in the Bush policy of refusing to recognize Lithuania as an independent state. But with her vigor and affability, the sturdy Prunskiene had indeed impressed Washington. Further flights took her to Britain, France, and West Germany throughout May.

On her arrival home, Lithuania seemed to back down even as the two other Baltic states grew bolder. While pro–Soviet demonstrators stormed the parliament buildings in Tallinn, Estonia, and Riga, Latvia, the independence laws in Lithuania were suspended. The move gained Prunskiene entry to the Kremlin, and on May 17 she met with Gorbachev. Afterward she declared that the talks had been a big step forward. A week later, Gorbachev promised that Lithuania could be independent in two years if it suspended the declaration of independence. This step it was not ready to take.

There was hope in June that a Bush-Gorbachev summit might produce some resolution, but none came. The energy embargo remained in place, but without too much grumbling, people had dusted off their bicycles to save gasoline. Still, the effect on the economy was serious. Newsprint ran short, and newspapers were reduced to half size; factories frequently shut down for want of raw materials. Many places were without hot water. When Prunskiene convinced the Supreme Council to suspend the declaration of independence as long as formal negotiations were going on with the Kremlin leadership, Gorbachev resumed the shipments of oil and natural gas after 74 days. The end of the embargo, however, still left Lithuania with a multitude of economic problems. Behind the doors of government, Prunskiene and Landsbergis frequently wrangled over what steps should be taken. She advocated quicker steps toward a market economy. They also differed about the pace of independence. Landsbergis was the more militant as Prunskiene, a moderate pragmatist, pleaded for compromise and reconciliation with Moscow. But for Landsbergis himself she often had sharp words of criticism.

Prunskiene's trips in June took her to Greece and Poland. She visited Finland in July, Czechoslovakia in September, and Sweden in October. Landsbergis, too, was traveling widely.

At home it was Prunskiene who gained the greater popularity, which discomfitted Landsbergis, who did not easily brook rivals. In a manner reminiscent of Milka Planinc's accolades, admirers tried to call the strong-jawed prime minister "Lithuania's Thatcher" or the "Iron Lady of the East." Prunskiene did not like the comparison. "If I had been made of iron," she said, "I'd have been broken a long time ago. Lithuania needs a firm hand, but not one made of iron." Later she would add, "Mrs. Thatcher is Mrs. Thatcher. My name is Prunskiene." She was more willing to accept another title, "Amber Lady," which fitted her hazel eyes.

Soviet and Lithuanian negotiating teams met in October, and discussions seemed ready to begin. Then the Kremlin demanded that Lithuania join the talks on forming a new union treaty according to Gorbachev's plan. Landsbergis refused.

Prunskiene attended an historic joint session of the three Baltic parliaments in Vilnius in December to firm up the drive toward independence.

The session adopted appeals to world parliaments, to the Fourth USSR Congress of People's Deputies, to all those who lived in the Baltic states, and to Soviet military personnel who were quartered in the three states to recognize the programs for national independence. The session further reaffirmed equal rights for national minorities. An interparliamentary working group among the three also was established.

Meanwhile the Supreme Council passed laws absolving Lithuanian youths of any obligation to serve in the Soviet army. In January of the new year, 1991, the Soviet commander for the Baltic military district informed Landsbergis that paratroopers would be installed in all three Baltic states to enforce the draft and to round up conscientious objectors.

The same day, January 7, Prunskiene learned that she had brought down a firestorm of criticism on her head by announcing sweeping price hikes for products purchased from other republics that were meant to be a step toward broad economic reform. Pensioners and low-income workers were given extra pay, but factory workers received no increases.

Anger and resentment rose to fever pitch. An estimated 5,000 demonstrators, organized by the pro–Moscow "Jedinsvo," streamed toward Parliament Square, but were finally driven away with fire hoses.

As pressure on her mounted, Prunskiene flew to Moscow to hold a half hour meeting with Gorbachev. They discussed the Soviet roundup of draft evaders in Lithuania, and he told her that the conflict would have to be resolved by talks between the Soviet Defense Ministry and Lithuanian representatives. When she asked whether she could assure her people that force would not be used against them, Gorbachev answered, "You cannot give them any assurances that I have not given you."

She returned to Vilnius the same day to hear that frightened parliamentarians had overthrown her price increases. Promptly Prunskiene resigned. In her speech to the deputies she cited differences with the Supreme Council over economic reforms and her wish to avoid confrontation with the Kremlin whenever possible. "Our views have conceptual differences. They began to differ for the first time in May and June when the policy of negotiations with the Soviet Union was being formed. We avoided a crisis then, but now the crisis has come." She was succeeded by Gediminas Vagnorius as prime minister, but remained a member of Parliament.

Prunskiene went home to be comforted by her husband, Algimantis Tarvidas, the director of Expo-Centrum in Vilnius, whom she had married in 1989. She and Prunskiene had been divorced several years before. As she explained, "Adjustment of differences is essential; otherwise your sovereignty becomes a burden you have to carry alone." She was now a grandmother of three.

To her unhappiness, her popularity, once so high, reached its low ebb after her resignation. She was bitterly criticized for having left office at a time of Lithuania's worst internal crisis in less than a year, for the day after her departure, Soviet soldiers stormed into the Vilnius broadcasting center. Thirteen unarmed civilians were killed, and mourning was intense as crowds filed by their bodies.

In February, Prunskiene paid a visit to Prague where, during an interview, she explained that tensions between her and her cabinet on one side and Landsbergis and his supporters in the Supreme Council on the other had triggered her resignation. In another interview she said that she would not have stepped down had she been certain of Landsbergis's support of her economic reforms.

Nine months after she resigned as prime minister, Boris Yeltsin and his reformers gained the upper hand in Moscow, and the Soviet Union recognized Lithuania's independence and that of Estonia and Latvia. Then with stunning immediacy, the USSR broke up and became the Commonwealth of Independent States. Understandably, the three Baltic states chose to remain outside that grouping.

Prunskiene had stayed in Parliament, but in the fall of 1992 she did not stand for reelection after a parliamentary commission leveled charges that in the early 1980s she had worked with the KGB or Soviet secret police. Although she vehemently denied the accusation, her supporters realized that months of legal maneuvering might lie ahead. Meanwhile as a consultant she stayed active within the business community.

VIOLETA CHAMORRO

*President of Nicaragua
(1990–   )*

When she became president in 1990, Violeta Chamorro set out to bring peace, prosperity, and reconciliation to a divided Nicaragua. But the problems of reconstruction have proved far more formidable than she and her advisers envisioned.

One of seven children of Carlos and Amelia Barrios, wealthy landowners, she was born on October 18, 1929, in Rivas, a small town 18 miles from the Costa Rican border. Her childhood on a sprawling cattle ranch she later described as carefree. She was sent to a Catholic high school in San Antonio, Texas, for two years and then to Blackstone College in Southside, Virginia, where she took secretarial courses. Never fluent in English, she dropped out of classes and came home when her father died in 1948.

In Managua, the Nicaraguan capital, the lovely, brown-eyed girl, tall and model slim, met 24-year-old Pedro Joaquín Chamorro, whose appeal was instant, not the least because of his adventuresome life. His family name reverberated through Nicaragua's political history. Fruto Chamorro, his great-uncle, had been the first president (1853–55). Subsequently, three other Chamorros at four different times occupied the office, the last one in 1926. Pedro's father was the publisher of *La Prensa,* the city's only afternoon daily. In 1944, while studying law, Pedro had participated in a student uprising against the dictatorial Somoza regime, which by way of punishment exiled him and his family and closed *La Prensa* for a time. While his parents settled in New York City, Pedro finished his law studies in Mexico City.

In 1948, when he and Violeta became acquainted, he had just returned home and was helping his father at the reopened *La Prensa* and using an incisive political pen to attack the government constantly. He had also just founded the National Union of Popular Action to protest 12 years of tyrannical rule. With their progressing courtship, Violeta was caught up in his impassioned opposition to General Anastasio Somoza Garcia, familiarly called Tacho. As the leader of the 14,000-man National Guard and with the backing of the U.S. government and the business establishment, Tacho had staged a coup in 1936 and "won" election as president of Nicaragua. Immediately he had begun to enrich himself at the country's expense. Within three years he called a Constituent Assembly to draft a new constitution, which extended the presidential term from four to six years, but reiterated the traditional constitutional injunctions against reelection and the candidacy of the incumbent's relatives or appointees. The assembly then transformed itself into the national Congress for the next eight years and decreed a similar term for Somoza.

Somoza belonged to the Liberal party, whereas the Chamorros had long been attached to the Conservative party. Actually, party names reflected heritage, rather than political behavior. The Conservatives were large landowners and supporters of an active governmental role for the Roman Catholic church; the Liberals, merchants and owners of small businesses, believed that the church should concern itself only with religious matters. Pedro said that he considered himself a "social Christian." In 1947 Somoza had reached the end of his eight-year term, but had continued to rule the country through his puppets. Human rights abuses were rampant; opposition parties and trade unions were violently suppressed.

Violeta married Pedro Chamorro in 1950. That year Tacho was reelected president, following the death of his successor, Víctor Román y Reyes. Pedro assumed the duties of publisher of *La Prensa* after his father died in 1952.

In 1954 Pedro joined the Interno Frente (Internal Front) to work toward democracy and social reform. The Somoza regime continued to represent pure oligarchy, laced with open, rampant corruption that contributed to widespread and hopeless poverty. Participation in a 1954 rebellion brought Pedro Chamorro a jail term of two years, but he was able to spend the second year under house arrest.

Three months after *La Prensa*'s publisher was released and returned to his newspaper duties, Somoza was assassinated. That night, coming back from a party, Violeta and Pedro were arrested, and he was charged

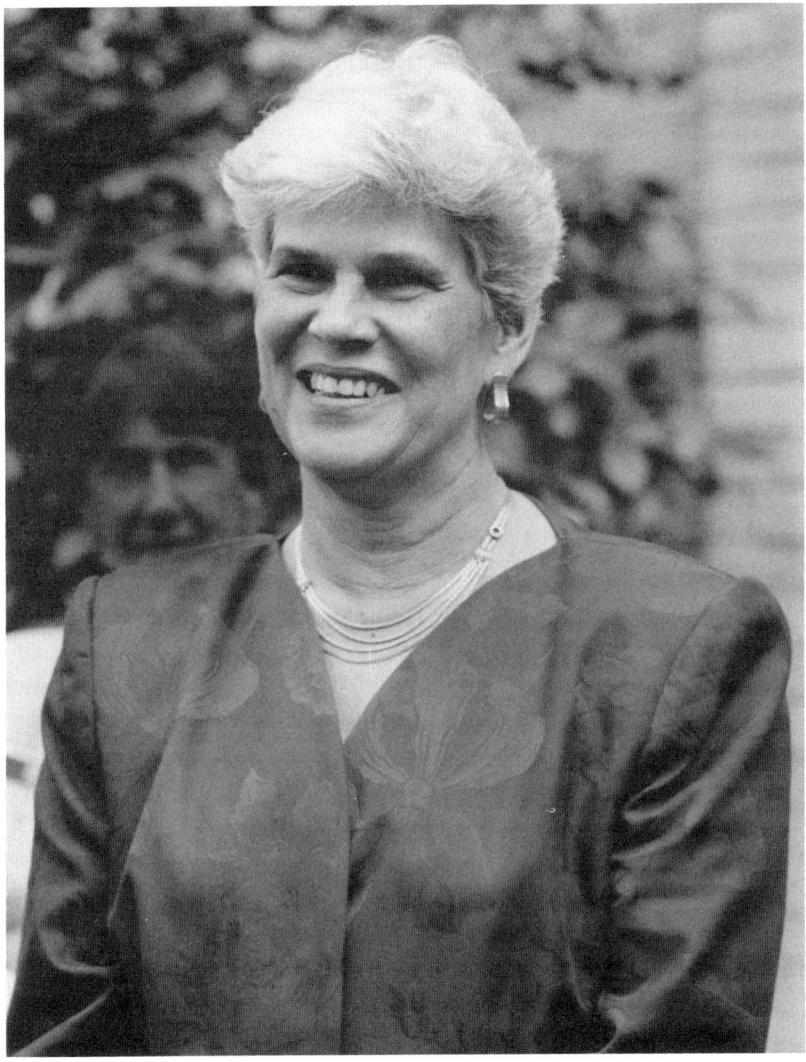

Violeta Chamorro: courtesy Embassy of Nicaragua, Washington, D.C.; photograph by Rebecca Hammel.

with conspiracy in the murder. She was not held, but Pedro was brought before a military court, which determined that he had known of the murder conspiracy and failed to report it. The court banished him for 40 months to the small town of San Carlos del Rio on the southern shores of Lake Nicaragua.

Violeta and Pedro had four children: Pedro Joaquín, Jr. (Quinto); Claudia; Cristiana; and Carlos. A fifth child, María de los Angeles, had died shortly after birth. Convinced that her place was by her husband's side, Violeta joined him after leaving the youngsters in the temporary care of her mother-in-law, with whom she and Pedro had been living. In San Carlos del Rio, Violeta looked for a house to which she could bring her family, but stopped her search when her husband told her he was determined to escape to Costa Rica by way of the San Juan River, the border between the two countries. One night they fled in a small boat, with Pedro rowing mightily to escape searchlights sweeping across the water. After three hours they entered a tributary of the river and felt safe. Once they had settled in San José, they were reunited with their children.

Somoza had been succeeded by his son Luis, and the power structure remained in place. Pedro remained fiercely antagonistic; while working for *Prensa Libre* (Free Press), he finished a book, *Bloody Stock: The Somozas*. He also organized a resistance movement. To solicit arms from Fidel Castro, who had just overthrown Fulgencio Batista, he went to Cuba, but met with no success. Although he considered himself a civil coordinator, rather than a military leader, Pedro decided that he must fight, and Violeta did not stop him. The exiles planned to link up with resistance forces inside Nicaragua. After one and a half months of training, Pedro became the leader of the first unit. Violeta would later hear how once inside Nicaragua this unit had been pursued by the National Guard, fired on by machine guns, and bombarded from the air.

After 15 days, Pedro surrendered and was again imprisoned in Managua, where Violeta brought the children. While she waited for him, she pasted together scraps of writing that visitors were able to smuggle out of the prison; they became the pages of her husband's new book, *Diary of a Prisoner*. At his trial, a tribunal accused Pedro Chamorro of organizing a rebellion with Castro's help and sentenced him to nine years of imprisonment. Violeta was stoic.

Whatever his reasons, Luis Somoza declared a general amnesty in June 1960. Out from behind bars, Pedro went right back to thundering in the pages of *La Prensa* against the feigned democracy, the inequalities, and the backwardness of Nicaragua. In 1963 *La Prensa* launched a literacy campaign: "One who does not know how to read is the one who cannot see, and it is necessary to take the blindfold off our brothers."

Attempting to make "a bridge for democracy," Luis Somoza announced the same year that the constitutional ban on reelection and a law forbidding the candidacy of an incumbent's blood relatives would be enforced. So he nominated René Schick, whom he expected to follow his dictates. But Schick surprised everybody by showing a certain independence. When Schick died of a heart attack, the ex-president saw to it that his replacement toed the mark.

The Chamorros reacted with dismay when they learned that Luis Somoza's brother, General Anastasio Somoza Debayle (Tachito), would run for the presidency in 1967. A 24-hour protest followed the declaration. Pedro was not among the demonstrators, but again Violeta saw her husband carted off to prison because at the *La Prensa* office "evidence" was found against him for plotting to overthrow the government through terrorist activity. This time, however, Violeta welcomed him home in 45 days. As expected, Tachito won the election; Luis Somoza died of a heart attack before his brother could be inaugurated.

Stubbornly *La Prensa* continued to assail the malfeasance and nepotism of the Somoza government. In 1972, Anastasio Somoza's term ended. Abiding by the rule that he could not succeed himself, he turned over power to a three-man triumvirate, secure in the knowledge that as commander of the armed forces and leader of the Liberal party, he was still Nicaragua's strong man.

That December a devastating earthquake hit Managua, killing 10,000, leveling 80 percent of the buildings, and leaving 300,000 homeless; *La Prensa*'s buildings and its principal rotary press were also destroyed. Undaunted, Pedro rescued his equipment and reopened the paper in a sheet-metal building in March 1973. Meanwhile he wrote a short novel, *Richter 7,* about the horror, confusion, and sorrow of his people, feelings that Violeta fully shared. Rebuilding would take years and would invite unchecked corruption.

The 1974 election returned Anastasio Somoza as president. Now, more than ever, he suppressed all stirrings of opposition, especially criticism by the press, by means of censorship and travel restrictions. That same year Pedro founded the Democratic Union of Liberation (UDEL), bringing together all the Somoza opposition. As he organized meetings in the rural areas, he and Violeta became intimately acquainted with the peasants' difficulties. Another novel, *Jesus Marchena,* about one such humble farmer, was set in Violeta's home area.

Pedro had never voted because he had been in prison or exile during all elections but one, against which he organized a boycott. But he could express his opposition in writing. Over the next few years his political rhetoric grew even more inflammatory. Therefore, he knew that he was in greater danger than ever, and he often told Violeta that he expected to be killed.

The fateful day came on January 10, 1978, when she was in Miami shopping for a trousseau with her younger daughter Cristiana, who was engaged to Antonio Lacayo, a young engineer who had studied in the United States. At the hotel Violeta received an urgent telephone call from her brother-in-law, Jaime Chamorro, who, out of respect for her feelings, reported only that there had been a serious accident. "No," she said, "they killed him." Then Jaime told her the story. That morning three gunmen had intercepted Pedro while he was driving to work and peppered him with bullets. He had died within minutes.

Violeta rushed home to bury her husband of 27 years. As the body lay in state at *La Prensa,* thousands mourned while international protests rained in on the government. In spite of her grief, she had to appear strong. Now she faced a special challenge, for she had inherited the mantle of publisher of *La Prensa.* But while looking to the future, she would not part with the bullet-riddled Saab, which Pedro Joaquín had been driving; she ordered it placed in the patio of the Chamorros' white stucco house. His blood-stained clothes were on display in a glass case inside the residence.

General opinion was that Anastasio Somoza had hired the assassins. Just two days before they struck, Pedro had received a written threat responding to an editorial he had written about Tachito's alleged connection with a Cuban doctor who was shipping blood obtained from poor Nicaraguans to the United States at considerable profit.

Outraged members of the UDEL called for a general strike, and 75 percent of industry and business complied. Thereupon Somoza imposed a state of siege, steadfastly refusing to resign. Before long he lifted it, but revolution was in the air. As Jaime Chamorro said, Pedro's murder ignited a national insurrection. The moderate opposition now sought closer ties with revolutionary organizations. Most prominent was a guerrilla group composed of peasants, urban workers, and students. Initially rural based, it called itself the Sandinista Liberation Front (FSLN). Founded in 1967, it had taken its name from General Augusto César Sandino, a rebel leader, who had fought domestic wrongdoing and intervention by the U.S. Marines. He had been captured in 1934 and subsequently executed by the U.S.-trained National Guard under the command of General Anastasio Somoza García.

The Chamorro family lent $50,000 to the Sandinistas in August 1979. That month 25 armed Sandinistas took over the National Palace while Congress was in session. Holding 1,500 hostages, they demanded the release of political prisoners, ransom, and safe conduct.

Although Somoza gave in to their demands, he set out to destroy their outposts. The first strike had ended, but another one began. Meanwhile the Sandinistas began distributing arms widely. As outlying cities fell to them, Somoza met them with renewed fighting and summary executions of those with Sandinista sympathies.

Somoza waited until June for a vengeful attack against *La Prensa*, which was staffed by a great many Chamorros. As publisher, Violeta usually visited the offices every day, but she was not present when National Guardsmen fired at the building from their vehicles and poured gasoline over it while rockets flew down from the sky. Faced with ashes and debris, the Chamorros resolutely moved their newspaper to the city of León and rented a press. With help from the Inter-American Press Association and a West German bank, *La Prensa* was able to return to Managua the next year.

In the summer of 1979 the revolution moved closer to Managua. Somoza had hoped for U.S. help, but it was not forthcoming, especially after his bomb attacks on his own people and the murder of an American television newsman. He resigned in July and fled to Miami. Two days later the Sandinistas seized Managua. The revolution had left bitter scars—10,000 dead and almost half a million homeless.

Doña Violeta, the "noble widow," who combined strength of character, courage, and elegance of person, was asked to join a provisional junta to exercise executive power within the new Sandinista-dominated Government of National Reconstruction. Most prominent among the members was Daniel Ortega. Later, she explained her reasons for joining the junta: "They told me that they needed me. They needed the name of my husband, and the name of *La Prensa*. It wouldn't have been patriotic to refuse."

She stayed in the junta only nine months, resigning "for health reasons." Actually she was disgusted with "an excessive militarism, an exaggerated Cuban pressure, and less and less interest in democratic ideas." Quickly the Sandinistas had begun to redistribute land and to nationalize large industries.

Although *La Prensa* had been satisfactorily rebuilt, the same forces that divided the country now created an ideological split within the

Chamorro family. Violeta's brother-in-law, Xavier Chamorro, left the staff and founded a pro–Sandinista newspaper. Her son Carlos became editor of the official Sandinista party paper. Her daughter Claudia also joined the Sandinistas. But Cristiana and Cristiana's husband Antonio and brother Quinto refused to do so. Somehow, outside politics, the family kept close ties because of Doña Violeta, the enduring symbol of home.

Somoza had sought refuge in Paraguay, where he was assassinated in the fall of 1980. But his spirit lived on in an opposition army, made up of members of the National Guard and other supporters who fled to Honduras, setting up bases from which to mount a counterrevolution in Nicaragua. They would become known as the Contras. President Ronald Reagan, in his ardent anti–Communist phase, was convinced that the Sandinistas were bringing communism to the western hemisphere and threw his support to the "freedom fighters." As his administration became committed to funding the Contras, bitter debate filled the halls of Congress. For the next couple of years the fighting escalated.

In 1984 the Sandinistas won national elections, and Daniel Ortega became president of Nicaragua. *La Prensa* vigorously protested the press censorship he imposed and the rising military allocations forced by the civil war. Frequently he shut down the newspaper for short periods. Then in 1986, the year Claudia married the Nicaraguan ambassador to Spain, *La Prensa* was boarded up for 15 months. Violeta used the time to write opinion pieces for various journals, asking western democracies to demand "a civilized government in Nicaragua, based on the right to free elections and respect for the fundamental rights of man." In a "Letter to Ortega," published in the *New York Times,* she said, "The grave crisis affecting Nicaragua must be resolved among ourselves, the Nicaraguans, without the interference of Cubans, Soviets, or Americans." Her son Quinto had become a Contra leader based in Miami.

As the civil war dragged on, the U.S. Congress cut down on aid to the Contras, and the White House resorted to sending covert funds and supplies. At last in 1989, Oscar Arias, president of Costa Rica, persuaded the presidents of the Central American countries to sign an accord aimed at bringing regional stability. In return for a promise that a plan would be devised for disarming and repatriating the Contras, Ortega pledged that Nicaragua would hold free elections in February 1990. He set the stage by lifting censorship and guaranteeing opposition parties equal television time and the opportunity to solicit funds from abroad.

The National Opposition Union (UNO), a coalition of 14 anti–Sandinista parties, aided by U.S. funding, chose the widely respected Doña Violeta as the candidate to oppose Ortega. Virgilio Godoy, a leading Sandinista critic, was picked as her running mate. Chamorro's son-in-law, Antonio, ran her campaign, stressing her dream of reconciling the Sandinistas and the Contras.

The representative of the Socialist Democratic party in the UNO political council was Alfredo César, an aggressive business leader who had served on the junta, had deserted to the Contras and then, after some adroit switching, had become a democratic leader in Nicaragua. He was also Lacayo's brother-in-law.

During the campaign, a newspaper in Honduras published a letter, ostensibly written by César on UNO letterhead, urging the Contras to disarm. Since the UNO was trying to get rid of any link to the Contras, its leadership was up in arms. César denied authorship to no avail. Because of his shifting allegiances in the past, he was dismissed from the UNO council. But Doña Violeta took the bold step of appointing him her personal adviser. By 1991 he would be president of the National Assembly.

Her campaign was not slick like Ortega's. César advised her to keep to a simple slogan, "UNO! Yes, it can change things," which proved more powerful than the FSLN's "Everything will be better."

A handsome grandmother who disdained coloring her salt-and-pepper hair, Chamorro presented a striking figure on the platform. She usually dressed in white; sometimes she rode through villages in a white-canopied wagon. Her appearance and her strong religiosity, so evident in her speeches, helped link her in people's minds with Mary, the mother of Jesus. But talking into public microphones was not easy for her. She evoked new sympathy when she fractured her kneecap and appeared in a wheelchair or on crutches. Seldom departing from her message of hope and national reconciliation, she won a six-year term with 55.2 percent of the vote.

She was still on crutches for her inauguration on April 25. Standing behind home plate at the baseball stadium, Chamorro took her oath from Miriam Argüello, the new president of the National Assembly. After Ortega had placed the blue-and-white presidential sash over her shoulder and each had kissed the other on the right cheek, she invoked Pedro's memory. "This is the hour that his blood has borne the fruit of his dreams. We have reached the promised land. This is the Nicaragua sought by the exiles expelled by dictators. This is the Nicaragua without tyrants, without ideologies that destroy reality, without lies that conceal our history."

Throughout the ceremony, Sandinista supporters jeered her, and UNO fans jeered back. Plastic bags of water were even thrown at Chamorro and Ortega. Both head of state and head of government, she had several important announcements: There would be general amnesty for all political crimes, including those of her husband's assassins. Lacayo would be minister of the presidency, her chief adviser. (Despite the staff's cries of compromising *La Prensa*'s independence, Lacayo's wife Cristiana would remain editor of the paper and defend her mother's government against right-wing opposition.) All partisan banners would be removed from public buildings and monuments. Land titles given to peasants by the Sandinista land reforms would be respected, but measures that legalized the seizure of other properties would be reviewed.

The most controversial announcement was that Humberto Ortega, Daniel's brother, would stay as army commander. Chamorro's rationale was that keeping him in office would lessen Sandinista opposition to her government.

But Contra rebels, who had cleared their base camps in Honduras and marched into Nicaragua, ready to hand over their guns to a United Nations peacekeeping force, protested Humberto Ortega's appointment. For weeks Doña Violeta had to negotiate, twice through all-night talks. After one of these sessions she hospitably invited the negotiators to her house for breakfast. Throughout, she had firmly insisted that the Contras must be the first to demilitarize.

By June she had disarmed the last of the 17,000-member Contra force and persuaded the Sandinista army, Central America's largest, to trim its ranks to 28,000. She also abolished military conscription.

That July, reacting to stabilization measures, protesters staged widespread strikes, which ballooned into violent street fighting. Chamorro called out the army and finally resolved the matter through negotiation. In September she staged a ceremonial farewell to arms. After watching 15,000 automatic rifles being dumped from giant trucks into a pit, she tossed red flowers over the guns, then stood back as hoses poured concrete on the tomb. That same month, the Sandinistas began a crippling strike to resist layoffs, wage cuts, and the government's attempts to sell state companies.

Her symbolism, however, did not bring political peace. The Sandinistas still controlled the army and the police. In some parts of the country their word remained law. Chamorro's supporters often had to seize highways, bridges, and police stations. The Contras also caused trouble. Toward the end of the year they formed an alliance with the right wing of the UNO and staged a regional uprising that Chamorro again ended through negotiations. Eventually an accord was signed, placing the Contras in demilitarized zones and turning in their remaining arms to the United Nations.

The economic picture was equally gloomy. War battered, the Sandinistas had turned over cash reserves of $3 billion, a $13 billion foreign debt, and a financial morass exacerbated by the state-owned banking system and more than 400 state-owned companies. Ominously, the Sandinistas kept their power in the trade unions, where they could veto any economic recovery plan Lacayo devised.

Within a year the UNO party leaders became disillusioned with Chamorro, accusing her of forging an alliance between her clan and the Sandinistas and faulting her for denying a post in her cabinet to the vice-president. Besides Lacayo, with his executive power as minister of the presidency and chief of staff, relatives and friends occupied key government posts — chairman of the central bank; home minister; and ambassadors to France, Venezuela, and the United States. UNO further complained that Chamorro and Lacayo had not made any dent in the distribution of riches: 70 percent of Nicaraguans lived below the poverty line.

As the government's economic underpinnings remained shaky, Doña Violeta realized that, like Daniel Ortega, she would constantly have to travel the world, hat in hand. Her foreign minister, Enrique Dreyfus, complained that the international community had forgotten the little country that had been a focus of Cold War rivalry. Especially overwhelming were overdue debts to the World Bank and the International Development Fund. In May 1991, Chamorro became the first Nicaraguan president in 52 years to visit the United States. While in Washington she pleaded for at least ten years of financial aid. President George Bush assured her of American help, but was not specific. She and Lacayo both hoped that recovery could be speeded by exiles who felt a strong pull to return to their homeland. But the country had a long way to go.

Taking stock of her first year, she told an interviewer at the Casa Presidencia: "I imagine they are going to ask, 'What have you done?' and I will say with great pride, that I stopped a war, reconciled everyone, gave an amnesty so Nicaraguans can return home and a free press so everyone can say whatever he wants."

But by 1992 a stable society had not materialized. Nicaragua had been beset by bad luck; a long-lasting drought; a devastating volcanic eruption; and a collapse in the world markets for cotton and coffee, the only important exports. To economic stagnation was added a constant turn to violence in the countryside.

Chamorro bristled when her opponents said she was not in charge. "I only make pacts with God," she declared, "Nobody governs me. I make the first decision and the last." Meanwhile her loyal supporters kept seeing the "great conciliator" as a symbol of new hope.

MARY ROBINSON

President of Ireland
(1990–)

Inaugurated at Dublin Castle toward the close of 1990, Ireland's first woman president was acclaimed as a herald of social tolerance and political sophistication in her socially conservative country. For 20 years, Mary Robinson had built an impressive reputation in the Irish Senate and in Irish and European courts, where she frequently argued against values associated with the Roman Catholic church to which she belonged.

In 1989 she was chosen "Man of the Year" in politically male-dominated County Mayo in northwestern Ireland, an honor this outspoken feminist particularly appreciated. She was born in Ballina, one of the county trade centers, on May 21, 1944, to Dr. Aubrey Bourke, a general practitioner, and the former Tessa Donnell, also a physician. Among four boys, Henry, Oliver, Adrian, and Aubrey, she was the only girl. Her childhood has been described as idyllic.

The Bourkes sent their daughter to a private school in Paris and then to Mount Anville, an Irish private school, where she graduated with honors. Intensely idealistic, the girl dreamed of becoming a lawyer like one of her grandfathers, who had a "passionate commitment to justice."

At prestigious Trinity College (University of Dublin), predominantly Protestant, Mary obtained a B.A. in French and an LL.B., again with honors. One of her law school classmates was Nicholas Robinson, destined to be her husband.

After Trinity came an American interlude, a year at Harvard to pick up an LL.M. in 1968. The civil rights movement and the student radicalism sweeping the United States particularly excited her. "There was a great questioning of the values of society," she later said. "Everything was up for examination."

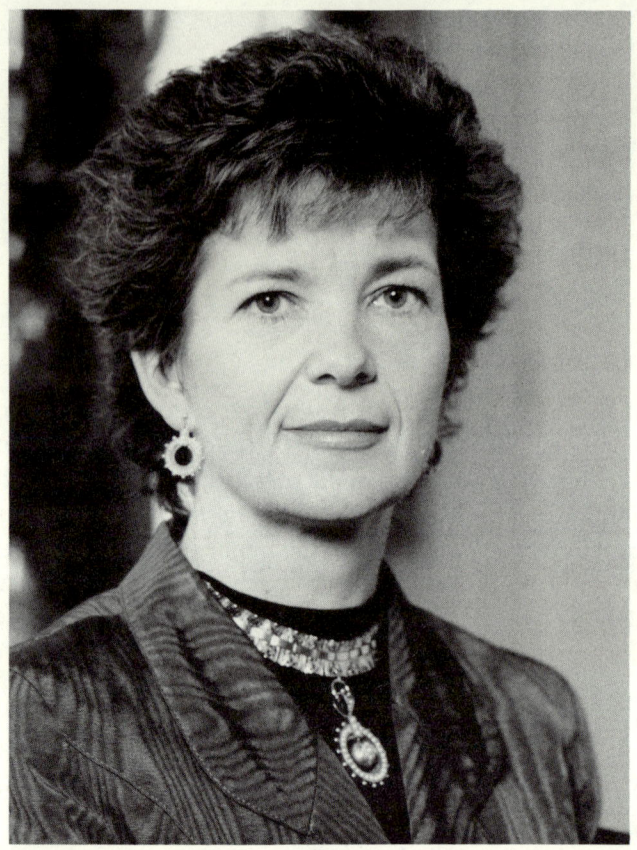

Mary Robinson: courtesy Office of the President, Dublin, Ireland.

On returning to Dublin at the age of 25, the shy, serious Mary Bourke became the youngest law professor in the history of Trinity College. She was Reid Professor in constitutional and criminal law. That same year she was chosen one of the three Dublin University constituency candidates for the Seanad Éireann, the upper house of the Oireachtas (Parliament). Running on the ticket of the Labour party, she won the seat, which she would hold for 20 years. She was the first Catholic to represent Trinity. The Seanad's powers were limited to introducing legislation in the Dáil (lower house) and delaying laws endorsed by the Dáil for up to three months, but Mary, also the youngest member of the upper house, believed that in the Seanad chambers she could work for liberal causes.

Nicholas Robinson, now a solicitor in Dublin, had been actively courting her, and she agreed to marry him in December 1970. But because of his Protestant religion, her staunchly Catholic parents refused to attend the wedding. Later, however, they would happily accept Nicholas into the family. The Robinsons' first child, Tessa, was born in 1974. William arrived in 1975 and Aubrey in 1982. Thanks to household help, the loving mother kept her career on track.

In the Seanad, where she was adept at sparking discussions, and in the courtroom, Mary Robinson concentrated on the legal rights of Irish women. Assiduously she attacked the laws that eliminated the inheritance rights of illegitimate children, barred women from jury duty, and gave women legislators fewer pension benefits than their male counterparts. Another issue that riveted her attention was divorce, prohibited by the constitution of 1937. Mary's compassion for people led her to introduce legislation to legalize divorce because she was deeply concerned with "second relationships" that produced children. But she well knew the odds against achieving any kind of breakthrough in an overwhelmingly Catholic country. Nor could she hope for any kind of success for her bills calling for maternity benefits and day care centers.

In 1971, Ireland entered the European Community, and Robinson had a new goal, nudging the Irish Establishment closer to social values established by the EC. Outside the Seanad and the Trinity classrooms, she continued to use lawsuits as her favorite weapon.

Once, on the way to the courtroom in a taxi, her client, Josie Airey, understandingly aware of Robinson's indifference to personal appearance, whipped out a needle and thread to mend the fallen hem of her lawyer's dress. Unruffled by the incident, Robinson argued the Josie Airey case so successfully that Ireland was found in breach of the European Convention on Human Rights. The end result was a national system of civic legal aid.

Having worked her way through the lower courts, Robinson lost a big case before the Irish Supreme Court in 1983, when she challenged an 1861 law ordering life imprisonment for sodomy. But five years later in Strasbourg, France, the European Court of Human Rights, which hears cases only after all national remedies have been exhausted, gave her the palm of victory, and the Irish government finally agreed to introduce laws to comply with its verdict.

Also in 1983, on the floor of the Seanad, she argued for hours against a proposed constitutional amendment banning abortion. She claimed that in equating the right to life of the fetus with that of the mother, the amendment would violate the European Convention on Human Rights, which she had highlighted during the Airey case. The amendment passed, but Robinson's intellectual challenge inspired progressive forces to organize better and plan new strategies.

Because of her own mixed marriage, she was one of the few Irish Catholic politicians who refused to castigate the Protestants in Northern Ireland. In 1984 she attended the Airlee House Conference held near Warrenton, Virginia, that had been called by advocates of a peaceful resolution to the 15-year civil war in Ulster between the Protestant majority and the Catholic minority. The negotiations resulted in an Anglo-Irish agreement that gave Ireland a small consultative role in the affairs of Ulster, and Ulster the right to choose its own political destiny. Robinson joined the Ulster firebrand, the Reverend Ian Paisley, in charging that the accord represented a first step in unifying the Irish republic and the British province. When the Labour party supported the Airlee agreement, Robinson resigned her membership.

By 1985 the progressive forces she had inspired were able to pass legislation permitting condoms and germicides to be purchased without prescriptions. Actually, Robinson had introduced such a bill during her first year in the Seanad, but owing to an extremely busy schedule she could not be on the floor during the new legislative debate.

Among all her honors, Robinson was perhaps most proud of her membership in the International Commission of Jurists, a body of distinguished human rights lawyers. She also sat on the board of the Common Market Law Review, the European Air Law Association, and other legal bodies. As a member of the Seanad, she had served for many years on the Oireachtas Joint Committee on European Community legislation and had emerged as an acknowledged international authority on European law.

Richard Spring, the leader of the Labour party, which Robinson had not rejoined, raised many hackles in 1990 when he nominated her as the party's candidate for president. The term was for seven years. An ardent feminist running against the candidates of male-dominated parties? Patrick Hillery, the president, was retiring, but it was expected that the Fianna Fáil (Soldiers of Destiny) party would again prevail. For 17 years its candidate had run uncontested. In 1990 it picked Brian Lenihan, the most popular politician in the country, celebrated for his invariable comment, "No problem."

Although surprised by her selection, Robinson decided to accept the challenge. The presidency is largely a ceremonial post, its power restricted to calling elections when a ruling party loses in Parliament. But she believed that it could offer her a symbolic forum on many issues that concerned her. Polls, however, predicted overwhelming defeat. She was called a 100 to 1 outsider.

Running as the candidate of both the Labour party and the Workers' party, Robinson began her campaign in County Mayo, her home region. She followed her advisers' suggestion to spruce up her image with a new closely cropped style for her reddish brown hair and designer suits for her tall, slender figure. To general surprise, she loosened up considerably and appeared witty, handsome, and charming as she traveled across the country in a campaign bus that blared the musical theme "Mrs. Robinson" from the American movie *The Graduate*. Carefully scripted, she was nonetheless outspoken, directing her appeal to women, young people, the poor, the handicapped, the unemployed — to those who she thought were left out of Irish politics. She kept saying, "You have a voice. I will make it heard." Many times she called for an end to the constitutional ban on abortion, for wider access to contraceptives, and for the legalization of homosexuality. Never was she afraid to criticize "the patriarchal, male-directed presence of the Roman Catholic Church" for holding back women's rights.

Campaigning for six months instead of the usual six weeks, Robinson rose in the polls. Soon she benefited even more from a scandal involving her rival, Lenihan. During a television news interview, former Prime Minister Garrett FitzGerald disclosed that after the fall of his government in 1982, Lenihan had improperly tried to get President Hillery to allow Fianna Fáil to form a government. Lenihan issued a denial even though the *Irish Times* produced a tape recording in which he admitted having telephoned Hillery. Quickly Prime Minister Charles Haughey, fearful of an uproar over his closest ally, saved his coalition government by dismissing Lenihan from the cabinet.

Watching its candidate dip in the polls, Fianna Fáil began to portray Robinson as an agent of abortion, homosexuality, and promiscuity and as a mother who had only a passing interest in her children. She replied, "My views are known. What I would represent is more space and more pluralism and more tolerance." Her family-oriented image was not tarnished.

Lenihan regained support, however, and in the first round of voting won 44.1 percent of the vote to Robinson's 39.9 percent. The third candidate, Austin Currie of the main opposition Fine Gael party, received 17 percent. According to an intricate election rule, the third candidate's votes were awarded to whichever candidate voters had selected as their second choice. So Robinson ended with 52.8 percent to Lenihan's 47.2 percent.

Robinson hailed her victory as a "great, great day for Irish women." To her enthusiastic supporters she said, "The women of Ireland instead of rocking the cradle rocked the system." She then noted that her triumph occurred on the first anniversary of the collapse of the Berlin Wall. "Something has crumbled away in Ireland too. We were up against the might and the money and the very effective machinery of the greatest political party in the country, and we beat them."

During the inaugural ceremony on December 3, Robinson said that she would try to reduce "the troubles" in Ulster. "I will seek to encourage mutual understanding and tolerance between the different communities on this island." Despite the traditional apolitical role of the Irish head of state, she wanted to be more than a figurehead. She promised to work on broad issues like the continuous emigration of young people from Ireland and to make the presidential mansion in Phoenix Park the showcase of national pride.

All other Irish presidents had gone to private Sunday Mass in the official residence. But two weeks after her swearing in, Robinson attended Mass in Ballymun, the most deprived section in Dublin, to call attention to the poor. As one of her aides explained, the president could not make statements without the government's approval, but she could sit and listen. Soon after, she was advised to refuse an invitation to speak at a prestigious lecture series in London. Good humoredly, she described her pullback as "teething adjustment."

In July 1991, Robinson savored a feminist victory. Before her election she had worked for eight years as special counsel to SIPTU, a women's union. The legal battle involved 105 women acting as advisers to female farm workers who were paid 20 percent less than their male counterparts. The Labour Court recognized Robinson's earlier effective arguments and backdated pay increases to January 1, 1981. Totaling $2 million, it was the biggest equal-pay award ever given to Irish women.

When she went to the United States in October, however, she could not discuss this significant event. The president of Ireland travels abroad only with the permission of the prime minister and must not talk about any political issues. Robinson told Americans that she recognized these restrictions. "As president," she said, "I don't have personal opinions." Still they saw her as a representative of a changing Ireland.

To mark her first anniversary as president, Mary and Nicholas Robinson stood together before press photographers to cut a cake. The occasion was the Challenging Images conference, focused on people with disabilities. When Robinson entered the conference room, she was accompanied by Donal Toflan, the first disabled appointee of the Council of State, who received a standing ovation. She told her audience that during the past year she had been personally enriched by seeing many disabled people fulfill their potential. Admitting that she herself had a disability, the problem of being unable to tell left from right, she laughingly added that it had not impeded her political life.

As well as being an advocate for the handicapped, Nicholas was the administrator of the Irish Center for European Law, an authority on historical preservation, and chairman of the Irish Architectural Archives.

To the president's dismay, the tragic plight of a 14-year-old rape victim brought international embarrassment to Ireland early in 1992. Like an estimated 5,000 women and girls who go to Britain each year for an abortion, the teenager wanted to leave for London. But when her parents asked if the fetus could be displayed at the rapist's trial, the plans for the secret trip became known, and Irish officials issued an injunction banning the girl from departing. Disconsolate, she threatened to commit suicide.

Rapidly the case became the pretext for protest marches, a matter of public debate, and the subject of opinion polls in Ireland and diplomatic conversations abroad. The Dublin High Court upheld the injunction, but within a few days the Irish Supreme Court overthrew it. Then the girl disappeared from the headlines. It was presumed that she went to London.

Many Irish women remembered that in 1983 Mary Robinson had mounted a decidedly legalistic challenge to the antiabortion amendment. But as president she had not been able to speak out on the case. She could only say that it had caused her nation "universal anguish and concern." But she took hope when the new prime minister, Albert Reynolds, promised to press for the legalization of abortion.

By autumn 1992 a political crisis pushed the abortion issue to the forefront. Reynolds quarreled with his coalition partner, Daniel O'Malley of the Progressive Democrats, who pulled out of the coalition. When

Reynolds lost a vote of confidence in the Dáil, a snap election was necessary.

It was then decided to hold a simultaneous referendum liberalizing the antiabortion constitutional provisions. Three amendments were offered to the voters. The first permitted abortions when necessary to save the life, as distinct from the health, of the mother. The second allowed travel to other countries for whatever purpose, including abortion, without fear of legal prosecution. The third declared that abortion information could be circulated throughout the country.

The first measure failed decisively; the second and third amendments passed. In the election itself no party gained a majority.

It has not bothered Mary Robinson that she has no political power. To a British newspaper reporter, who asked if her activities were purely symbolic, she said:

> Symbols can be extremely important, when they have a possible practical relevance. If organizations and individuals make contact in a much more concerted way, then that ceases to be a pure symbol. It becomes a mood, and something with a momentum of its own.
>
> And it becomes then a significant encouragement to greater political willingness to reach out for structures that bring about peace and reconciliation. So although a great deal of the approach and the language and the direction of it will be using symbolism and not speaking in the normal political language, there's a lot more substance to it.

KHALEDA ZIA

*Prime Minister of Bangladesh
(1991–   )*

Khaleda Zia was another widow-by-assassination who entered political life after the untimely death of her husband. When she became prime minister of Bangladesh, she faced enormous challenges and did not expect miracles.

The third of five children of Iskandar Majumdar, a businessman, and his wife Taiyaba, a social worker, she was born on August 14, 1945, in Dinajpur, a town in the north of East Bengal. Historic times for British India lay just ahead. In 1942 Britain had proposed making India an independent dominion within the British Commonwealth of Nations, but the Muslim League demanded a divided India. In 1946 it forcibly called for the establishment of a new nation, Pakistan, to be carved out of the Muslim areas. After bloody riots, Britain agreed to a partition along Hindu and Muslim lines.

The day after Khaleda's second birthday, Pakistan (Land of the Pure) was created a British dominion consisting of two territories, the East Wing (East Bengal) and the West Wing, with 1,000 miles of Indian territory between them. A day later, August 16, India became an independent dominion. Bad feelings between Hindus and Muslims persisted, however, and an undeclared but bloody war between India and Pakistan broke out, lasting until 1949.

In 1956, when Khaleda was 11, Pakistan became a republic. Under a new constitution, which stressed a belief in Islamic teachings, the country was divided into two provinces, East and West Pakistan, the old East and West wings. Each had a governor, ministry, and legislature, and each had equal representation in the National Assembly.

Khaleda's family continued to live in East Pakistan, with its proud

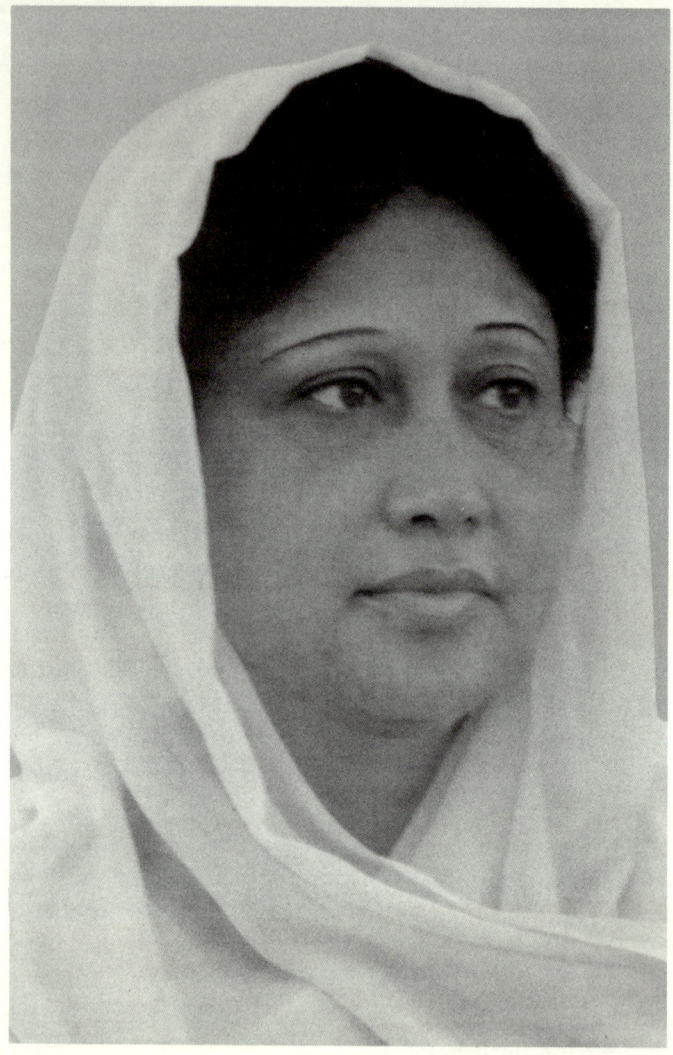

Khaleda Zia: courtesy Embassy of Bangladesh, Washington, D.C.

heritage of the Bengali (Bangla) language and culture, particularly its literature. Bangla would soon become an issue. Mohammed Ali Jinnah, leader of the Muslim League and first governor-general, had hoped one language, Urdu, would help unite the country's two wings, but Bengali nationalists stubbornly held on to their native tongue.

The Bengalis had little else. From the beginning, the federal government in West Pakistan neglected East Pakistan, where millions of workers had long been pushed into subsistence agriculture, dominated by jute and rice. It was a sad land beset by fierce storms, crushing poverty, malnutrition, and disease.

The first president of Pakistan was Major General Iskander Mirza. Three weeks after taking office, he abrogated the constitution and declared martial law in October 1958. The minister of defense, General Mohammed Ayub Khan, sent him into exile and instituted military rule. Later, by means of an engineered election, he would become president and establish a parliamentary government ruled by his own party.

Khaleda received a liberal, English-language education, five years primary, five years secondary, and two years higher secondary. At 15 she married 24-year-old Zia-ur Rahman, a dashing captain in the Pakistani army, who served in the first East Bengali Regiment. She had just passed her matriculation examination from Dinajpur Government School, and it was agreed that she should continue her studies at Surendranath College, also in Dinajpur.

Meanwhile East and West Pakistan grew further and further apart. In 1963, Sheikh Mujib-ur Rahman took over as leader of East Pakistan's dominant party, the Awami League, and became an ardent spokesman for political autonomy. At a conference of the eastern and western chapters of the league, he presented a controversial six-point political program for a confederated Pakistan. But after his supporters called a general strike, Ayub Khan interpreted the Mujib program as a call for independence and firmly rejected it.

Khaleda joined her husband in West Pakistan in 1965, ready to assume her domestic role. Then war broke out with India over the disputed province of Kashmir. Zia served as commander of the Khamkaran sector, but was home again in two months after hostilities ceased. In the next few years Khaleda was busy rearing their two sons, Arafat and Tariq, and like her husband, showing great interest in politics and sports. Zia was a dedicated athlete.

By this time Ayub Khan had grown vastly unpopular. Protests and riots continued throughout Pakistan, and in 1969 he announced that he would not run in the 1970 election. As police and the military stood by, helpless to control the near-anarchy, he resigned, and the commander-in-chief, General Agha Muhammad Yahya Khan, took charge.

The beautiful land of East Bengal had long been known for its natural disasters, the worst of which were tropical storms surging in from the vast Bay of Bengal. On November 13, 1970, a cyclone hit the mid-coastal lowlands and the constantly shifting low-lying islands or *chars*, where landless sharecroppers lived in bamboo-and-thatch huts. The death toll was estimated at 250,000 or more. Bengalis, including the Rahmans, were angered that Yahya Khan waited two days to inspect the devastation and then stayed only 24 hours.

In spite of this massive tragedy, plans went ahead for the first free election in more than ten years. On December 8, 1970, Mujib-ur Rahman and the Awami League won a majority in the National Assembly. The other big winner was Zulfikar Bhutto from West Pakistan. More than ever, East Pakistan felt exploited and deliberately impoverished by West Pakistan, and Mujib believed he had a mandate to improve the lot of his unhappy province.

Yahya Khan went to the East Pakistan capital, Dacca, in March 1971 to discuss terms under which the National Assembly would accept a new constitution and form a civilian government. Again Mujib presented his conditions that would lead to the creation of a federal state with the powers of the national government limited to defense and foreign affairs, but both Yahya Khan and Bhutto rejected them.

Fearful of a Bengali revolt and hating Mujib, Yahya Khan was determined to crush him. Even as the talks proceeded at Dacca, his troops were moving eastward. On March 25 they struck brutally at the University of Dacca, a center of nationalism, and then began moving around the surrounding area, killing indiscriminately. Bengali troops fought back; a leader in their ranks was Zia-ur Rahman, who had been among the first officers of the Pakistani army to join the revolt. On the 26th a radio message from a makeshift, clandestine station at Chittagong proclaimed "the independent sovereign republic of Bangladesh." Two days later the "voice of independent Bangladesh" announced that "Major Zia" would form a new government with himself as president. Mujib meanwhile had been arrested and flown to West Pakistan. From his prison cell he let it be known that he considered Zia's self-appointment brash, and the major quickly yielded his office.

The scene in East Pakistan was grim. Hard on the heels of the Pakistani army, non–Bengali vigilantes were brutalizing the countryside, burning, looting, destroying. In stark terror, millions of Bengalis poured over the frontier to India.

That April, leaders of the Awami League who had escaped to India gathered at a special ceremony just inside East Pakistan to proclaim formally their province independent and set up a Bangla Desh (Bengal State) government. (Dacca would now be spelled Dhaka.) Disturbed by the swarms of refugees, India began training guerrillas to be infiltrated into West Pakistan. During the "war of liberation," Major Zia commanded his "Z" force, and Khaleda, as the wife of a prominent enemy leader, was arrested and detained by the occupation army.

Knowing that India would soon be on the warpath, Yahya Khan launched preemptive strikes against Indian airfields on December 3. The next day India invaded East Pakistan and two days later recognized Bangladesh. Yahya Khan's army was no match for the Indian troops, and on December 16, Pakistani military forces in East Pakistan surrendered. The same day, Khaleda was released from prison.

Pressured by civilian leaders and the military, Yahya Khan resigned as president and was succeeded by Bhutto. Mujib's adherents then declared him president in absentia of Bangladesh and demanded his release.

Mujib returned on January 10, 1972, and a million people joyously shouted, "Glory to the Father of the Nation!" Zia, however, was not so sure he deserved the cheers. International aid came quickly for the ravaged land, the United States giving one-third of it. But shortages remained critical, and inflation doubled and tripled. The new nation was described as an international basket case.

In November the Constituent Assembly adopted a constitution to go into effect on the first anniversary of the surrender of West Pakistan. Elections were set for March 1973. After a year Mujib's Awami League was showing signs of corruption and divided goals, but the *Bangabandhu* (friend of Bengal), as he was called, won overwhelmingly. Closer to the seat of power, however, his enemies faulted him directly for making all decisions, even the most trivial. His relatives were said to be enriching themselves from the treasury.

Meanwhile Zia's military career prospered. That year he became a brigadier and then a major general. In 1974, soldiers were deeply involved in fending off disaster. Floods, starting in June, left more than 1,000 dead and millions homeless. Tons of rice were lost, and vast quantities of jute, the primary export, were destroyed. On top of the floods, a cyclone swept in from the Bay of Bengal severely damaging property. Mujib's answer to the distress was to exert more personal authority. At the end of the year, after three members of the Awami League were murdered, he suspended the constitution. Then in January 1975 he relinquished his post as prime minister to become president with absolute power. His next step was to abolish all political parties except his Awami League.

Conditions only grew worse, however. For the second straight year there was a cholera epidemic. And thousands died of starvation in spite of heavy infusions of foreign cash and other aid.

Mujib's popularity had faded with disaster. On August 15 a so-called majors' plot brought about the assassination of the president; his wife; his three sons; his brother; and his nephew, one of the most hated men in government. Triumphantly, Radio Dhaka announced that the regime of "corruption, injustice, and autocracy" had ended. At once the minister of commerce, Khandakar Muchtaque Ahmed, was sworn in as president, and the majors moved into the presidential palace. Zia was now chief of staff.

Another coup followed in November, led by a Mujib loyalist, Brigadier Khali Musharraf, who installed Chief Justice Abut Sadat Mohammed Sayem as president. When Musharraf promoted himself to major general, he replaced Zia as chief of staff.

Only two days later, Musharraf was killed in a firefight with agitators from a leftist movement. Frail and elderly, Sayem became chief martial law administrator; Zia regained his post as chief of staff, became a deputy chief martial law administrator, and took up the portfolios of finance, home affairs, industry, and information.

By November 1976 he had made himself chief martial law administrator, but downplayed his military posture, preferring to appear in civilian dress. Nevertheless he took great care to consolidate his position in the army. Major General Hossain Mohammad Ershad, an officer on the rise, was made the deputy army chief of staff. Khaleda saw her husband constantly on the move, traveling through the country and preaching his "politics of hope," the slow liberalization of Bengali politics. Everywhere he urged people to work harder and produce more.

When Sayem resigned in April 1977, Zia-ur Rahman took over as president. But Khaleda remained in the background at home, while her husband promoted an ambitious political and economic program that emphasized rural development. On the heels of this manifesto he scheduled a referendum on his presidency and won 98.9 percent of the vote. To give his administration a nonmilitary appearance, he chose Supreme Court Justice Abdul Sattar as his vice-president.

Zia was successful in establishing public order, but he did not entirely control the military. In September 1977, Japanese Red Army terrorists hijacked a Japan Airlines plane and forced its landing in Dhaka. While Zia fixed his attention on negotiating with the terrorists, a soldiers' mutiny broke out in Bogra, but was quickly stopped. During a second revolt in Dhaka, the mutineers attacked the Rahman residence, terrifying Khaleda and her sons. After the mutiny was put down, Zia did some housecleaning among his staff.

"To pave the way for democracy," he announced that elections would be held in April 1978. Simultaneously he lifted the ban on political parties. As the candidate of the Jatiyo Gantranak Dal–National Front, he won almost three-quarters of the vote. Then, combining the two parties, he founded the Bangladesh Nationalist party (BNP) with Sattar as chairman.

Over the next three years Zia justified his ongoing martial law by saying it had reduced corruption, shortages, and inflation. He did not mention that the press was muzzled, that opposition political activity was restricted, and that the jails were filled with thousands of political prisoners. A deeply religious Khaleda had welcomed his alteration of the constitution to reflect "complete trust and faith in mighty Allah," rather than Mujib's emphasis on secularism.

Zia's adherents applauded his plans to develop natural gas, the nation's only major resource, with help from abroad. The United States government, which gave most of the aid for his project, urged him to begin a family-planning program, but Muslim clerics prevented him from carrying it out.

Khaleda would always live with the pain of what happened on the night of May 30, 1981. As Zia-ur Rahman and two aides lay asleep in an army guest house in Chittagong, they were brutally gunned down; six bodyguards were also slain. The alleged mastermind of the killings was Major General Manzur, the army commander in Chittagong, who was angry over a projected transfer to a noncommand position elsewhere. A few days later, a devastated Khaleda watched her husband of 21 years being buried in a plot in front of Parliament.

Vice-President Sattar became acting president. When he called for elections in six months, rumors began to fly that Zia's widow and Mujib's eldest daughter, Sheikh Hasina Wajed, would be candidates. Both however, turned down the proposition that they run. Thus Sattar had only political unknowns as opponents and won easily.

It was not long until army officers came to believe that Sattar was also ineffectual. When Sattar tried to limit the influence of the military in the government, Ershad, the deputy chief of staff, stepped in forcibly. Engineering a coup in March 1982, he dismissed Sattar, suspended the constitution, dissolved the National Assembly, and abolished political parties. As chief martial law administrator, he assumed full powers, although Abdul Fazed Muhammad Ahsanuddin Chowdhury became acting president.

After the coup, Sattar remained in charge of the day-to-day activities of the BNP and appointed Khaleda Zia vice-chair. The first public opposition to martial law came 11 months later, in February 1983, when students demonstrated in the streets but were dispersed. By December the acting president was dismissed, and Ershad assumed the presidency.

Sattar, an octogenarian, retired from political life in 1984, and Khaleda Zia took over as party chair. An election within the party in August confirmed her in her position. Now she was often referred to as Begum Khaleda.

Forgetting his earlier ties to Zia, Ershad made the BNP a prime target of attack. Khaleda Zia, who was often involved in street protests, therefore arranged a seven-party alliance, which launched an unrelenting campaign against the Ershad regime. The goal was to get Ershad to step down and hand over power to a neutral caretaker government that would hold free elections.

Women were a rarity in Bangladesh politics. Other than Khaleda Zia, the only powerful woman was the leftist Sheikh Hasina Wajed, who headed the Awami League. The two disliked each other, but managed to place their parties at the core of a 32-party grouping called the Movement for the Restoration of Democracy, which demanded an end to martial law, the scheduling of parliamentary elections, and the release of political prisoners. Its chief weapon was the calling of strikes.

Ershad's power gained steadily, and by 1985 a general referendum supported his administration. Khaleda Zia and Hasina Wajed and their followers boycotted the elections of May 1986, which gave the pro–Ershad Jatiyo party a majority in Parliament. Soon after, Ershad was elected president. Barely a month following his victory, Parliament passed the Seventh Amendment to the constitution, ratifying all the actions of his martial law administration; with everything in place, he withdrew martial law and restored the constitution in full.

Still, Begum Khaleda and Sheikh Hasina, who both had been placed under house arrest several times, attacked the regime with all the fervor they could muster. They had boycotted the 1986 elections, and they planned to boycott those of 1988. In October they finally sat down together to plot a final campaign to get rid of the one man who controlled the police, the army, and the administration. The result was a series of mass street demonstrations in November that became known as the Siege of Dhaka. Ershad then declared a state of emergency. Khaleda, Hasina, and other leaders were again arrested but later released.

Street fighting continued nonetheless. Trying to portray himself as a democratic leader, Ershad offered to hold early presidential and parliamentary elections, but the BNP and the Awami League, still the dominant opposition parties, flatly refused to participate, saying that Ershad should resign. Because of the two parties' boycott, only elections for local governments were held.

On July 12, opposition forces began a 26-day campaign to force Ershad out. A nationwide protest followed on July 29, but he hung on stubbornly. Countries on which Bangladesh depended for aid now began pressuring him to restore civil rights. Again the country suffered from massive monsoon rains, and he was criticized for dealing ineffectively with the crisis.

Finally, on December 5, 1990, the information minister announced Ershad's resignation. After celebrating in the streets, the opposition parties chose Shahabuddin Ahmed, the chief justice, to head a caretaker government. He rescinded the emergency powers Ershad had decreed and promised early elections. The ex-president and his wife were arrested.

The worldwide press noted that two dead men were locked in electoral battle in February 1991. The Awami League and the BNP displayed only the portraits of Mujib-ur Rahman and Zia-ur Rahman on their campaign posters, and campaign speeches dwelt only on the qualities of the two charismatic but departed leaders, who were not related to each other. Zia's widow and Mujib's daughter were ignored.

The BNP emerged as the winning party; the Awami League, despite Hasina Wajed's prediction of a huge majority, was left far behind. Begum Khaleda Zia, however, had to wait until March 20 to take her oath of office. Ahmed, the interim president, was reluctant to appoint her and decided that the BNP first had to prove its strength in the newly elected National Assembly that would not meet until the first week in April. But when Hasina Wajed, still smarting from her defeat, threatened to send her supporters to the streets if Khaleda Zia were prime minister, Ahmed decided that further delay would be unproductive, and the former housewife moved into office.

Under the prevailing presidential form of government, the prime minister did not control the legislature, but led a council of 11 ministers, supported by 21 junior ministers, who "advised" the president. Begum Khaleda did not overstate the problems the council faced. Because of an autocratic government and plundering, she said, "all institutions have been devastated and the society corrupted. So we have a very onerous task."

One hundred thirteen million Bengalis were crammed into a country the size of the state of Wisconsin. The economy was fragile, industry was underdeveloped, and infrastructural facilities were inadequate. Food production, in spite of Green Revolution seeds and techniques introduced in the 1980s, failed to keep pace with the zooming population. Poverty was enormous.

In its first weeks, Begum Khaleda's government attempted to undertake market reforms to privatize the state-dominated economy, a step that provoked violent reactions from labor unions affiliated with the Awami League. Clashes between the opposition and armed student groups affiliated with the government broke out, and the attempts to undertake free-market reforms and impose fiscal discipline proved painful.

Then on April 30, Khaleda's attention was sharply diverted from the economy, when a devastating cyclone took the lives of more than 100,000 Bengalis. She flew over the hardest-hit areas by helicopter; desperately she appealed for international aid. Help did pour in, and the United States sent eight warships carrying swarms of helicopters and landing craft and about 7,500 troops. But relief and development agencies were not optimistic about quick solutions for the long-destitute country.

Observers agreed that Begum Khaleda Zia had successfully overcome the first real test of her leadership. Now she and the BNP began working to switch from the presidential to the parliamentary form of government. The National Assembly endorsed the new system, which was then approved in a nationwide referendum. On September 19, 1991, she took over as chief executive.

Allowing complete freedom of the press and expression, she set new priorities for revitalizing the economy: the achievement of self-sufficiency in food production in the quickest time and an emphasis on small and cottage industries. The Zia government also paid attention to containing the population explosion and to effecting mass literacy, women's development, and environmental protection.

Like her late husband, Begum Khaleda Zia began to crisscross the country to talk with people. In her soft sari and veil, she might take up a shovel to inaugurate a canal-digging program and open mills, factories, or educational institutions. Thursday evenings she reserved for listening to public grievances. It was reported that some nights she walks through the city streets, even in the slums, to listen and learn.

She has little time for her hobbies—reading, gardening, and listening to music. When her physicians complained about her overlong workdays, she invariably replied, "There are so many thoughts, there are so many problems to be solved, and there is no time to lose." But she remains an optimist.

EDITH CRESSON

*Prime Minister of France
(1991–92)*

François Mitterand called his political protégée "mon petit soldat." She was loyal, she was combative; he could deploy her in rough political terrain. In 1991, during his second presidential term, he gave her the greatest challenge of her career, the job of prime minister of France. But "la battant," the fighter, as she was called, lasted only for ten difficult months in that post.

She was born on January 27, 1934, in the fashionable Parisian suburb of Boulogne-Billancourt, to Gabriel and Jacqueline Campion. Two brothers would follow her. A Socialist, Gabriel was a tax inspector; thanks to her family, his wife was well off. So the Campions could afford a summer house, special vacations in Jersey, and an English nanny for Edith.

At the beginning of 1940, under the government of Paul Reynaud, Gabriel Campion was posted as a financial consultant to the French embassy in Belgrade, Yugoslavia. By spring the embassy was filled with foreboding. In September 1939, France and Britain had declared war on Nazi Germany, following its blitzkrieg of Poland, but there had been little action. Then in May the Germans rolled into France through Holland and Belgium. Edith heard her mother's friends constantly ask, "What is happening? Will France fight back?"

By the middle of June there was disheartening news. Lacking armored divisions and air power, France had fallen, and Paris had been occupied. Rather than surrender, Reynaud resigned and was replaced by a World War I hero, Marshal Henri Philippe Pétain, who signed an armistice. France was divided into two zones, the occupied zone north of the Loire River and the "free" zone to the south. By July the Belgrade embassy was representing a new government. The octogenarian Pétain

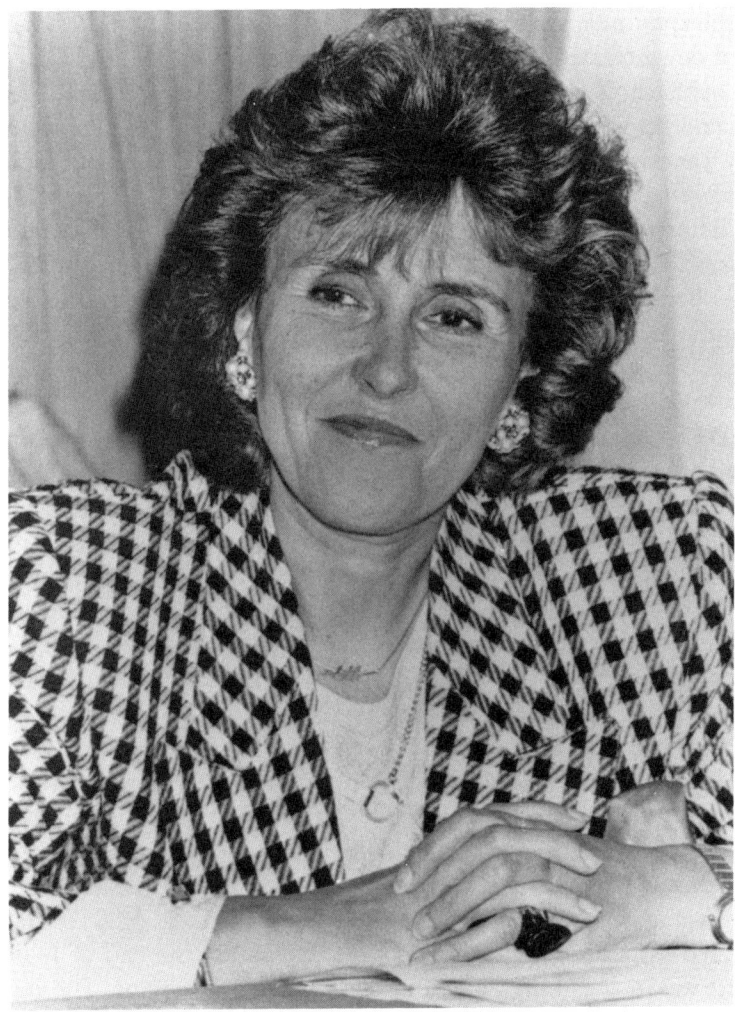

Edith Cresson: courtesy Embassy of France, Washington, D.C.

moved to Vichy, the Third Republic was declared dead, and he was made chief of staff of the Government of Unoccupied France. At his shoulder stood the unscrupulous Pierre Laval, who urged more and more collaboration with the enemy.

With the new year, tensions also ran high in Belgrade. Prince Paul, the regent, was reported to be negotiating with the Nazis. As protesters filled the streets, seven-year-old Edith stepped out on the balcony of the

Cresson apartment and with the help of her four-year-old brother Harold tossed down cigarettes carrying the embassy insignia.

In March, Yugoslavia joined the Axis, and the military ousted Prince Paul and his government. Fearing a German invasion, the French embassy was closed. Shortly before the Germans marched in, the Campions joined other embassy families fleeing the city.

After reaching France, Gabriel settled his family in Thonon-les-Bains, a spa in the French Alps, not far from the better-known Évian-les-Bains, both of which were located on Lake Geneva. Edith was placed in a communal school and then enrolled as a boarder at the convent of Sacre Coeur. She saw little of her beloved father because he had taken an obscure post in occupied Paris.

As a result of the Allied invasion of North Africa, the Germans overran all of France in 1942, rendering Pétain and Laval powerless. Men and women of all political persuasions formed an heroic resistance movement, but only a small fraction of the total populace participated. Some resistance fighters went into exile. General Charles de Gaulle, whom Reynaud had made undersecretary of war in the desperate days of June 1940, established a Free France movement in London and won support from the Allies. The same year the French fleet scuttled itself at Toulon to prevent being seized by the Germans.

One of Edith's friends, a young resistance Jew in Thonon, was seized by German officers and sent to a concentration camp from which he never returned. His fate affected her deeply. She was often ill in the chilly corridors of Sacre Coeur, and to regain her health she was sent during vacations to stay with an Alsatian resistance family in nearby Publier.

Two months after D-Day, 1944, Paris was liberated, and De Gaulle returned as head of a provisional government. By the end of 1944 all France was free, and the Campions could finally come home. The Fourth Republic was proclaimed in 1946. But because a new constitution did not provide for a strong executive, as De Gaulle insisted, he retired to his country estate. Shaky coalition governments rapidly succeeded each other, but with the help of the U.S. Marshall Plan the national economy was rebuilt. Women were enfranchised.

At 15, Edith was sent to Dupanloup, a religious school near the Bois de Boulogne, that catered to daughters of the bourgeoisie. She chafed at the strict rules and believed she was missing out on too much of the world. To allay her boredom, she read "all of Zola, all of Stendhal, all of Balzac, all of Proust."

Dutifully she attended the parties and balls typical of her parents' social circles, but became convinced that she wanted a more meaningful life. She considered her mother a "Japanese vase" and could not bear the thought of becoming one herself. "One of the most obvious characteristics of the bourgeoisie is the boredom it produces," she would write in her autobiography. During this period, Gabriel and Jacqueline Campion went to Morocco, where he worked in the French embassy. Moroccans, like Tunisians, were clamoring for independence. They would finally achieve it in 1956, two years after the fall of Dien Bien Phu, which ended French power in Indochina.

On leaving Dupanloup at the age of 17, Edith, an exemplary student, had no difficulty being admitted to the Women's School for Advanced Commercial Studies (HEC) in Paris, where she continued her excellent record. She passed her vacations with the family of a Norman banker, who had opened the top floor of his mansion to HEC students for respites in the country.

With her business degree in hand, she took her first job as a secretary in the sales department of the Worth perfumery in Paris. Before long, she said that being a secretary there was like being a housemaid. Next she worked for Bernard Lafay, a conservative deputy in the National Assembly, who was trying to form a new party.

In 1958 the war of independence in Algeria violently divided the French people and threatened civil war. So an appeal was made to De Gaulle to return to public life. That summer the heroic-sized general attained the premiership and designed a constitution that gave immense powers to the president. The constitution was approved in September, and the Fourth Republic became the Fifth Republic. De Gaulle was elected president in December and promised to resolve the Algerian crisis through negotiations. The Algerians would achieve their independence in 1962.

Edith had no political affiliations. Although she was sympathetic to the Algerians, her mind was on other matters. She had fallen in love with Jacques Cresson, an executive with the Peugeot auto company, whom she had met in 1958 at a surprise party in Neuilly. As he later told the story, he was captured by her pretty face and vivacity, but thought she could look more stylish. During their courtship, he gave her two assignments: learn how to dress well and learn to love Mozart. Edith did both. They were married on December 26, 1959, and would become the parents of two daughters, Nathalie and Alexandra.

When Peugeot sent Jacques to Nantes for 2½ years, Edith began teaching history and French at a normal school there. In 1961 the Cressons attended the French Exposition in Moscow, their trip made more interesting because of Jacques's fluency in Russian. Jacques's French-born father had been a surgeon in St. Petersburg, sometimes treating members of the czar's family, but with the Russian Revolution Dr. Cresson and his Russian wife had escaped to France.

Nantes was only a short distance from Angers; near that city, the senior Cressons had lived in a country mansion, Le Tertre, where Jacques had spent his childhood. Edith became greatly attached to the old house in Anjou and to the family gatherings held there. She learned how to make special Russian dishes for Christmas and Easter and said she would hand on to her daughters the holiday traditions from St. Petersburg. She claimed that her love for the historic old province was so great she had become an Angevin.

She and Jacques moved back to Paris, where she enrolled in the Institute of Demography. As she later wrote, for the first time she was taking a course of studies that really interested her. To gain her doctorate in demography from her old school, the HEC, she decided to research the lives of Breton farm women and base her thesis on 500 interviews.

The presidential election of 1965 was historically important. For the first time a chief executive was to be chosen by popular vote; previously, the president had been picked by an electoral college consisting of members of the National Assembly and Senate. In 1962 De Gaulle had initiated a constitutional amendment for this procedure. Paulette Moreau, Edith's friend from their days at Dupanloup, got her involved in the campaign of François Mitterand, a non–Communist leftist, who was running against De Gaulle. A literary esthete in his student days on the Left Bank, Mitterand had become a dynamic and wide-ranging politician, who had moved through the ranks from Right to Left and was running under the banner of a party he had founded, Organization of Republican Institutions. Welcomed to headquarters, elegant Mme. Cresson was set to work licking envelopes, typing, and preparing packets of posters and brochures. Soon she attracted notice with her enthusiasm and organizational ability. Mitterand forced 75-year-old De Gaulle into a runoff, but lost narrowly in the second round. Edith joined his party and began to look on him as a man of destiny.

In 1968, when both daughters were in school close to the Cresson apartment and household help was available, she felt ready to resume a professional career. She took a job with a bureau of economic studies and for one project was sent to Algiers with about ten engineers. As the party entered the hotel, where a room had been reserved for each, the hotel keeper protested, "There is one too many." Then pointing to Edith Cresson, he said, "This woman. Whom is she with?"

Since his return in 1958, De Gaulle had tried to make France the leader of Europe. He had developed nuclear weapons and arrogantly asserted an independent foreign policy. But his countrymen were angry over inflation, unemployment, the lack of housing, the old-fashioned educational system, and rigid government control over the media. In May 1968, striking workers and student rioters paralyzed Paris and threatened to topple the government.

To save his regime, De Gaulle offered a national referendum and promised to resign if it went against him. His further pledge of elections within 40 days ended the 19-day strike. Speaking with the old fire in his television appeal, the president won back his support, and the referendum gave him a massive vote of approval. In the general election in late June, the Gaullists gained an absolute majority in the National Assembly.

Within a year the general called for a referendum on some minor constitutional changes he wanted to make. Taking the defeat of the measures as a personal affront, he resigned in April, leaving his post to an interim president until the June elections, when Georges Pompidou, his former prime minister, was elected.

Edith had worked actively with Mitterand and his party since 1965. Six years later, the Organization of Republican Institutions merged with a variety of Socialist splinter groups to form the new Parti Socialiste (PS) with Mitterand as first secretary. In 1974 Mitterand ran again for the presidency. (Pompidou had died in office in April, and elections were held in May.) Again Cresson showed her commitment to his banner. Mitterand won the first round, Valéry Giscard d'Estaing, a conservative non–Gaullist, the second round. Within a year, at the Socialist Congress in Pau, Mitterand sponsored Cresson's nomination for membership in the party.

Immediately she was asked to run for the National Assembly from Châtellerault, a conservative bastion in the department of Vienne that was close to Le Tertre. She staged a vigorous fight that earned Mitterand's praise, but lost. Instead, she became the PS's national secretary for Youth Organizations. That year her autobiography, *Avec le Soleil,* was published.

Since she was only 41, many were puzzled why she had written it so early in her political career. In 1977 she was elected mayor of Thure, also in the Anjou region.

Next, in 1979, Cresson was elected to the European Parliament and served on its agricultural commission. Overlapping her duties in Strasbourg, she took an additional post as her party's national delegate for environmental matters from 1980 to 1981, when she left the Parliament.

Edging out Giscard, Mitterand won his third bid for the presidency in 1981 and was bolstered by a big Socialist majority in the National Assembly. There were four main parties in France: the Socialist party; the conservative Réassemblement pour la République (RRP), founded by de Gaulle; Union pour la Démocratie Française (UDF); and the French Communist party. Vindicating her earlier defeat, Cresson was elected deputy from the department of Vienne.

Mitterand cited her agricultural expertise and combative skills when he asked Prime Minister Pierre Mauroy to appoint her as his minister of agriculture, considered the hot seat in the cabinet. Cresson spent two days considering the offer, then made up her mind after her daughter, who was studying agronomy at Montpellier, wrote a letter urging her to accept. She had never been one to refuse a challenge.

Although the appointment fueled anger among the farmers, Cresson indicated that she understood why: "They are such conservatives and women haters that giving them a woman as minister and a Socialist on top of that amounted to provocation." Her challenge to the National Farmers' Federation (FNSEA) monopoly and her reforms of the highly protected agricultural market only exacerbated the farmers' anger. Deriding her married name, which is also the French word for watercress, surly farmers carried posters demanding weed-killers for her. The worst episode occurred during a trip to Calvados. Though pelted with mud and rotten fruit and tomatoes, she did not shrink from facing down her noisy enemies. Finally gendarmes whisked her away by helicopter. Within government circles, however, Cresson was given credit for her vigorous promotion of French agricultural products in world markets and for raising farm incomes 10 percent.

Meanwhile, she had set her sights on becoming mayor of Châtellerault. Her campaign style was forceful and appealing, and her victory was especially impressive to her party, since she was one of the few Socialists to win any kind of election in 1983. As mayor, she presided over her daughter Nathalie's wedding in the Town Hall.

Mitterand had begun his seven-year term with a flurry of promises to nationalize banks and industries. But, almost half way through their targets, the Socialists had aborted their program in favor of a strong market-oriented agenda that much resembled that of their right-wing rivals.

Advised by Mitterand, the new prime minister Laurent Faubius selected Cresson as minister of external trade and tourism. Meanwhile she remained mayor of Châtellerault. With her outspoken ways, she at once angered the travel industry by defending the government's austerity program, which discouraged foreign travel because the franc was weak. Ever the chauvinist, Cresson declared, "France is a magnificent country. To encourage people to travel in France is not protectionism."

French Socialists had begun blending pragmatism with their party's traditional values, and Mitterand himself gave considerable recognition to business achievement. The name of Cresson's department was changed in 1984 to industrial restructuring and external trade. One of her main tasks was to take charge of the major industrial companies that had been nationalized, nine out of 15. The ailing iron and steel industry presented an especially difficult challenge. She astonished some old-time Socialists when she began favoring the practice of allowing nationalized companies to obtain capital from the private market by selling "certificates of investment." Cresson said that it was unnecessary for taxpayers to support companies that could obtain their own financing. But for all her probusiness tone, she argued that nationalization had been effective because governmental infusions of capital had helped various industries modernize. In addition, she said, the Socialists were the most suited to bring about modernization because they could best explain it to the workers.

She was also supposed to encourage private industry and trade. Cresson rode a French motor scooter to work to prove that French models were as good as the popular Japanese ones. At Le Tertre she preferred a bicycle, which she pedaled so fast that Jacques Cresson complained that he had to go by motor scooter to keep up with her. When he mentioned her cycling speed, he often spoke of swimming, one of her favorite sports. He had learned to accept her habit of going so far out into the Atlantic that she would disappear from view for several minutes at a time.

To encourage investment, Cresson pleaded for tax breaks for business. She chartered planes for dozens of French executivies to show their wares in New York and Tokyo. On such tours she also promoted French fashion; she herself wore outfits lent by the leading couturiers.

To an English interviewer she admitted, "I probably had to work harder than a man to prove myself. Still, the advantages outweigh the disadvantages—people are much nicer to you. Sometimes I feel that men are being condescending, but that amuses rather than irritates me. I am not a feminist in the normal sense. Men are only indispensable in one area—one's private life."

Cresson was reelected deputy from Vienne in 1986, a year in which the Socialists lost their parliamentary majority. The Gaullist leader, Jacques Chirac, who had been prime minister from 1974 to 1976 under Giscard, took the post again and began a period of "cohabitation" with Mitterand. He stayed two years, undoing some of the Socialists' nationalization.

Mitterand was reelected for a second term of seven years in 1988 and at the same time gained a Socialist prime minister in Michel Rocard, who made Cresson minister of European affairs. Now her Japan bashing, which had gone on since 1983, reached its peak. "Japan is an adversary that must be stopped," she warned. "It does not play by the rules." Then in her blunt way she called the Japanese ants. Without pause, she asked other countries to follow France's lead in restricting Japanese car imports to 3 percent. Meanwhile she engaged in important negotiations with European leaders to plan for a unified, borderless economic union in the 1990s. France held the presidency of the European Community from July 1989 to January 1, 1990.

Feeling she had accomplished her task, she resigned in the fall of 1990 to join Groupe Schneider, a French manufacturer of electrical equipment. After only six month, however, she left corporate sales to accept her old friend Mitterand's invitation to form a government. Rocard had failed to muster majorities in the National Assembly, and the president believed he was straying too much from the Socialist line. When Mitterand was asked to explain his choice of a woman as prime minister, he said he needed Cresson's experience in trade matters as France prepared for the forthcoming elimination of European trade barriers. He was making this issue the pillar of his policy for the rest of his term. He was convinced, he added, that Cresson's combination of Socialist sentiment and strong rapport with business leaders would attract both the Right and the Left in the National Assembly. Traditionally, the French president takes charge of foreign policy, and the prime minister administers domestic affairs.

Cresson's impressive credentials, however, were momentarily forgotten in the controversy that surged around her appointment. A woman heading the French government! With characteristic aplomb, however, she shrugged off the criticism. To assure continuity, she kept the leading ministers in the Rocard government. But she named three women to cabinet posts: Martine Aubry (labor), Frederique Breden (youth and sports), and Edvige Avice (cooperation and development). Other women were asked to serve as deputy ministers and undersecretaries.

One of her first decisions was to drop the customary weekly breakfast meetings at the Matignon Palace with the "elephants," the leading lights of the Socialist party. "I'm not one of the elephants," she said, "and when I want to see them, I'll see them."

With her eye on the high unemployment figures, Cresson listed revitalizing French industry and improving workers' skills as her main objectives. Despite her vision of consolidating all bureaucracies dealing with economic, industrial, trade, and telecommunications matters in a single superministry of economic affairs, based on the Japanese pattern, she began to challenge the Japanese even more aggressively. The new department did not materialize.

As prime minister, she traded barb for barb in the National Assembly. To reporters she gave her views on almost everything, including the "sexual inhibitions" of American and British men. Polls quickly showed that her popularity was slipping. A daily television show "Babette," featuring puppets, satirized her as Amarotte, the sexy, slavish creature of Mitterand. Angrily Cresson denounced it as "grotesque, brainless, a synthesis of all stereotypes of women." She added, "This goes beyond the limit."

Michele Barzach, a former health minister, commented that the program had never been so horrible to anyone before. "This attitude — that women who succeed at the top level in politics must have done so through seduction is so pervasive among men that they dismiss the reaction of many women to the show as hysterical and paranoid."

A month after her installation in the Matignon, Cresson felt forced to increase social security taxes to plug the gaping deficit in the health system.

Jacques Cresson, submitting good-naturedly to interviews, wryly remarked that he had joined the Denis Thatcher club. But he emphasized that unlike his British counterpart, he did not accompany his wife on her travels. In the Margaret Thatcher tradition, however, Edith Cresson, when in Paris, prepared his breakfast each morning. The Cressons continued to gather with their daughters, sons-in-law, and grandchildren at Le Tertre for relaxing weekends. At Christmas and Easter, Edith prepared the Russian dishes she had learned as a bride.

Another crisis for Cresson arose in January 1992, when opposition leaders and certain members of the Socialist party asked Mitterand to dismiss his prime minister. A furor had arisen over the secret entry into France of the Palestinian terrorist leader, George Habash, who had come for treatment of a heart condition. Mitterand dismissed the matter as a "puffed-up soufflé" and refused to act. The Habash affair, however, served as a lightning rod for accumulated frustration, resentment, and impatience over the long years of Mitterand's tenure.

Sensing an approaching storm, Mitterand fired four senior civil servants and an adviser, who he said were responsible for the internationally embarrassing incident. Still, Center-Right opposition parties proposed a censure vote aimed at condemning the political and moral crises gripping the country.

After Mitterand called a special session of the National Assembly, Socialist members fought for days, but finally rallied around Cresson. The Assembly's 26 French Communists refused to join in the vote, which required an absolute majority. Thereupon Cresson led the Socialists in a pep rally in which she listed the accomplishments of their party during the Mitterand period. It was described as one of her best speeches.

But in regional elections on March 24 and 29, the Socialist party made its worst showing in 24 years, finishing third behind the ultraright National Front party in the Île de France region around Paris. The prime minister shouldered much of the criticism. During her ten rocky months in office, her popularity had fallen from 65 to 20 percent. Most obviously, a sagging economy and her often intemperate remarks had helped bring her to this low ebb. Mitterand found himself under extreme pressure to rebuild the Socialist image before parliamentary elections scheduled for March 1993. The obvious sacrifice was Cresson. On April 2 she resigned and was replaced by Finance Minister Pierre Bergevoy, who formerly had served as chief of staff.

She left graciously, speaking no bitter words about having been abandoned. But Antoinette Fouque, president of a women's rights group, the Women's Alliance for Democracy, took up the cudgel. Cresson's quick ouster, she noted, probably retarded the advancement of women in French politics. Fouque blamed a "media hate campaign," with sexist overtones, for many of Cresson's problems. Beyond the

"Babette" show, Edith had frequently been forced to respond to unsubstantiated claims by the opposition that she had had an affair with Mitterand. Other feminists joined with Fouque in saying that French male politicians would never have been subjected to the same kind of questioning about their private lives.

Edith Cresson was still mayor of Châtellerault. Unspoken was what lay over the horizon.

HANNA SUCHOCKA

*Prime Minister of Poland
(1992–   )*

Solidarity, the independent trade union movement, which changed Poland's political landscape in the 1980s, played an important role in Hanna Suchocka's rise to the prime minister's office in 1992. To Lech Wałęsa, its founding father and Poland's current president, however, she has no close ties. But she has two links to an earlier prime minister, Ignace Jan Paderewski, the famed concert pianist and composer. Beyond the law and politics, music is central to Suchocka's life; her chosen instrument is the piano. And her grandmother, Anna (Czajkowska) Suchocka, a deputy in the first Polish parliament after the restoration of independence, served as minister of women's affairs in Paderewski's short-lived government in 1919. Beset by partisan wrangling, Paderewski stayed in office only ten months. Suchocka, on the other hand, began her tenure by leading a coalition of seven parties.

She was born on April 3, 1946, in Pleszew, close to Poznań (formerly Posen) in western Poland. Her parents, Józef and Wanda (Baczkowka) Suchoccy, ran a pharmacy that had been established by her grandfather, Stanisław Suchocki,* a former lecturer on pharmaceutical botany at the University of Poznań. His politically active wife Anna and their equally active daughter Maria (Mita) campaigned continually for equal rights for women. For a time Mita was president of the National Association for Female Catholic Youth.

The year before Hanna's birth, Poland had begun to fall into the Communist orbit, one more step in a tragic and complicated history extending over almost two centuries. Before her first birthday a People's

---

**Polish usage is Suchocka (feminine), Suchocki (masculine), Suchoccy (couple).*

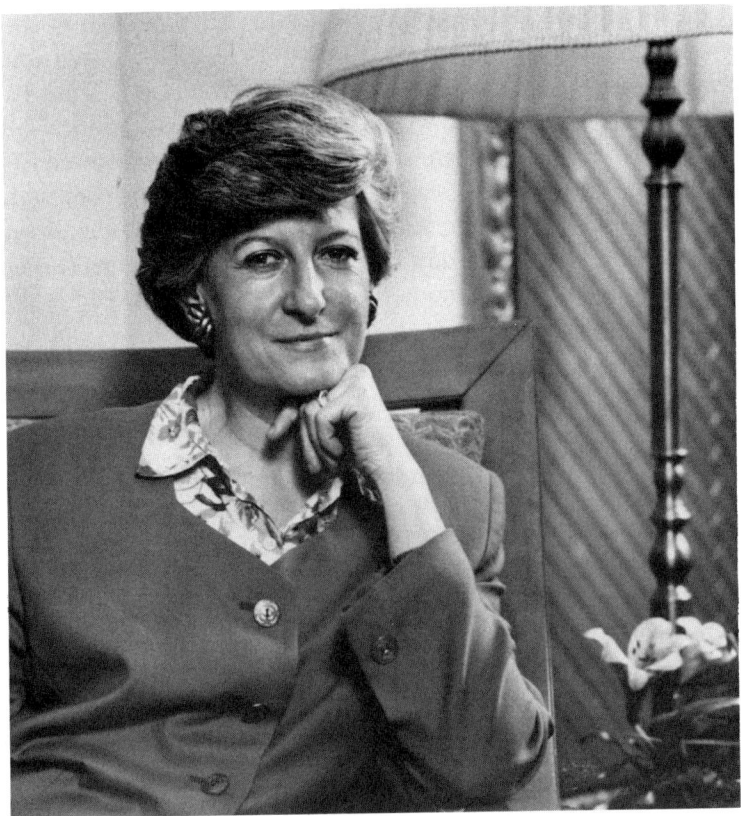

Hanna Suchocka: courtesy Consulate General of Poland, New York; photograph by Cezary Slomiński.

Republic had been established that was dominated by the Polish Workers party under Władisław Gomułka. When Hanna was two, a small amount of anti-Communist resistance had been suppressed, and a reconstituted Communist party, the Polish United Workers party (Polska Zjednoczona Partia Robotnicza — PZPR), a merging of the Polish Workers party with the Polish Socialist party, was in full control, thanks to the presence of Soviet soldiers and security police. Gomułka was dismissed.

After the PZPR took over, the new primate of Poland, Stefan Cardinal Wyszynski, tried to make accommodations with the Communists. But with the onset of a campaign against the practice of religion, he was kept under house arrest for almost three years.

As in the Suchoccy home, where Hanna's sister Elzbieta was born in

1949, the bitter national history inspired fervid patriotism in households everywhere. Poland, long in a federation with Lithuania, was split among Austria, Prussia, and Russia during the First, Second, and Third Partitions in 1772, 1793, and 1795, when it ceased to exist as a political entity and its name disappeared from maps. National identity, however, was not lost. In 1807 Napoleon I created the puppet Grand Duchy of Warsaw out of the Prussian partition, with the king of Saxony as the absentee duke. Following Napoleon's downfall, the Congress of Vienna (1814–15) altered the boundaries once more. Prussia kept the western part of its acquisition (Grand Duchy of Posen); Austria stayed in Galicia; and Russia gained central Poland, including Warsaw, and organized it as the constitutional Kingdom of Poland with the czar as king.

In 1831, with the ill-fated November Rising, Poles drove the Russians out of Warsaw and proclaimed independence. But the czar's soldiers recaptured the capital city the next year. Thereafter the constitution of the Congress Kingdom was suspended. Posen (now Poznań) lost its autonomy in 1848. Again in 1863 a revolution against the Russians broke out, only to fail. Representing the new German Empire after 1871, the Germans stayed on in western Poland.

This unfortunate history continued into the 20th century. Polish territory became a prominent battleground during World War I, and Poles were drafted into the Austrian, German, and Prussian armies. The Austrian-German offensive drove the Russians back beyond the old borders in 1915, and Germany introduced an "independent," short-lived Kingdom of Poland in 1916 without naming its ruler or boundaries. As the war raged on and as the Russian empire collapsed in revolution, Allied powers began to discuss Poland's future. President Woodrow Wilson made the nation's rebirth one of his Fourteen Points. After the Allied victory in 1918, the independent republic of Poland, with much of its territory restored, was born.

Józef Pilsudski became chief of state and minister of defense. An independence-minded activist in the Polish Socialist party, he was the founder of the Polish Legions that had operated with the Austrians against the Russian army. In an attempt to establish Poland's eastern borders in 1919–20, he led his legions against the Red Army and the forces of Lithuania and the Byelorussian and Ukrainian Soviet Republics. With Allied help, the Poles were victorious, and almost all their eastern frontier was returned. Pilsudski quit politics temporarily in 1922, but in 1926 used military force to overthrow the government. Until his death in 1935, he moved in and out as premier, but kept the real power in his hands even when he was not in office. A "colonels' regime," made up of his close followers, succeeded him.

All too soon the darkest chapters in national history began to be written. On September 1, 1939, using blitzkrieg tactics, Adolf Hitler attacked Poland, causing Britain and France to declare war. Just a month before, the Nazi Reich and the Soviet Union had signed a secret protocol of nonaggression, which envisaged a joint attack on Poland and the division of territory. On September 17, Soviet troops struck Poland from the east. The campaigns were fierce and brief, since the Western Allies did not fire a shot in Poland's defense. Thus western Poland fell under Nazi, and eastern Poland fell under Soviet, occupational forces. Atrocities abounded on both sides.

But relations between Josef Stalin and Adolf Hitler worsened, and in June 1941, with their Operation Barbarossa, the Nazis invaded the Soviet Union, and Poland came under German control. Polish Jews were killed in gas chambers and burned in furnaces; other Poles were sent to forced labor camps. The Warsaw Rising was another unsuccessful Polish attempt to liberate the city. Then in 1944 the Soviet army, savoring its victory at Stalingrad, entered Poland and, with the help of the Polish underground, drove out the Germans. Soon after, a pro–Communist Polish Committee of National Liberation was set up in Lublin. But under Stalin's brutal policies, suffering only intensified.

Although a Polish government in exile existed in London, after the war the Lublin Committee was recognized as the provisional government. Under the Yalta and Potsdam agreements among the chief Allies, Poland's prewar territory to the east was transferred to the Soviet Union. By way of compensation, Poland was given most of the land east of the Oder and Neisse rivers that Germany had held, but in the process the Poles lost more than they had gained. This vast series of territorial transformations led to frequent social disruptions.

Such had been the turbulent events conditioning the lives of Hanna's parents and their forebears. They would ultimately inspire the rise of Solidarity, which, in turn, made possible her political success. History was constantly discussed in the comfortable Suchoccy house, attached to the pharmacy. Religion, poetry, and music were also important. The family called their home "the house with the piano." Later Suchocka would say, "My mother was an intellectual. She knew by heart the poetry of two Polish masters: Jan Kochanowski and Adam Mickiewicz. We learned from her what is the best. We believed in values, self-discipline, and human dignity." Many of their values were derived from their deep-rooted affinity with the Catholic church, which was entrenched in the national consciousness.

Using the Soviet blueprint as a model, the new regime dominated the political system and dictated economic and social policies. Industries were nationalized, and accordingly the pharmacy was "modernized," with the family grieving over the removal of fine wood paneling and the disposal of porcelain mixing bowls and expensive medical jars. As in wartime, shortages, inflation, and shabby consumer goods characterized the economy.

Primate of Poland since 1948, the year Gomułka was suddenly dismissed, Stefan Cardinal Wyszynski tried to reach a state of accommodation with the Communists. But with the onset of a campaign against the practice of religion, he was placed under house arrest in 1953. Poles, however, continued to go to church.

When Hanna was ten, a workers' uprising in nearby Poznań typified the widespread mood of discontent. For three days, workers rose against harsh working and depressed living conditions, the continual presence of Soviet troops, and the Polish Communist regime.

Although the army put down the revolt, that year there was hope that a more independent Polish communism might develop with the return of Gomułka. One of Gomułka's first acts was to release Cardinal Wyszynski, who, for the next two decades, would pursue a cautious course toward the regime, seeking conciliation or compromise when necessary.

During the Gomułka era, Hanna was graduated from high school and studied law at Poznań University, finishing in 1968. By that time, however, Gomułka had become highly unpopular. Hanna joined the faculty of law, but after a year her contract was not renewed because she refused to belong to the PZPR, which controlled or sponsored all legally organized activities except the church, although its membership actually was less than 7 percent of the population.

Suchocka now joined the small Democratic party (Stronnictwo Demokratyczne—SD), which had been created by the Communist government to act as a puppet alternative to the Sejm, the unicameral national legislature. She spent the next three years at the Institute of Home Industries and Crafts and then returned to Poznań University to prepare for her doctorate.

In spite of the optimism Gomułka had engendered in 1956, the economy had steadily deteriorated. Angry over sudden price increases, workers in Gdańsk and other Baltic ports rose in rebellion in December 1970. As soldiers fired into the crowds, 23 men fell dead. Pleading ill health, Gomułka then stepped down, and Edward Gierek was named party chief in his place, ending the strikes. Initially Gierek reaped praise for helping to modernize the Polish economy.

During the early 1970s, Suchocka went abroad. In Leyden she attended a symposium on American law sponsored by Columbia University; at the Institute for Public Law at Heidelberg University she participated in one on human rights. She obtained her doctoral degree in constitutional law in 1975.

Toward the middle of the decade, Cardinal Wyszynski, who had confined his activities to defending Catholic religious practices, began disputing with the Gierek government over constitutional changes that he thought threatened civil rights. The Polish church also backed the riots over food prices in 1976, urged clemency for those arrested, and sent church offerings to them. It gained extra strength when Karol Cardinal Wojtyla, archbishop of Kraków, was elected pope as John Paul II in 1978.

Suchocka was chosen SD representative to the Sejm in 1980. It proved to be a momentous year with Polish workers setting the stage for a new revolution. After the government announced increases in meat prices in July, factory workers in Warsaw, Tczew, and Łódź began striking for higher wages. When wage hikes up to 15 percent were promised, the strikes were quickly settled.

But the fever had caught on. It reached its high point at the huge Lenin Shipyard in Gdańsk (formerly Danzig) in mid-August. There workers on an early shift sat down on their jobs after reading leaflets demanding the reinstatement of a woman crane driver who had been fired for militantly opposing the management. Another immediate demand was a general cost-of-living increase. Just as the manager was talking to the dissidents, a labor activist and unemployed electrician named Lech Wałęsa, who had been hoisted over the fence, jumped up on the bulldozer where the manager was standing and called for an occupation strike by the 16,000 workers. Within a day other shipyards in Gdańsk and in Gdynia joined in.

Quickly an Inter-Factory Strike Committee, headed by Wałęsa, began using a courier system to enlist other workers in the Baltic area, where strikes were spreading. After the Inter-Factory Strike Committee worked out a list of 21 demands, worried government officials met with the committee negotiators, and the Gdańsk Agreement was signed by the end of the month. Workers, who won the right to establish independent trade unions and to strike, were also promised an increase in the minimum wage and welfare benefits, as well as reforms in health services and pension systems. An especially important government concession was that from then on management leaders in all state enterprises would be elected on the basis of ability alone. In a vulnerable position, Gierek was replaced by Stanisław Kania as party secretary.

Ten days later, Wałęsa and his associates sat in a shabby Warsaw hotel and founded the "independent, self-managing trade union," Solidarity (Solidarność), actually a federation. Disputes soon flared, however, over the union's legal registration. After weeks of serious crisis, Solidarity was finally registered in November. Meanwhile, strike committees all over the country adopted the main outlines of the Gdańsk Agreement, and Solidarity turned into a national movement for democracy in which the intelligentsia and workers combined their talents and strengths and worked together. Suchocka became a special adviser on Solidarity's legal problems. Support came also from the Roman Catholic church, but Cardinal Wyszynski cautioned against violence.

In December 1980, Solidarity planned a special ceremony to commemorate the 23 men killed in the 1970 Gdańsk rebellion. The ceremony was billed as a "national unity" gathering, and government officials and trade unionists watched Wałęsa light an eternal flame at a 140-foot steel structure erected for the occasion.

Quickly, however, the "national unity" mood evaporated. Always hiding behind black spectacles, General Wojciech Jaruzelski, the defense minister who became prime minister in February, grew increasingly nervous over Moscow's unhappiness with the concessions. The understanding had been that the government should carry out the reforms demanded by Solidarity while the federation concerned itself with trade union matters.

Cardinal Wyszynski died in May and was succeeded as primate by Archbishop Józef Glemp, who promised to continue the church's mediating role between the PZRP and Solidarity.

As the year wore on, the economy showed no improvement, and the government moved too slowly on reforms. During September and October, the union federation held its first national congress in two sessions, packing them with patriotic pageantry, recitations, and passionate calls for restructuring the nation toward democracy and subjecting economic reform to public control. In the next few months, however, the government seemed unprepared to compromise on any issue. As food shortages led to further strikes, Kania stepped down as party leader and was replaced by Jaruzelski, who retained his post as prime minister.

Wałęsa urged moderation, but radicals within Solidarity pressed the leadership to make demands for a new trade union law, free elections, free media access, and a halt to harassment. Believing that the goals were so political that they threatened the PZPR's monopoly of power and well aware of what had happened in Hungary in 1956 and in Czechoslovakia in 1968, Jaruzelski resolved to prevent any Soviet intervention. Therefore, on December 12, 1981, he struck back by declaring martial law and interning Wałęsa and other Solidarity leaders. Underground Solidarity was established soon afterward.

The next autumn, when a bill disfranchising Solidarity was introduced in the Sejm, Suchocka, a member of the Sejm Commission of Legislative Works, voted against it and other punitive measures. When the legislation passed, the SD party court promptly suspended her from the Sejm. Returning to academic life, she lectured at Lublin Catholic University and later worked at the Institute of Law in Poznań.

With the disappearance of Solidarity as a legal entity, Wałęsa was released. Under his leadershsip the underground movement kept its goals alive through a provisional coordinating commission of former leaders, secret cells, provisional factory committees, and various clandestine publication networks. Martial law was lifted in July 1983. Within a few months Wałęsa was awarded the Nobel Peace Prize. Later he donated his prize money to an emergency fund for health care, social welfare, and education.

Suchocka left the SD party in 1984. That year the murder by the secret police of Father Jerzy Popiełuszko, a young radical priest, gave Solidarity a new sense of mission even as it remained underground.

Wałęsa and his advisers believed they could be openly active again in 1988 after Soviet President Mikhail Gorbachev had introduced *glasnost* (openness) and *perestroika* (restructuring) to the Soviet Union. Stung by a harsh recession, brought on by too heavy borrowing from Western banks, Communist leaders and Solidarity, aided by Pope John Paul II, reached a "roundtable agreement," which allowed a freer political atmosphere. A 100-seat Senate with veto power was added to the Sejm; 35 percent of the seats in the Sejm were to be open to the alternative parties;

65 percent were reserved for the Communists and their allies. The old Communist constitution of 1952 was hastily amended, establishing a presidency. The president, also commander in chief, could dissolve the Sejm and call new elections only under certain circumstances, initiate his own legislation, veto Sejm measures, impose martial law when the Sejm was not in session, and ratify international agreements. The prime minister had to countersign all bills of major importance. To general rejoicing, the roundtable also announced that Solidarity was legalized.

Parliamentary elections in June 1989 resulted in a landslide for Solidarity-backed candidates, including Suchocka, one of those picked by the Civic Committee, Solidarity's political arm. The Sejm elected Tadeusz Mazowiecki, well-known magazine editor and member of the moderate Solidarity wing, as prime minister and Jaruzelski as president. Then it renamed the Polish People's Republic the Republic of Poland.

Like all countries that threw off the Communist yoke, Poland suffered from economic dislocation. Initially Mazowiecki's government, on advice from the International Monetary Fund, sought to bring about economic reform through shock therapy. Price subsidies on foodstuffs and manufactured goods were removed, and many state-owned small businesses were sold to private owners and workers' collectives. No changes were necessary in agricultural control, for Poland had always maintained private ownership of most farmland, in contrast to the neighboring countries in the Eastern bloc. At first the results were dismaying: Unemployment rose, and industrial prices and output fell.

With the overwhelming Solidarity victory, the PZPR was officially dissolved in early 1990. By summer, Wałęsa's supporters were organized into the Center Bloc; several of his rivals had formed the Democratic Union, which Mazowiecki headed and Suchocka joined.

A split then developed between Wałęsa and Mazowiecki, who both announced they would run for president toward the end of 1990. A third candidate was Stanisław Tyminski, who had left Poland to pursue a successful business career in Canada and Peru. Mazowiecki, for whom Suchocka voted, finished third and resigned as prime minister. Wałęsa then won a runoff election against Tyminski and resigned as head of Solidarity. He became president in December 1990 for a six-year term and asked the Sejm to appoint Krzysztof Bielecki prime minister. Running as a candidate of the Democratic Union in 1991, Suchocka was reelected to the Sejm for a four-year term.

Wałęsa, who quarreled frequently with many of his old allies, wanted a powerful presidency and felt frustrated by his inability to deliver the reforms he had promised. An ardent admirer of Charles De Gaulle, who had established an executive presidency, he looked longingly at the French model. Bielecki was succeeded by a human rights lawyer, Jan Olszewski, who made little progress. Economic conditions had worsened in spite of a promise that 50 percent of the foreign debt would be canceled. By May 1992 the splintered Sejm had passed no significant legislation.

Wałęsa fought hard to keep his third prime minister, Waldemar Pawlak, who garnered little support after he was named in June 1992. Since the Sejm was made up of 29 political parties, forming a cabinet seemed an almost impossible undertaking. As his own popularity sagged, the president claimed that he was a victim of popular disillusionment with politicians in a climate of economic hardship. Pending the adoption of a new constitution, which was expected to be a lengthy process, he felt his hands bound, his possible powers largely undefined.

After days of deadlock over Pawlak, a quiet, studious farmer, a coalition of eight parties, including nationalist right-wingers, Christian Democrats, and proponents of a free market, brought Suchocka's name forward. Suchocka had gained respect as an expert on constitutional and human rights law and as deputy chair of Poland's delegation to the Council of Europe. In the Sejm, however, where she had helped sponsor an antiabortion bill, she had not been particularly prominent. At first she was taken aback. "To see my name as a candidate for prime minister seems a little surrealistic." Poland has sometimes been cited by human rights groups for discrimination against women.

The coalition could command a parliamentary majority, and somewhat reluctantly Wałęsa decided to send her nomination to the Sejm. After meeting with him, a smartly tailored Suchocka told the press: "I think that as a woman I had a better chance of forming a government because women often eliminate conflicts. I agreed to become a candidate for prime minister because I believe that after all these conflicts and arguments, we need a government of national agreement."

In early July the Sejm dismissed Pawlak; voted in Suchocka, whose coalition partners had dropped to six; and then approved her cabinet. After she won, parliamentary deputies swarmed around her, kissing her hand in traditional Polish fashion. When asked why her cabinet included no women, she said, "None of the coalition parties presented a woman candidate. If I could, I would propose a few women because it is easier to work with women. They are reliable and conscientious." She added, "I am not afraid of working with men. I have always moved in a man's world."

From the beginning Suchocka promised to reduce the role of the government in the economy, to make the private sector unrestricted, and to help free enterprise. Generally she advocated education and health reforms.

Unmarried, she lives alone in a Warsaw apartment and relaxes from the chaotic political marketplace by playing her piano and taking her dog for walks. But she is in close touch with her married sister Elzbieta Gajewska, a lawyer in charge of the foreign investment division of the Chamber of Commerce in Poznań. As soon as Hanna took over her official duties, Elzbieta informed smiling reporters with disarming directness that the prime minister had one weakness: devouring three heads of lettuce every day. When a German interviewer asked Suchocka how she could eat that many heads of lettuce in view of the omnipresent pollution, she answered that she had eaten lettuce for years and that on some days she consumed only two heads. The persistent interviewer then wondered why a widely respected specialist had been replaced by a less knowledgeable man as minister of the environment, and Suchocka explained that the appointment had been made by one of the coalition partners. Environment, she insisted, would be her deep concern, and she promised to keep careful watch.

Dietary habits aside, Elzbieta said more: "My sister is more feminist than I. Without any hesitation she tells you her age and in public counts her gray hairs." But in her antiabortion stand, rooted in her loyalty to the Catholic Church, Suchocka does depart from feminist doctrine.

Supporters point out that Hanna Suchocka is a politician who wants to reconcile and unify, not antagonize, and that she has a charming way of saying to opponents, "But you will help. You can't refuse, can you?"

She knows, however, that moving a previously centralized economy toward market capitalism and the closest possible integration with Western Europe is a task of unprecedented dimensions for the Sejm, the president, and the prime minister.

SELECTED BIBLIOGRAPHY

Sirimavo Bandaranaike

Manor, James. *The Expedient Utopian: Bandaranaike and Ceylon.* New York: Cambridge University Press, 1989.
Seneviratne, Maureen. *Sirimavo Bandaranaike. The World's First Woman Prime Minister.* Colombo, Sri Lanka: Hanta Publisher, in association with Laklooms, 1975.

Indira Gandhi

Abbas, Khwaja Ahmed. *Indira Gandhi: Return of the Red Rose.* Bombay: Popular Prakashan, 1966.
———. *That Woman.* Delhi: Indian Book Co., 1973.
Alexander, M. K. *Madame Gandhi: A Political Biography.* North Quincy, Mass.: Christopher Publishing House, 1969.
Ali, Tariq. *An Indian Dynasty: The Story of the Nehru-Gandhi Family.* New York: G. P. Putnam's Sons, 1983.
Bhatia, Krishna. *Indira: A Biography.* New York: Praeger, 1974.
Birla, K. K. *Indira Gandhi: Reminiscences.* Delhi: Vikas, 1987.
Brecher, Michael. *Nehru's Mantle. The Politics of Succession.* New York: Praeger, 1966.
Carras, Mary. *Indira Gandhi in the Crucible of Leadership.* Boston: Beacon Press, 1979.
Gandhi, Indira. *Letters to a Friend, 1950-1984,* Selected, with commentary, from correspondence with Dorothy Norman. London: Weidenfeld & Nicolson, 1986.
———. *My Truth.* Delhi: Vikas, 1981.
———. *On People & Problems.* London: Hodder & Stoughton, 1983.
———. *Speeches and Writings.* New York: Harper & Row, 1973.
Gandhi, Sonia, ed. *Freedom's Daughter. Letters Between Indira Gandhi and Jawaharlal Nehru.* London: Hodder & Stoughton, 1989.

Gupte, Pranay. *Mother India. A Political Biography of Indira Gandhi.* Charles Scribner's Sons, 1992.
———. *Vengeance: India After the Assassination of Indira Gandhi.* New York: W. W. Norton & Co., 1985.
Hutheesing, Krishna. *Dear to Behold: An Intimate Portrait of Indira Gandhi.* New York: Macmillan Co., 1969.
———, and Alden Hatch. *We Nehrus.* New York: Holt, Rinehart, & Winston, 1967.
Kalhan, Promilla. *Kamala Nehru: An Intimate Biography.* Delhi: NIB Publishers, 1990.
Malhotra, Inder. *Indira Gandhi.* London: Hodder & Stoughton, 1989.
Masani, Shakuntala. *The Story of Indira.* Delhi: Vikas, 1974.
Masani, Zareer. *Indira Gandhi: A Biography.* New York: T.Y. Crowell, 1976.
Mohan, Anand. *Indira Gandhi: A Biography.* New York: Meredith, 1967.
Nehru, Jawaharlal. *Autobiography.* London: Bodley Head, 1936.
Sahgal, Nayantara. *Indira Gandhi—Her Rise to Power.* New York: Unger, 1978.
Vatudeo, Uma. *Indira Gandhi: Revolution in Restraint.* Delhi: Nikos, 1974.
Willcoxen, Harriet. *First Lady of India: The Story of Indira Gandhi.* Garden City, N.Y.: Doubleday & Co., 1969.

Golda Meir

Agress, Eliahu. *Golda Meir: Portrait of a Prime Minister.* New York: Sabra Books, 1969.
Mann, Peggy. *Golda: The Life of Israel's Prime Minister.* New York: Coward, McCann, Geoghegan, 1971.
Martin, Ralph G. *Golda Meir, the Romantic Years.* New York: Charles Scribner's Sons, 1988.
Meir, Golda. *A Land of Our Own. An Oral Autobiography,* ed. by Marie Syrkin. New York: G. P. Putnam's Sons, 1973.
———. *My Life.* New York: G. P. Putnam's Sons, 1975.
———. *This Is Our Strength.* ed. by Henry M. Cristman. New York: Macmillan Co., 1962.
Meir, Menahem. *My Mother Golda Meir: A Son's Evocation of Life with Golda Meir.* New York: Arbor House, 1983.
Shenker, Israel, and Shenker, Mary, eds. *As Good as Golda: The Warmth and Wisdom of Israel's Prime Minister.* New York: McCall, 1970.
Slater, Robert. *Golda, The Unnamed Queen of Israel. A Pictorial Biography.* Middle Village, N.Y.: Jonathan David, 1979.
Syrkin, Marie. *Golda Meir. Israel's Leader.* New York: G. P. Putnam's Sons, 1969.

_____. *Golda Meir. Woman with a Cause.* New York: G. P. Putnam's Sons, 1963.

Isabel Perón

Alexander, Robert J. *Juan Domingo Perón: A History.* Boulder, Colo.: Westview Press, 1979.
Barnes, John. *Evita, First Lady: A Biography of Eva Perón.* New York: Grove Press, 1975.
Crasweller, Robert D. *Perón and the Enigmas of Argentina.* New York: W. W. Norton & Co., 1987.
Main, Mary. *Evita: The Woman with the Whip.* New York: Dodd, Mead, 1980.
Page, Joseph A. *Perón, a Biography.* New York: Random House, 1983.
Turner, Frederick C., and Miguens, José, eds. *Juan Perón and the Reshaping of Argentina.* Pittsburgh, Penn.: University of Pittsburgh, 1983.

Margaret Thatcher

Bruce-Gardyne, Jock. *Mrs. Thatcher's First Administration: The Prophets Confounded.* London: Macmillan Co., 1984.
Cole, John. *The Thatcher Years.* London: BBC Books, 1987.
Donoughe, Bernard. *Prime Minister.* London: Jonathan Cape, 1987.
Gardiner, George. *Margaret Thatcher: From Childhood to Leadership.* London: Kimber, 1975.
Hall, Stuart, and Jacques, Martin. *The Politics of Thatcherism.* London: Lawrence & Wishart, 1983.
Harris, Kenneth. *Thatcher.* Boston: Little, Brown, & Co., 1988.
Jenkins, Peter. *Mrs. Thatcher's Revolution. The Ending of the Socialist Era.* Cambridge, Mass.: Harvard University Press, 1988.
Junor, Penny. *Margaret Thatcher.* London: Sidgwick & Jackson, 1983.
Kavanagh, Dennis. *Thatcherism and British Politics: The End of Consensus.* Oxford, England: Oxford University Press, 1987.
_____, and Seldon, Anthony, eds. *The Thatcher Effect: A Decade of Change.* Oxford, England: Oxford University Press, 1989.
Lewis, Russell. *Margaret Thatcher. A Personal and Political Biography.* London: Routledge & Kegan Paul, 1975.
Mayer, Allen J. *Madame Prime Minister: Margaret Thatcher and Her Rise to Power.* New York, Newsweek Books, 1979.
McFadyeen, Melanie, and Renn, Margaret. *Thatcher's Reign.* London: Chatto & Windus, 1984.
Minogue, Kenneth, and Michael Biddess. *Thatcherism: Personality and Politics.* New York: St. Martin's Press, 1987.

Murray, Patricia. *Margaret Thatcher*. London: W. H. Allen, 1980.
Ogden, Chris. *Maggie, An Intimate Portrait of a Woman in Power*. New York: Simon & Schuster, 1990.
Pearce, Edward. *Looking Down on Margaret Thatcher*. London: Hamish Hamilton, 1987.
Riddell, Peter. *The Thatcher Government*. London: Robertson, 1983.
Smith, Geoffrey. *Reagan and Thatcher*. New York: W. W. Norton & Co., 1991.
Thatcher, Carol. *Diary of an Election*. London: Sidgwick & Jackson, 1983.
Thatcher, Margaret. *In Defense of Freedom*. London: Aurum Press, 1986.
Walters, Alan. *Britain's Economic Renaissance: Margaret Thatcher's Reforms 1979–1984*. Oxford, England: Oxford University Press, 1986.
Young, Hugo. *The Iron Lady: A Biography of Margaret Thatcher*. New York: Farrar, Straus, Giroux, 1989.
————, and Sloman, Anne. *The Thatcher Phenomenon*. London: BBC Books, 1986.

Maria de Lourdes Pintasilgo

Pintasilgo, Maria de Lourdes. *As minhas respostas (My Answer)*. Lisbon: Dom Quixote, 1985.
————. *Dimensoes da mudança (Dimensions of Change)*. Lisbon: Afrontamento, 1985.
————. *Imaginar a Igreja (To Imagine the Church)*. Lisbon: Multinova, 1980.
————. *Les Nouveaux Feminismes: question pour les chrétians?* Paris: Editions du Cerf. 1980.
————. *Sulcos do nosso querer comum (Furrows of Our Common Ground)*. Lisbon: Afrontamento, 1980.

Gro Harlem Brundtland

Hirsti, Reidar, ed. *Gro — midt i livet (Gro — In the Middle of Life)*. Oslo: Tiden Norsk Forlag, 1989.
Johanssen, Kjell Chr., and Brunvand, Per. *Gro. Norges første kvinnelige statsminister (Gro. Norway's first woman prime minister)*. Oslo: Tiden Norsk Forlag, 1981.
Our Common Future (Brundtland Report). New York: Oxford University Press, 1989.

Corazon Aquino

Burton, Sandra. *Impossible Dream: The Marcoses, the Aquinos, and the Unfinished Revolution*. New York: Warner Books, 1989.

Buss, Claude A. *Corazon Aquino and the People of the Philippines.* Stanford, Calif.: Portable Stanford, 1987.
Chrisotomo, Isabelo T. *Cory: Profile of a President.* Quezon City, Philippines: J. Kriz, 1986.
Komisar, Lucy. *Corazon Aquino: The Story of a Revolution.* New York: George Braziller, 1987.
Mercado, Monina Allerey, ed. *People Power: An Eyewitness History: The Philippine Revolution of 1986.* Manila: James B. Reuter, S.J. Foundation, 1986.
Nadel, Laura. *Corazon Aquino: Journey to Power.* New York: Julian Messner, 1987.
Pedrosa, Carmen Vavano. *Imelda Marcos.* New York: St. Martin's Press, 1987.

Benazir Bhutto

Bhutto, Benazir. *Daughter of Destiny: An Autobiography.* New York: Simon & Schuster, 1989.
Muner, Muhammed. *From Jinnah to Zia.* Lahore, Pakistan: Vanguard, 1980.
Schofield, Victoria. *Bhutto, Trial and Execution.* London: Cassell, 1979.
Shahed, Javed Burki. *Pakistan under Bhutto.* New York: St. Martin's Press, 1980.

Violeta Chamorro

Edmister, Patricia Taylor. *Nicaragua Divided: La Prensa and the Chamorro Legacy.* Pensacola: University of West Florida Press, 1990.

Edith Cresson

Cresson, Edith. *Avec le Soleil* [autobiography]. Paris: J. C. Lattès, 1976.

Author's note: Presently there are no relevant books about Elizabeth Domitien, Vigdis Finnbogadóttir, Eugenia Charles, Milka Planinc, Maria Liberia-Peters, Ertha Pascal-Trouillot, Kazimiera Prunskiene, Mary Robinson, Khaleda Zia, or Hanna Suchocka.

INDEX

Abdullah ibn Hussein 41
Achdut Ha'avoda 47
Adams, Alvin P., Jr. 158
Aguinaldo, Emil 128
Ahmed, Fakhruddin 29
Ahmed, Khandakar Muchtaque 194
Ahmed, Shahabuddin 197
AIDS panic 157
Airey, Josie 183
Airlee House conference 184
Alexander I 112
Allfrey, Phyllis Shand 91
Allon, Yigal 47
American Revolution 89
Amnesty International 66
Antonio, Jorge 57
Aquino, Agopito 139
Aquino, Aurelia 132
Aquino, Benigno III 132, 138
Aquino, Benigno, Jr. 127, 130, 131, 132, 133, 134
Aquino, Benigno, Sr. 130, 131
Aquino, Corazon 127–140, 149
Aquino, Kristina 132, 138
Aquino, Maria Elena 127, 138
Aquino, Victoria 132, 138
Aramburu, Pedro 55, 58
Aranne, Zalman 40
Argüello, Miriam 177
Arias, Oscar 176
Aristide, Jean-Bertrand 159, 160
Armed Forces Movement (AMF) 83
Astridur 98
Atlee, Clement 42, 71, 72
Aubry, Martine 209
Avice, Edvige 209
Avril, Prosper 158

Awami League 27, 144, 191, 192, 193, 194, 196, 197, 198
Ayub Khan, Mohammed 25, 142, 144, 191

"Babette" show 209, 211
Baka, Jean 63
Balfour Declaration 37, 41
Bandaranaike, Anura 4, 11
Bandaranaike, Chandraka *see* Kumaranatunga, Chandraka
Bandaranaike, Sirimavo ix, 1–13
Bandaranaike, Sir Solomon Dias 2
Bandaranaike, Solomon West Ridgeway 1–6, 7
Bandaranaike, Sunetra 4
Bangladesh National Party (BNP) 195, 196, 197
Barios, Américo 56
Barrios, Amelia 169
Barrios, Carlos 169
Batista, Fulgencio 55
Beatrix, queen 124, 126
Begin, Menahem 50
Ben-Gurion, David 39, 42, 43, 44, 46
Bergevoy, Pierre 210
Berlin Wall 162, 186
Bernadotte, Folke 43
Bhutto, Benazir 141–53
Bhutto, Fauzia 148
Bhutto, Mir Murtaza 141, 146, 148
Bhutto, Nusrat Ispahni 141, 142, 145, 146, 147, 150, 151, 152, 153
Bhutto, Rehana 148, 153
Bhutto, Sanam 141, 144, 147, 148
Bhutto, Shah Nawaz 141, 146

Bhutto, Zulfikar Ali 141, 142, 144, 145, 146, 192, 193
Bielecki, Krzystof 220, 221
Bishop, Maurice 93
Boganda, Barthélmy 63
Bokassa, Jean-Bedel 62, 63–64, 65, 66, 67
Bourke, Adrian 181
Bourke, Aubrey (father) 181
Bourke, Aubrey (son) 181
Bourke, Henry 181
Bourke, Oliver 181
Bourke, Tessa Donnell 181, 183
Boutros-Ghali, Boutros 110
Bratteli, Trygve 101–102, 104
Brazauskas, Algirdas 163
Breden, Frederique 209
Brezhnev, Leonid 28
Brundtland, Arne Olav 102, 104, 106, 107, 109
Brundtland, Gro Harlem 101, 111
Brundtland, Ivar 102, 104
Brundtland, Jørgen 102, 111
Brundtland, Kari 102, 104
Brundtland, Knud 102, 104
Brundtland Report *see Our Common Future*
Bunche, Ralph 43
Bush, George 151, 165, 179

Caetano, Marcello 83, 84
Callaghan, James 75, 76
Campion, Gabriel 201, 202, 203
Campion, Harold 202, 203
Campion, Jacqueline 201, 202, 203
Campora, Hector 58, 59
Caribbean Basin Initiative 93
Caribbean Community and Common Market (CARICOM) 93
Carl XVI Gustav 110
Carlos I 82
Carlos, Adelino de Palma 85
Carrington, Lord 77
Castillo, Ramon S. 51
Castro, Fidel 172
Center Bloc 220
Center party (Norway) 109

Central Intelligence Agency (CIA) 94, 152
Centre for our Common Future 108
César, Alfredo 177
Ceylon Muslim League 4
Ceylon National Congress 4
Chamorro, Claudia 172, 176
Chamorro, Cristiana *see* Lacayo, Cristiana
Chamorro, Fruto 169
Chamorro, Jaime 174
Chamorro, Pedro Joaquín 169, 170, 171, 172, 173, 174, 177
Chamorro, Pedro Joaquín, Jr. (Quinto) 172, 176
Chamorro, Violeta 169–180
Chamorro, Xavier 176
Charles, Eugenia 82–94
Charles, John Baptiste (JB) 88
Charles, Josephine Delauney 88
Charles, Prince of Wales 78
Chetniks 113
Chinese border war with India 25
Chirac, Jacques 208
Chowdhury, Abdul Fazed Muhammad Ahsanuddin 196
Christian X 95
Christian Democrats 109
Churchill, Winston 70, 71
Cojuangco, Demetria Sumulong 127, 128, 130
Cojuangco, Jose 127, 128, 130
Cojuangco, Teresita 130
Columbus, Christopher 88, 91
Combone, Luckner 156
Committee of National Salvation 92
Communist Information Bureau (COMINTERN) 116
Communist party (Ceylon) 4, 7, 8, 10, 11; (India) 24
CONELEC 135
Congress party 23, 24, 26, 27, 28, 30, 31
Congress-I party 30, 31, 32
Conservative party (Britain) 68, 69, 70, 71, 72, 73, 74, 75, 80, 81; (Nicaragua) 170; (Norway) 104, 106, 109
Contras 176, 177, 178, 179
Cresson, Alexandra 203, 204, 210

Cresson, Edith 200–211
Cresson, Jacques 203, 204, 207, 209, 210
Cresson, Nathalie 203, 204, 206
Cresto, Isabel 52
Cresto, José 52
Currie, Austin 186

Dacko, David 63, 66, 67
Da Costa, Alfredo Nobre 86
Dahanayake, Wijaynanda 6
Damasco, Vincente 60, 61
Dayan, Moshe 44, 47, 49
De Gaulle, Charles 202, 204, 205, 206, 221
Democratic party of Sint Maarten (DPSM) 125
Democratic Union 220
Democratic Union of Liberation (UDEL) 173, 174
Desai, Morarji 25, 27, 29, 30, 31
Dewey, George 127
Dimetz, Simcha 33–34
Dominica Freedom party (DFP) 91, 92, 94
Dominican Labour party 90
Dominique, Max 156
Domitien, Elizabeth 62–67
Douglas, Michael 94
Douglas-Home, Sir Alec 73
Dreads 91, 92
Dreyfus, Enrique 179
Duvalier, François (Papa Doc) 154, 155, 156
Duvalier, Jean-Claude (Baby Doc) 156, 157, 160
Duvalier, Michele 157
Duvalier, Simone 156

Earth Summit 110, 111
Eden, Anthony 72
Eiriksdóttir, Sigridur 95, 96
Eisenhower, Dwight D. 5, 45
Elizabeth II 76
Enrile, Juan Ponce 132, 135, 136
Ershad, Hossain Mohammad 194, 196, 197

Eshkol, Levi 46, 47
European Air Law Association 184
European Community (EC) 76, 80, 87, 109, 110, 119, 183, 208
European Convention on Human Rights 183
European Court of Human Rights 183
European Economic Area (EEA) 110
European Free Trade Association (EFTA) 109, 110
European Monetary System (EMS) 80, 81
European Parliament 87, 110, 206

Falklands War 78, 79
Faubius, Laurent 107
Federal Government of the West Indies 91
Ferdinand and Isabella 88
Fianna Fáil party 184, 185
Fine Gael party 185
Finnbogadóttir, Vigdis 95–100
FitzGerald, Garrett 185
Five, Kaci Kullman 109
Flores Tascon, Francisco 56
Flores Tascon, Señora de 56
Foot, Michael 79
Fortunato, Leopold 78
Fouque, Antoinette 210
Franco, Francisco 55
French Communist party 206, 210
Frondizi, Arturo 55, 56

Gahal party 47
Gajewska, Elzbieta *see* Suchocka, Elzbieta
Galbraith, John Kenneth 144
Galbraith, Peter 144, 147
Gandhi, Feroze 18, 19, 20, 21, 23, 24
Gandhi, Indira 14–32, 70, 78, 119, 142, 145
Gandhi, Maneka 32
Gandhi, Mohandas K. (Mahatma) 3, 15, 18–19, 20, 21, 22, 23
Gandhi, Rajiv 14, 21, 22, 24, 30, 31, 32

Gandhi, Sanjay 22, 24, 30, 31
Gandhi, Sonia 32
Gardner, Ava 56
General Alliance 87
Gierek, Edward 217, 218
Gima 96
Giri, Varahagiri Venkata 27
Giscard d'Estaing, Valéry 65, 67, 205, 206
Glemp, Józef 218
Godoy, Virgilio 177
Gollapawa, William 9, 10
Gomez, Francisco da Costa 85
Gomułka, Władisław 213, 216, 217
Gonçalves, Vasco dos Santos 85
Goonetilloke, Sir Oliver 7
Gorbachev, Mikhail S. 80, 100, 162, 163, 164, 165, 167, 219
Graal *see* International Grail Movement
Green Revolution 198
Grenada invasion 93, 94
Guevara, Che 9
Guido, José María 56
Gultiere, Leopold Fortunato 78

Habash, George 210
Haig, Alexander 78
Hamburger, Regina 37
Harald, Crown Prince 109
Harlem, Gudmund 101, 102, 104
Harlem, Helle 102
Harlem, Inga Brynolf 101, 102, 104
Harlem, Lars 101
Harrison, Agatha 19
Haughey, Charles 183
Hazan, Yaacov 40
Heath, Edward 73, 74
Herald, Joe 54
Hermannsson, Steingrímur 99, 100
Herzl, Theodor 36
Heseltine, Michael 81
Hillery, Patrick 184
Hirsch, Ernst 126
Hitler, Adolf 40, 52, 112, 215
Hodgkin, Dorothy Crowfoot 70
Honsteen, Kirsten 107
Honychurch, Lennox 92
Houphouët-Boigny, Félix 67
Howe, Sir Geoffrey 80
Hukbalahaps (Huks) 131
Hurd, Douglas 81
Husain, Zakir 27

Icelandic Women's Liberation Movement 99
Illía, Arturo 56, 57
Indian National Congress 14–15, 17, 18, 20, 21, 23
Indo-Pakistani Wars (1948–49) 22; (1965) 25, 142, 191; (1971) 28, 144, 193
International Bank for Reconstruction and Development 8
International Commission of Jurists 184
International Conference of Women 145
International Development Fund 179
International Grail Movement (Graal in Portugal) 83, 86
International Monetary Fund (IMF) 85, 86, 220
Interno Frente 170
Irish Architectural Archives 187
Irish Center for European Law 187
Irish Republican Army (IRA) 79
Irish Supreme Court 183, 187
Irwin, Lord 18
Israel Labor party 47, 49, 50
Izhak Khan, Ghulam 152

Janata party 30
Jaruzelski, Wojciech 218
Jatiyo Gantranak Dal–National Front 195
Jatiyo party 196
Jayewardene, Junius R. 10–11, 12
Jewish Agency of Israel 41
Jewish National Council 42
Jinnah, Mohammed Ali 141, 190
John Paul II, Pope 217, 219

John, Patrick 91, 92, 93
Johnson, Lyndon B. 26
Joseph, Sir Keith 74
J P Movement 29
Junejo, Mohammed Khan 148

Kaddar, Lou 43
Kamaraj, Kumaraswamy 25, 26
Kania, Stanisław 218, 219
Kashmir 142
Kennedy, John F. 144
KGB 168
Kinnock, Neil 80
Kissinger, Henry 49
Kleveland, Åse 109
Kochanowski, Jan 215
Kolingba, André-Dieudonne 62, 67
Korean War 130
Korngold, Shamir (Sam) 34, 36, 37, 50
Korngold, Sheyna 33–34, 36, 37
Kosygin, Alexei 78
Kotelawa, Sir John 4
Krishna Menon, V.K. 23
Kumaranatunga, Chandraka 4, 12
Kumaranatunga, Vijaya 12

Laban People's Power party 133
Labor party (Israel) *see* United Labor party (old); Israel Labor party (new)
Labor party (Norway); 101, 102, 105, 106, 107, 108, 109
Labour party (Britain) 71, 73, 74, 75, 80; (Dominica-DLP) 94; (Ireland) 182, 184, 185
Lacayo, Antonio 174, 176, 177, 178, 179
Lacayo, Cristiana 172, 174, 176, 178
Lafay, Bernard 203
Lafontant, Roger 159, 160
Lahnstein, Anne Engen 109
Landsbergis, Vitautas 162, 163, 164, 165, 166
Lanka Mahila Samiti 3, 4, 5
Lanusse, Alejandro 58
La Prensa 169, 170, 172–173, 174, 175, 176, 178

Latortue, François 157
Laurel, Salvador 135, 137
Laval, Pierre 201, 202
Lavon affair 46
Lawson, Nigel 80
Laxness, Halldór Kiljan 98
League of Communists of Croatia (LCC) 116, 117
League of Communists of Yugoslavia (LCY) 116, 117, 119
Le Blanc, Edward O. 90, 91
Leganeur, Violène 159
Lenihan, Brian 184, 185
Levingston, Roberto M. 58
Liberal party (Nicaragua) 190
Liberia, Niels 122, 124
Liberia-Peters, Maria 121–126
Likud party 50
Lithuanian Communist party 162, 163, 164
Lithuanian Restructuring Movement (Sajudis) 162, 163
Lonardi, Eduardo 55
López Rega, José 57, 58, 59, 60
Luis, crown prince 82

Mabovitch, Blume 33, 34, 38
Mabovitch, Moshe 33, 34, 38
Mabovitch, Sheyna, *see* Korngold, Sheyna
Mabovitch, Zipke 33, 34, 38, 50
Macapagal, Diosbado 132
MacArthur, Douglas 129, 130
McKinley, William 128
Macmillan, Harold 72, 73
Magsaysay, Ramon 131
Mahawalatenne, Ratemahatmumaya 1, 2
Mahjana Eksath Peramuna (MEP) 5, 7
Major, John 81
Majumdar, Iskandar 189
Majumdar, Taiyaba 189
Manigat, Leslie 157
Manuel II 82
Mapai *see* United Labor party
Mapam party 47
Marcos, Ferdinand 127, 132, 133, 134, 135, 136, 137, 138, 139, 149

Marcos, Imelda 132, 133, 136, 138, 139, 140
Marshall Plan 202
Martina, Dominico 124, 125
Martínez, Carmelo 51
Martínez, María Josepha 51
Marxist People's Revolutionary Army 59
Mathai, M.O. 23
Mauroy, Pierre 206
Mazowiecki, Tadeusz 220
Meir, Golda 33–50
MESAN 63, 64, 66
Meyerson, Menahem 38, 39, 40, 41, 44, 45, 46
Meyerson, Morris 36–37, 38, 39, 40, 41, 44, 45
Meyerson, Sarah 38, 39, 40, 43, 44, 46
Mickiewicz, Adam 215
Mihailovic, Draza 113, 115
Mirza, Iskander 142, 191
Mitterand, François 80, 205, 206, 207, 208, 209, 210
Monteneros 61
Moreau, Paulette 204
Moros 132
Mota Pinto, Carlos Alberto da 86
Mountbatten, Lord Louis 22
Movement for the Restoration of Democracy 196
Movement to Restore Democracy (MRD) 146, 150
Moyne Commission 90
Mugabe, Robert 77
Mujib-ur Rahman *see* Rahman, Mujib-ur
Musharraf, Khali 194
Muslim League 27, 189
Mussolini, Benito 52, 82
Muzorewa, Abel 77

Nacionalista party 132
NAMFREL 135
Namphy, Henri 157, 158
Nanda, Gulzarilal 25
Napier, Elma 91
Napoleon I 67, 214

Narain, Raj 29
Narayan, Jayaprakash 29
Nasser, Gamal Abdel 44, 46, 47, 48, 117
National Association for Female Catholic Youth 212
National Commission on the Status of Women (Portugal) 84
National Farmers' Federation (FNSEA) 206
National Herald 21
National Liberation Front 115
National Opposition Union (UNO) 177, 178, 179
National People's party (NVP) 124, 125, 126
National Union of Popular Action 170
Neave, Aubrey 74, 79
Nehru, Jawaharlal 14–15, 17, 18, 19, 20, 21, 22, 23, 117
Nehru, Kamala Kaul 14, 15, 17, 18–19, 20
Nehru, Krishna (later Hutheesing) 14–15, 22
Nehru, Motilal 14–15, 17–18
Nehru, Swarup Rani 14, 15
Nehru, Vijaya Lakshmi *see* Pandit, Vijaya Lakshmi
Netherlands Antilles Movement (NAM) 124
New Jewel government 91
New People's Army (NPA) 132, 138
New Society Movement 133
Nixon, Richard 49
Nkomo, Joshua 77
Nordli, Odvar 104, 105
North Atlantic Treaty Organization (NATO) 98, 108
Nyalingappa, Siddavanahalli 27

Olav V 105
Olympic Committee 110
O'Malley, Daniel 187
Ongania, Juan C. 57
Organization for Economic Cooperation and Development (OECD) 86
Organization of American States (OAS) 91, 94, 160

Organization of Eastern Caribbean States (OECS) 88, 93
Organization of Petroleum Exporting Countries (OPEC) 108
Organization of Republican Institutions 204, 205
Ortega, Daniel 175, 176, 177, 178, 179
Ortega, Humberto 178
Our Common Future 108, 110

Paderewski, Ignace Jan 212
Paisley, Ian 184
Pakistan People's party (PPP) 144, 145, 146, 147, 149, 150, 151, 153
Pállson, Thorsteinn 100
Palma Carlos, Adelino de 85
Palme, Olav 85
Pandit, Lekha 21
Pandit, Vijaya Lakshmi Nehru 14, 21, 23, 29
Parat, Orna 50
Parti Socialiste (PS) 205, 206, 207, 208, 209, 210
Partisans 113, 115
Pascal, Louise Damanoy 154
Pascal, Thimocles 154
Pascal-Trouillot, Ertha 154–160
Patasse, Ange 66
Paul VI, Pope 60, 112
Paul, Evans 158
Paul, Prince 112, 201, 202
Pawlak, Waldemar 221
Pax Romana 83
Peel Commission 40
Pell, Claiborne 147
People's Front 115
People's United Front, *see* Mahajana Eksath Peramuna
Perez, Shimon 45, 49
Pérez de Cuellar, Javier 106, 110
Pérez Jiménez, Marcos 55
Perón, Eva (Evita) 51, 52, 53, 56, 57, 58, 59, 60, 61
Perón, Isabel ix, 51–61
Perón, Juan D. 51, 52–53, 54, 55, 56, 57, 58, 59, 60, 61

Peronist party 52, 55, 56, 57, 58, 59, 60
Pétain, Henri Philippe 200–201, 202
Peter II 112, 113, 114
Pilsudski, Józef 213–214
Pintasilgo, Amelia Ruivo da Silva 82
Pintasilgo, Jaime de Matos 82
Pintasilgo, Maria de Lourdes 82–87
Pioneer Women 39
Planinc, Milka 112–120, 166
Poale Zion 36, 37
Polish United Workers party (PZPR) 213, 216, 220
Polish Workers party 213
Pompidou, Georges 205
Popiełuszko, Jerzy 219
La Prensa see under L
Progressive Democrats 187
Prunskiene, Dayvita 161
Prunskiene, Kazimiera 161–168
Prunskiene, Raisa 161
Prunskiene, Vaidotos 161
Pym, Francis 78

Quadaffi, Muammar 66
Quexon, Manuel 128

Rabin, Yitzhak 49
Rafi party 46, 47
Rahman, Arafat 191
Rahman, Mujib-ur 27, 28, 144, 191, 192, 193, 195, 197
Rahman, Tariq 191
Rahman, Zia-ur 191, 192, 193, 194, 195, 196, 197, 198
Ram, Jagjivan 31
Ramalho Eanes, Antonio dos Santos 85, 87
Ramos, Fidel 135, 136, 140
Rastafarians *see* Dreads
Ratwatte, Barnes 1, 2
Ratwatte, Kumarihamy 1, 2, 3, 6
Reagan, Ronald 80, 88, 93, 100, 108, 136, 137, 176
Réassemblement pour la République (RRP) 205

Reddy, Neelam Sanjiva 27, 31
Reece, Gordon 74
Rehabi, Zechariah 43
Remez, David 38, 40, 41
Reyes *see* Román y Reyes
Reykjavik Theater Company 98
Reynaud, Paul 200
Reynolds, Albert 187, 188
Ridore, Irene 158, 159
Roberts, Alfred 68, 70, 71
Roberts, Beatrice 68, 71
Roberts, Muriel 68, 69–70
Robinson, Aubrey 183
Robinson, Mary 181–188
Robinson, Nicholas 181, 183, 187
Robinson, Tessa 183
Robinson, William 183
Roces, Joaquin 134
Román y Reyes, Víctor 170
Rowlett Acts 15
Rubashov, Shneur Zalman *see* Shazar, Zalman

Sá Carneiro, Francisco 87
Sadat, Anwar 48, 50
St. Louis Belland 158
Sajudis *see* Lithuanian Restructuring Movement
Salazar, Antonio Oliveira de 82, 83
Samis 105
Sandinistas 174, 175, 176, 177, 178, 179
Sandino, Augusto César 174
Santiago, Miriam Defensor 140
Sattar, Abdul 194, 195, 196
Sayem, Abu Sadat Mohammed 194
Scargill, Arthur 79
Schick, René 173
Senanayake, D.D. 4
Senanayake, Dudley 4, 6, 8, 10
Seraphine, James Oliver 92
Seven Years War 89
Sharett, Moshe 41, 44
Sharif, Nazar 153
Shastri, Lal Bahadur 24, 25, 142
Shazar, Zalman 40
Sin, Jaime 134
Singh, Charan 31

Sinhala Maha Sabha 2
SIPTU 186
Six Day War 47
Smetona, Antanas 162
Smith, Ian D. 77
Soames, Lord Christopher 77
Soares, Mario 85, 86
SOCACOM 63
Social Democratic Center 85
Solidarity 212, 218, 219, 220
Somorama, Talduwe 6
Samoza, Luis 172–173
Somoza Debayle, Anastasio (Tachito) 173, 174, 175, 176
Somoza García, Anastasio (Tacho) 170, 172
Spanish-American War 127
Spencer, Lady Diana 78
Spínola, Antonio de 85
Spring, Richard 184
Sri Lanka Freedom party (SLFP) 4, 6, 7, 8, 12
Sri Lanka People's party 12
Stalin, Josef 113, 114, 116, 215
Stambolic, Peter 117
Stankevicius, Pranas 161
Stankevicius, Ramantas 163
Stoltenberg, Thorvald 109
Stronnictwo Demokratyczne (SD) 216, 219
Subovic, Ivan 114, 115
Suchocka, Anna Czajkowska 212
Suchocka, Elzbieta 213
Suchocka, Hanna 212–222
Suchocka, Maria 212
Suchocka, Wanda Baczkowka 212, 275
Suchocki, Józef 212, 215
Sumulong, Juan 128
Syse, Jan 108, 109

Taft, William Howard 128
Tagore, Rabindranath 18–19
Taruc, Luis 131
Thant, U 46
Thatcher, Carol 72, 73, 74, 75
Thatcher, Denis 71, 72, 73, 79, 209
Thatcher, Margaret 68–81, 99, 107, 118, 166

Thatcher, Mark 72, 73, 74, 79, 89
Thorodssen, Gunnar 99
Thorvaldsen, Finnbogi Rutur 95, 96
Tito (Josip Broz) 113, 114, 115, 116, 117, 118, 120
Toflan, Donal 187
Tontons Macoutes 155, 156, 159
Trotskyite Equality party 10
Trotskyite People's Revolutionary Army 60
Trouillot, Ernst 156
Trouillot, Yantha 157
Trujillo, Rafael L. 55
Tyminski, Stanisław 220

U Thant 46
UNESCO 25, 85
UNIDO 135
Union pour la Démocratie Française 206
United Front 8, 10, 11
United Labor party (Mapai) 39, 46, 47, 50
United National party (UNP) 4, 6, 8, 10, 11
United Nations 5, 25, 42, 43, 45, 46, 47, 49, 77, 91, 94, 110, 111, 120, 137, 142, 151
Ustinov, Peter 32

Vagnorius, Gediminas 167
Vandor, Augusto 57
Ver, Fabian 134
Videla, Jorge Raphael 61
Vietnam War 26
Villard, Serge 159

Wainwright, Jonathan 129
Wajed, Hasina 195, 196, 197
Wałęsa, Lech 217, 218, 219, 220
War over Kashmir 142
Wathey, Claude 125
Watkins, Sir Alan 80
Weizmann, Chaim 37, 43
West Indies Associated States 90
White Paper of 1939 41, 43
Willoch, Kåre 106, 107
Wilson, Harold 25, 73, 74, 75
Wilson, Woodrow 214
Women's Alliance 100
Women's Alliance for Democracy 210
Workers' party 185
World Bank 179
World Commission on Environment and Development 106, 110
World War I 36, 37, 82, 95, 161, 162
World War II 4, 20, 21, 41, 70, 95, 107, 112, 128–129, 130, 214
Wyszynski, Stefan 213, 216

Yahya Khan, Agha Muhammad 28, 144, 145, 191, 192, 193
Yeltsin, Boris 167–168
Yishuv 41
Yom Kippur War 48–49

Zardari, Asif 150, 152
Zardari, Bilawal 150
Zardari, Hakim Ali 151
Zia, Khaleda 189–199
Zia ul-Haq 145, 146, 147, 148, 149, 150, 151, 153
Zia-ur Rahman *see* Rahman, Zia-ur